CAPTAIN AMERICA
★ THEATER O

WRITER
PAUL JENKINS

"AMERICA THE BEAUTIFUL"
ARTIST: GARY ERSKINE
COLORIST: CHRIS SOTOMAYOR

"A BROTHER IN ARMS"
PENCILER: JOHN MCCREA
INKERS: JAMES HODGKINS, ALLEN MARTINEZ & VICTOR OLAZABA
COLORISTS: ANDREW ELDER & SOTOCOLOR'S LARRY MOLINAR & CHRIS GARCIA

"TO SOLDIER ON"
ARTIST: FERNANDO BLANCO
COLORIST: MARTA MARTINEZ

"GHOSTS OF MY COUNTRY"
ARTIST: ELIA BONETTI
COLORIST: JORGE MAESE

LETTERERS: DAVE LANPHEAR & JARED FLETCHER
EDITORS: JEANINE SCHAEFER & LAUREN SANKOVITCH
EXECUTIVE EDITOR: TOM BREVOORT
COVER ARTIST: STEVE EPTING

CAPTAIN AMERICA CREATED BY JOE SIMON & JACK KIRBY

COLLECTION EDITOR: MARK D. BEAZLEY • **EDITORIAL ASSISTANTS:** JAMES EMMETT & JOE HOCHSTEIN
ASSISTANT EDITOR: ALEX STARBUCK • **ASSOCIATE EDITOR:** JOHN DENNING
EDITOR, SPECIAL PROJECTS: JENNIFER GRÜNWALD • **SENIOR EDITOR, SPECIAL PROJECTS:** JEFF YOUNGQUIST
SENIOR VICE PRESIDENT OF SALES: DAVID GABRIEL • **PRODUCTION:** JERRY KALINOWSKI
BOOK DESIGNER: SPRING HOTELING

EDITOR IN CHIEF: JOE QUESADA • **PUBLISHER:** DAN BUCKLEY
EXECUTIVE PRODUCER: ALAN FINE

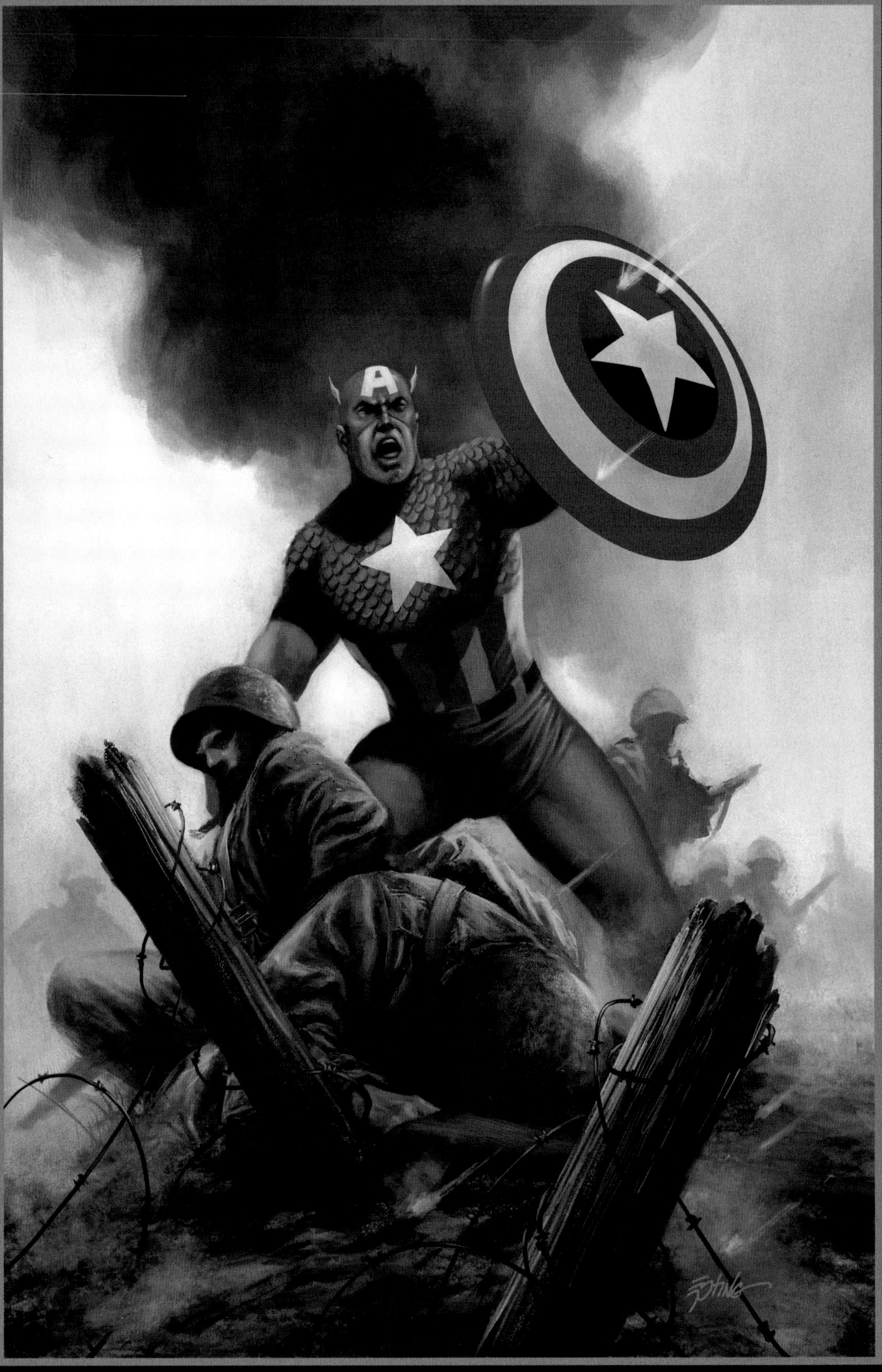

AMERICA THE BEAUTIFUL

NUMBER	RECEIVED BY	CHECK

In the dark days of the early 1940s, Steve Rogers, a struggling young artist from the Lower East Side of Manhattan, found himself horrified by the war raging overseas. Desperate to help, he was rejected by the US Army as unfit for service when he tried to enlist.

Undeterred, convinced this was where he needed to be, he was selected to participate in a covert military project called Operation: Rebirth. There, he was chosen by scientist Abraham Erskine as the first human test subject, and overnight was transformed into America's first Super-Soldier.

Enhanced to the peak of human perfection with superior strength, reflexes and speed, Steve Rogers now fights to protect the people and the country he loves from the forces that would destroy them as CAPTAIN AMERICA.

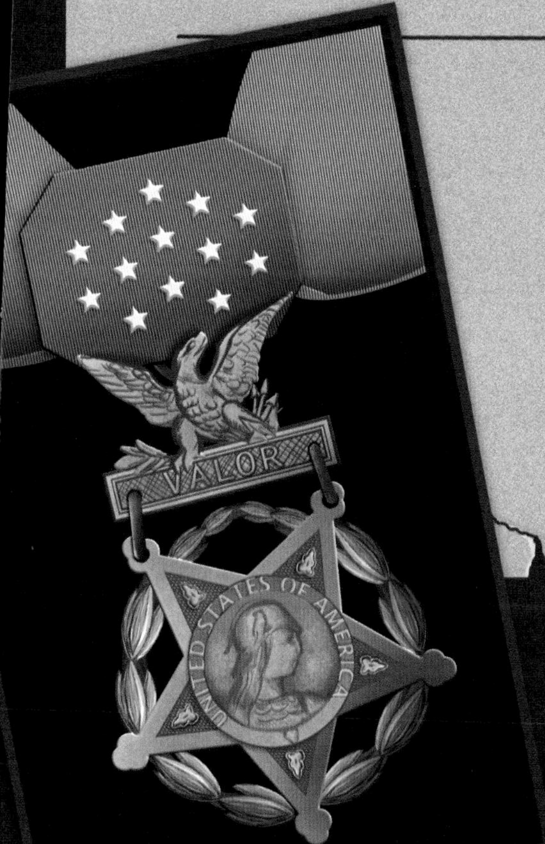
VALOR
UNITED STATES OF AMERICA

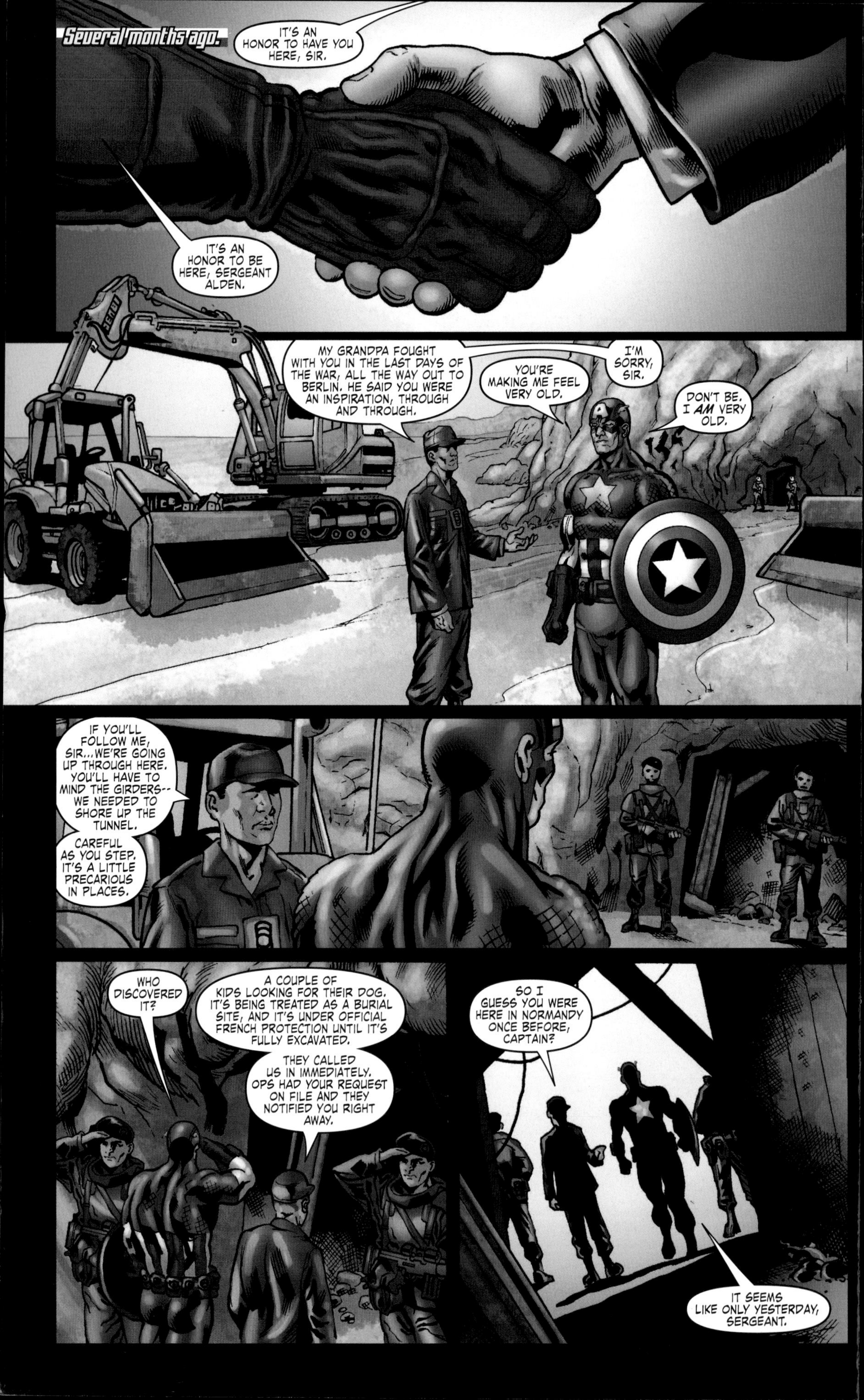
Several months ago.
IT'S AN HONOR TO HAVE YOU HERE, SIR.
IT'S AN HONOR TO BE HERE, SERGEANT ALDEN.
MY GRANDPA FOUGHT WITH YOU IN THE LAST DAYS OF THE WAR, ALL THE WAY OUT TO BERLIN. HE SAID YOU WERE AN INSPIRATION, THROUGH AND THROUGH.
YOU'RE MAKING ME FEEL VERY OLD.
I'M SORRY, SIR.
DON'T BE. I AM VERY OLD.
IF YOU'LL FOLLOW ME, SIR...WE'RE GOING UP THROUGH HERE. YOU'LL HAVE TO MIND THE GIRDERS-- WE NEEDED TO SHORE UP THE TUNNEL.
CAREFUL AS YOU STEP. IT'S A LITTLE PRECARIOUS IN PLACES.
WHO DISCOVERED IT?
A COUPLE OF KIDS LOOKING FOR THEIR DOG. IT'S BEING TREATED AS A BURIAL SITE, AND IT'S UNDER OFFICIAL FRENCH PROTECTION UNTIL IT'S FULLY EXCAVATED.
THEY CALLED US IN IMMEDIATELY. OPS HAD YOUR REQUEST ON FILE AND THEY NOTIFIED YOU RIGHT AWAY.
SO I GUESS YOU WERE HERE IN NORMANDY ONCE BEFORE, CAPTAIN?
IT SEEMS LIKE ONLY YESTERDAY, SERGEANT.

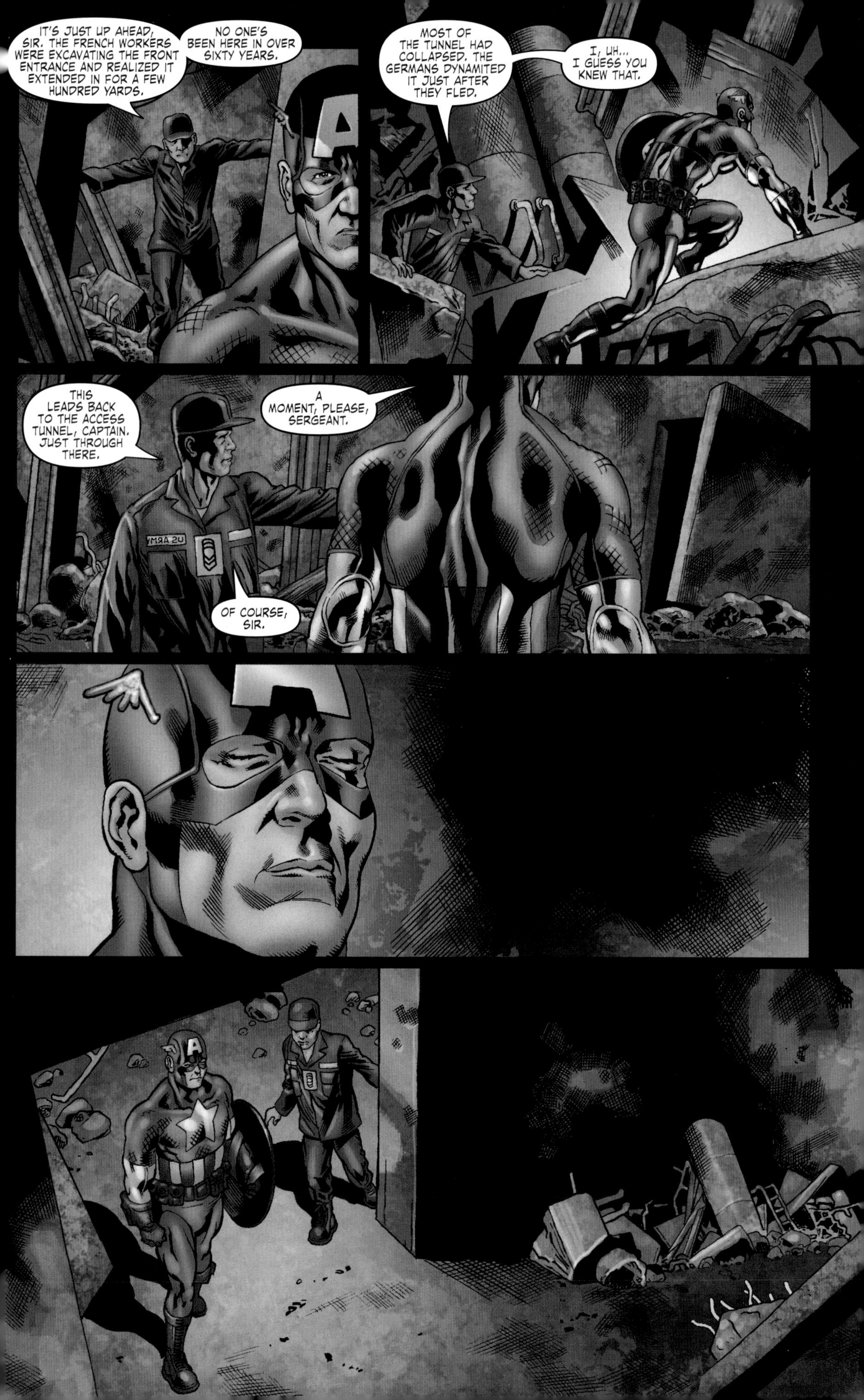
IT'S JUST UP AHEAD, SIR. THE FRENCH WORKERS WERE EXCAVATING THE FRONT ENTRANCE AND REALIZED IT EXTENDED IN FOR A FEW HUNDRED YARDS.
NO ONE'S BEEN HERE IN OVER SIXTY YEARS.
MOST OF THE TUNNEL HAD COLLAPSED. THE GERMANS DYNAMITED IT JUST AFTER THEY FLED.
I, UH... I GUESS YOU KNEW THAT.
THIS LEADS BACK TO THE ACCESS TUNNEL, CAPTAIN. JUST THROUGH THERE.
A MOMENT, PLEASE, SERGEANT.
OF COURSE, SIR.
US ARMY

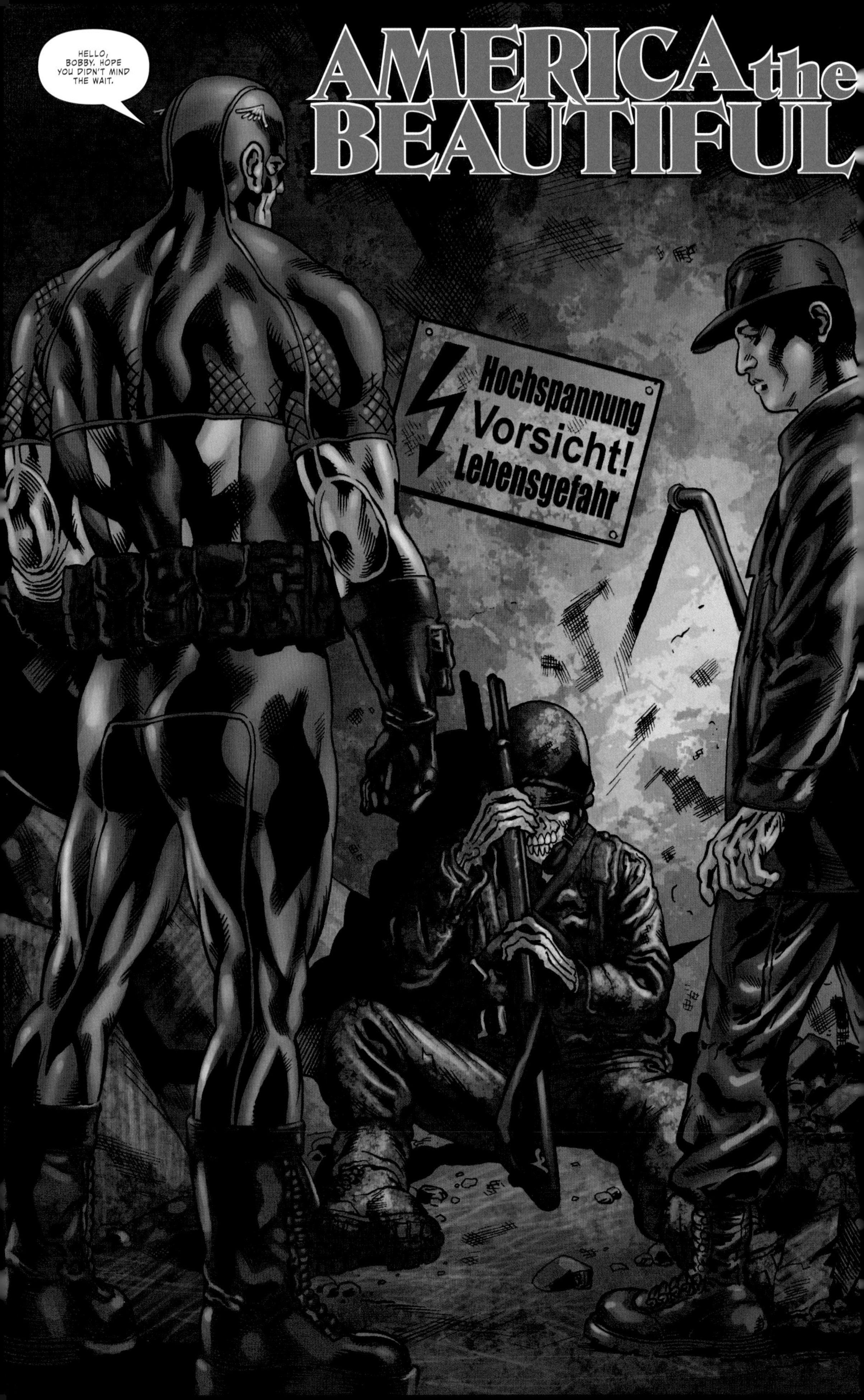
HELLO, BOBBY. HOPE YOU DIDN'T MIND THE WAIT.
AMERICA the BEAUTIFUL
Hochspannung
Vorsicht!
Lebensgefahr

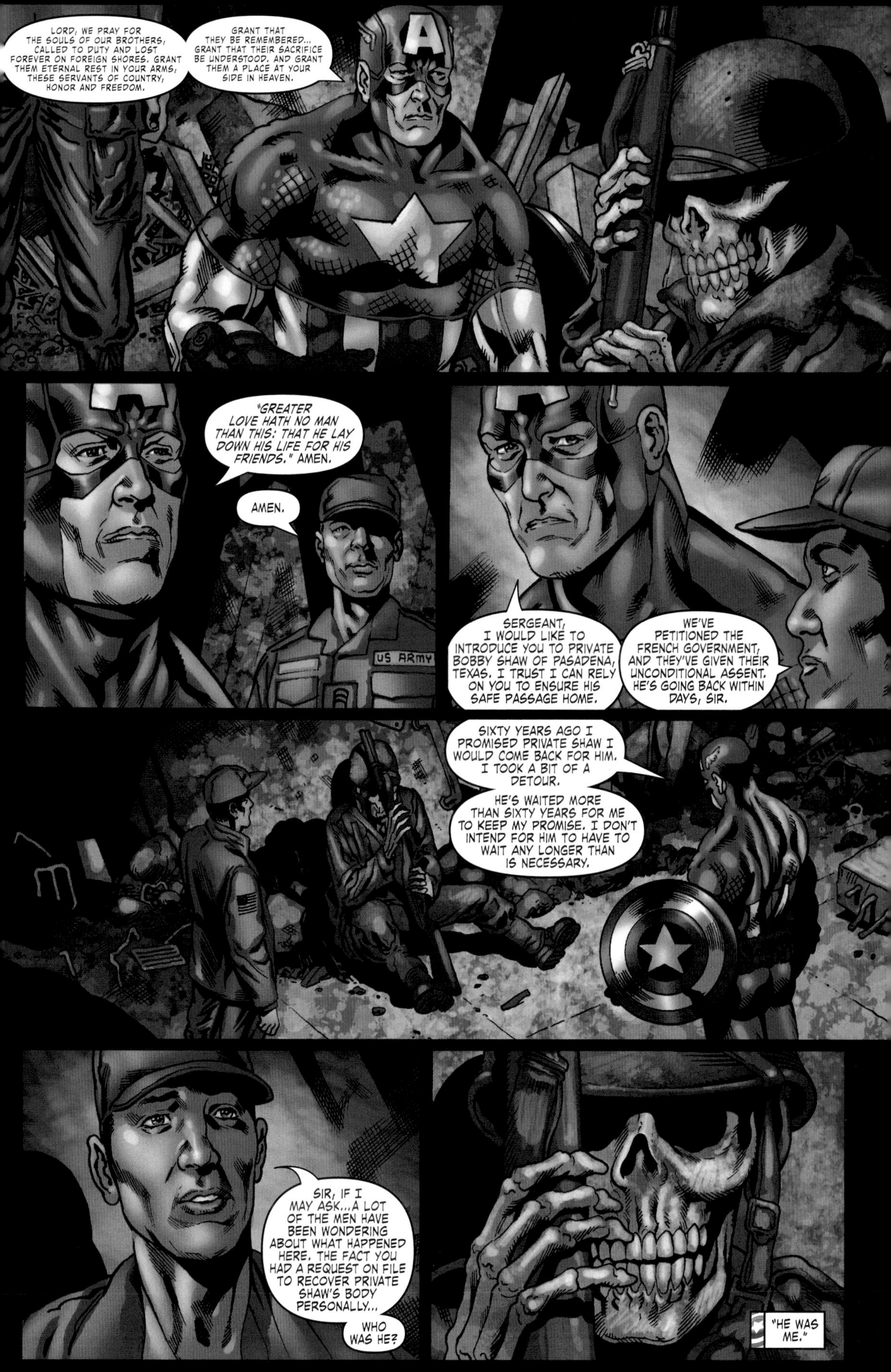
LORD, WE PRAY FOR THE SOULS OF OUR BROTHERS, CALLED TO DUTY AND LOST FOREVER ON FOREIGN SHORES. GRANT THEM ETERNAL REST IN YOUR ARMS, THESE SERVANTS OF COUNTRY, HONOR AND FREEDOM.
GRANT THAT THEY BE REMEMBERED... GRANT THAT THEIR SACRIFICE BE UNDERSTOOD, AND GRANT THEM A PLACE AT YOUR SIDE IN HEAVEN.
"GREATER LOVE HATH NO MAN THAN THIS: THAT HE LAY DOWN HIS LIFE FOR HIS FRIENDS." AMEN.
AMEN.
US ARMY
SERGEANT, I WOULD LIKE TO INTRODUCE YOU TO PRIVATE BOBBY SHAW OF PASADENA, TEXAS. I TRUST I CAN RELY ON YOU TO ENSURE HIS SAFE PASSAGE HOME.
WE'VE PETITIONED THE FRENCH GOVERNMENT, AND THEY'VE GIVEN THEIR UNCONDITIONAL ASSENT. HE'S GOING BACK WITHIN DAYS, SIR.
SIXTY YEARS AGO I PROMISED PRIVATE SHAW I WOULD COME BACK FOR HIM. I TOOK A BIT OF A DETOUR.
HE'S WAITED MORE THAN SIXTY YEARS FOR ME TO KEEP MY PROMISE. I DON'T INTEND FOR HIM TO HAVE TO WAIT ANY LONGER THAN IS NECESSARY.
SIR, IF I MAY ASK...A LOT OF THE MEN HAVE BEEN WONDERING ABOUT WHAT HAPPENED HERE. THE FACT YOU HAD A REQUEST ON FILE TO RECOVER PRIVATE SHAW'S BODY PERSONALLY...
WHO WAS HE?
"HE WAS ME."

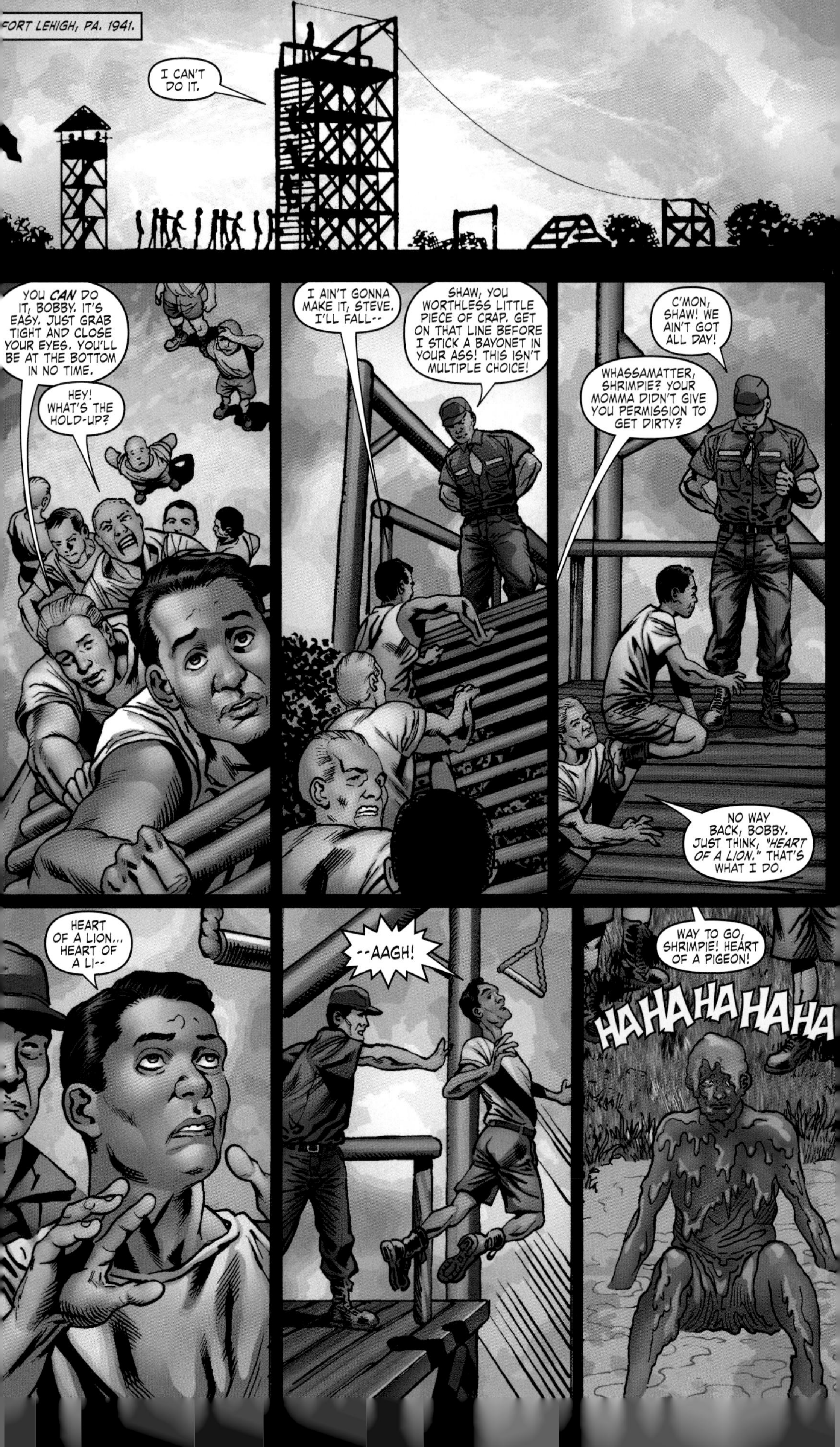
FORT LEHIGH, PA. 1941.
I CAN'T DO IT.
YOU CAN DO IT, BOBBY. IT'S EASY. JUST GRAB TIGHT AND CLOSE YOUR EYES. YOU'LL BE AT THE BOTTOM IN NO TIME.
HEY! WHAT'S THE HOLD-UP?
I AIN'T GONNA MAKE IT, STEVE. I'LL FALL--
SHAW, YOU WORTHLESS LITTLE PIECE OF CRAP. GET ON THAT LINE BEFORE I STICK A BAYONET IN YOUR ASS! THIS ISN'T MULTIPLE CHOICE!
C'MON, SHAW! WE AIN'T GOT ALL DAY!
WHASSAMATTER, SHRIMPIE? YOUR MOMMA DIDN'T GIVE YOU PERMISSION TO GET DIRTY?
NO WAY BACK, BOBBY. JUST THINK, "HEART OF A LION." THAT'S WHAT I DO.
HEART OF A LION... HEART OF A LI--
--AAGH!
WAY TO GO, SHRIMPIE! HEART OF A PIGEON!
HAHAHAHAHAHA

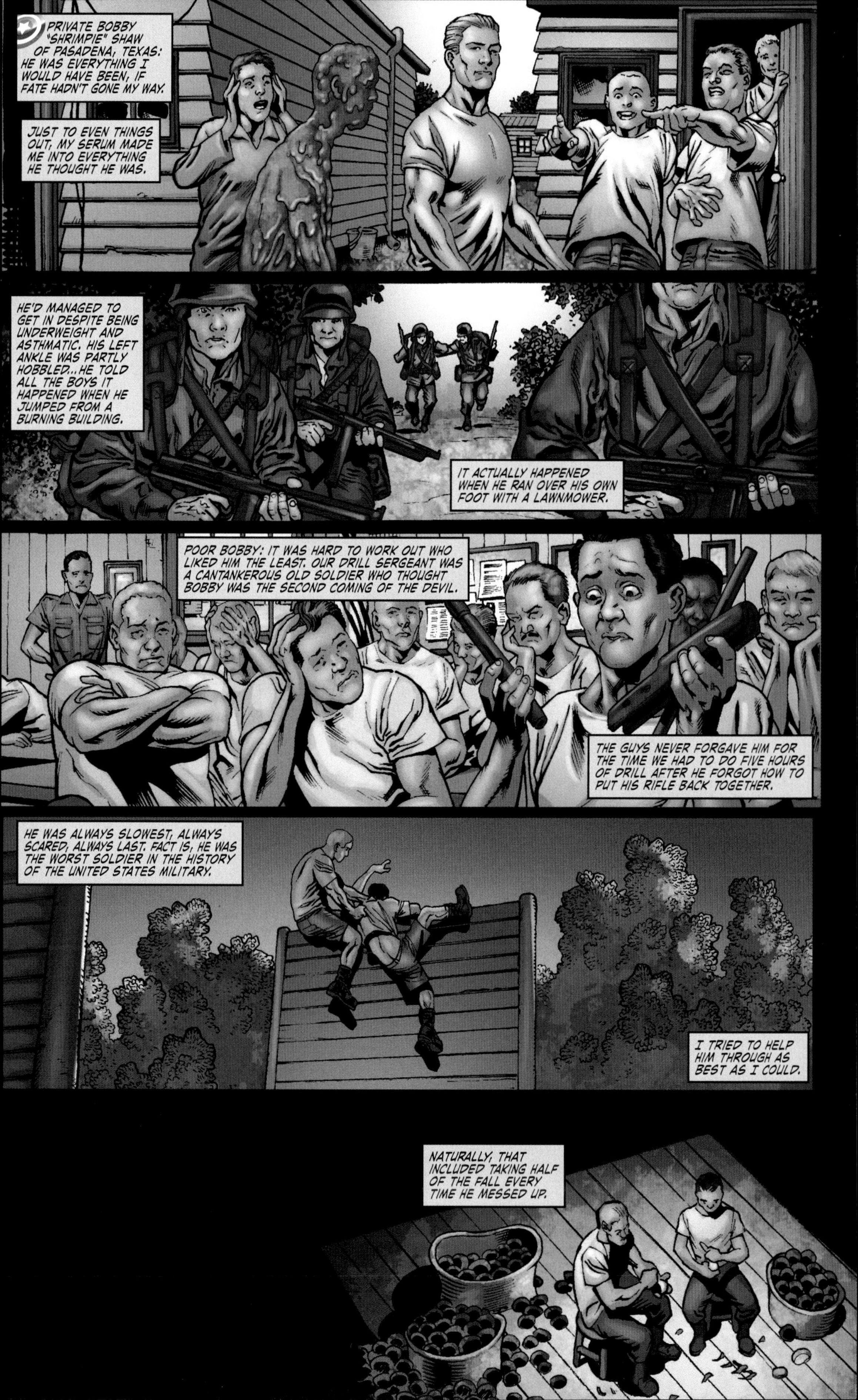
PRIVATE BOBBY "SHRIMPIE" SHAW OF PASADENA, TEXAS: HE WAS EVERYTHING I WOULD HAVE BEEN, IF FATE HADN'T GONE MY WAY.
JUST TO EVEN THINGS OUT, MY SERUM MADE ME INTO EVERYTHING HE THOUGHT HE WAS.
HE'D MANAGED TO GET IN DESPITE BEING UNDERWEIGHT AND ASTHMATIC. HIS LEFT ANKLE WAS PARTLY HOBBLED...HE TOLD ALL THE BOYS IT HAPPENED WHEN HE JUMPED FROM A BURNING BUILDING.
IT ACTUALLY HAPPENED WHEN HE RAN OVER HIS OWN FOOT WITH A LAWNMOWER.
POOR BOBBY: IT WAS HARD TO WORK OUT WHO LIKED HIM THE LEAST. OUR DRILL SERGEANT WAS A CANTANKEROUS OLD SOLDIER WHO THOUGHT BOBBY WAS THE SECOND COMING OF THE DEVIL.
THE GUYS NEVER FORGAVE HIM FOR THE TIME WE HAD TO DO FIVE HOURS OF DRILL AFTER HE FORGOT HOW TO PUT HIS RIFLE BACK TOGETHER.
HE WAS ALWAYS SLOWEST, ALWAYS SCARED, ALWAYS LAST. FACT IS, HE WAS THE WORST SOLDIER IN THE HISTORY OF THE UNITED STATES MILITARY.
I TRIED TO HELP HIM THROUGH AS BEST AS I COULD.
NATURALLY, THAT INCLUDED TAKING HALF OF THE FALL EVERY TIME HE MESSED UP.

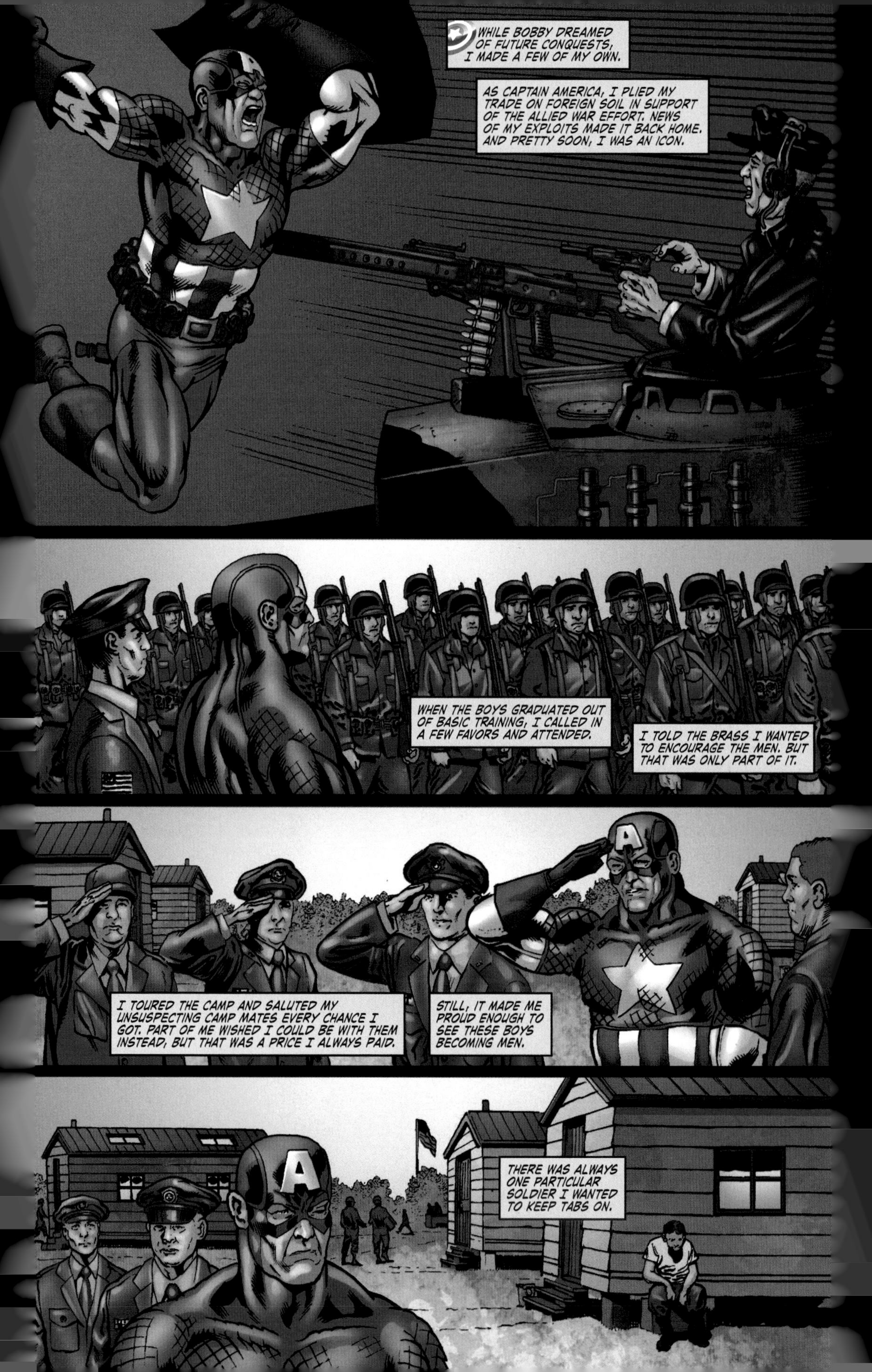
WHILE BOBBY DREAMED OF FUTURE CONQUESTS, I MADE A FEW OF MY OWN.
AS CAPTAIN AMERICA, I PLIED MY TRADE ON FOREIGN SOIL IN SUPPORT OF THE ALLIED WAR EFFORT. NEWS OF MY EXPLOITS MADE IT BACK HOME. AND PRETTY SOON, I WAS AN ICON.
WHEN THE BOYS GRADUATED OUT OF BASIC TRAINING, I CALLED IN A FEW FAVORS AND ATTENDED.
I TOLD THE BRASS I WANTED TO ENCOURAGE THE MEN. BUT THAT WAS ONLY PART OF IT.
I TOURED THE CAMP AND SALUTED MY UNSUSPECTING CAMP MATES EVERY CHANCE I GOT. PART OF ME WISHED I COULD BE WITH THEM INSTEAD, BUT THAT WAS A PRICE I ALWAYS PAID.
STILL, IT MADE ME PROUD ENOUGH TO SEE THESE BOYS BECOMING MEN.
THERE WAS ALWAYS ONE PARTICULAR SOLDIER I WANTED TO KEEP TABS ON.

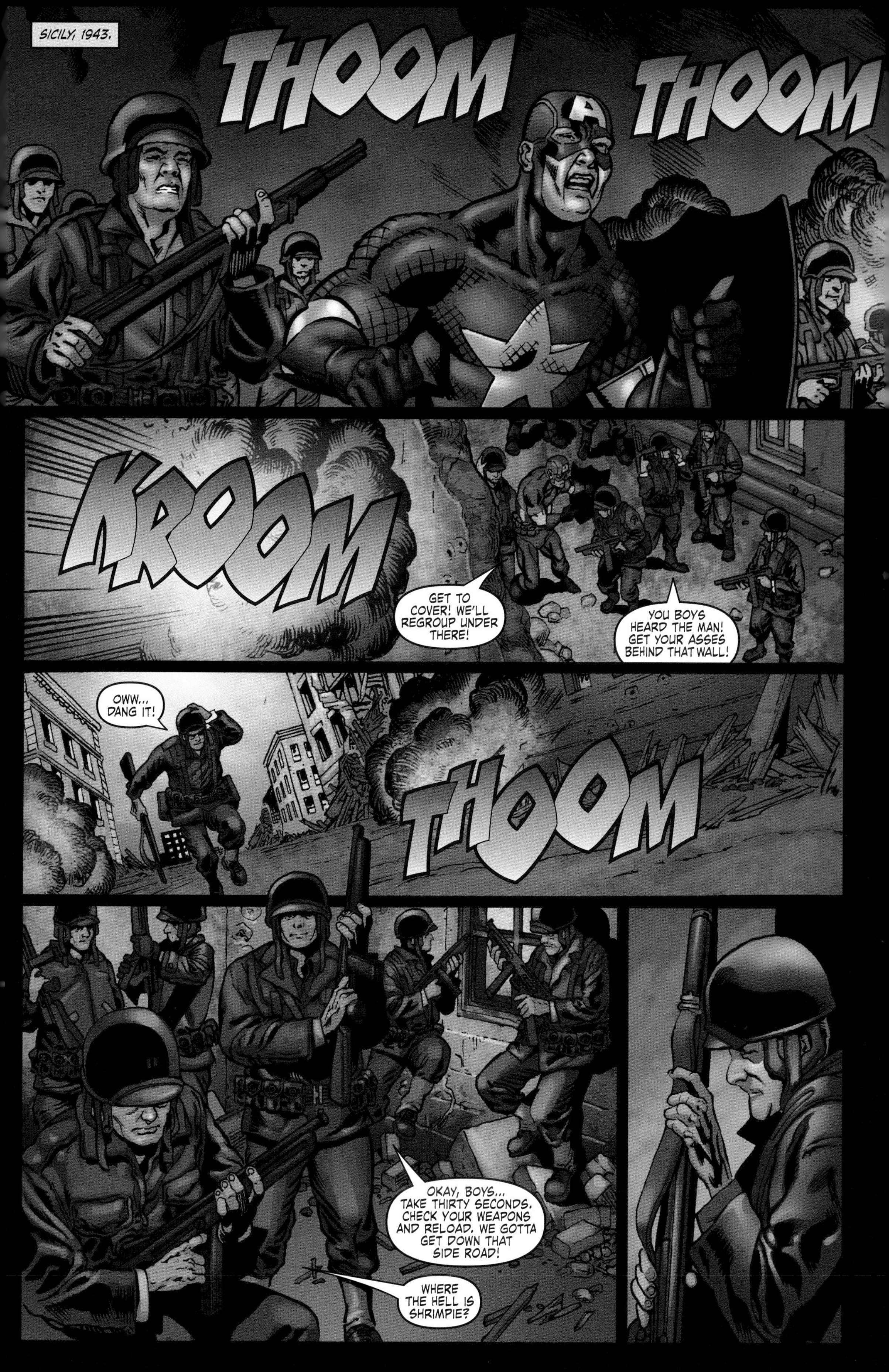
SICILY, 1943.
THOOM
THOOM
KROOM
GET TO COVER! WE'LL REGROUP UNDER THERE!
YOU BOYS HEARD THE MAN! GET YOUR ASSES BEHIND THAT WALL!
OWW... DANG IT!
THOOM
OKAY, BOYS... TAKE THIRTY SECONDS. CHECK YOUR WEAPONS AND RELOAD. WE GOTTA GET DOWN THAT SIDE ROAD!
WHERE THE HELL IS SHRIMPIE?

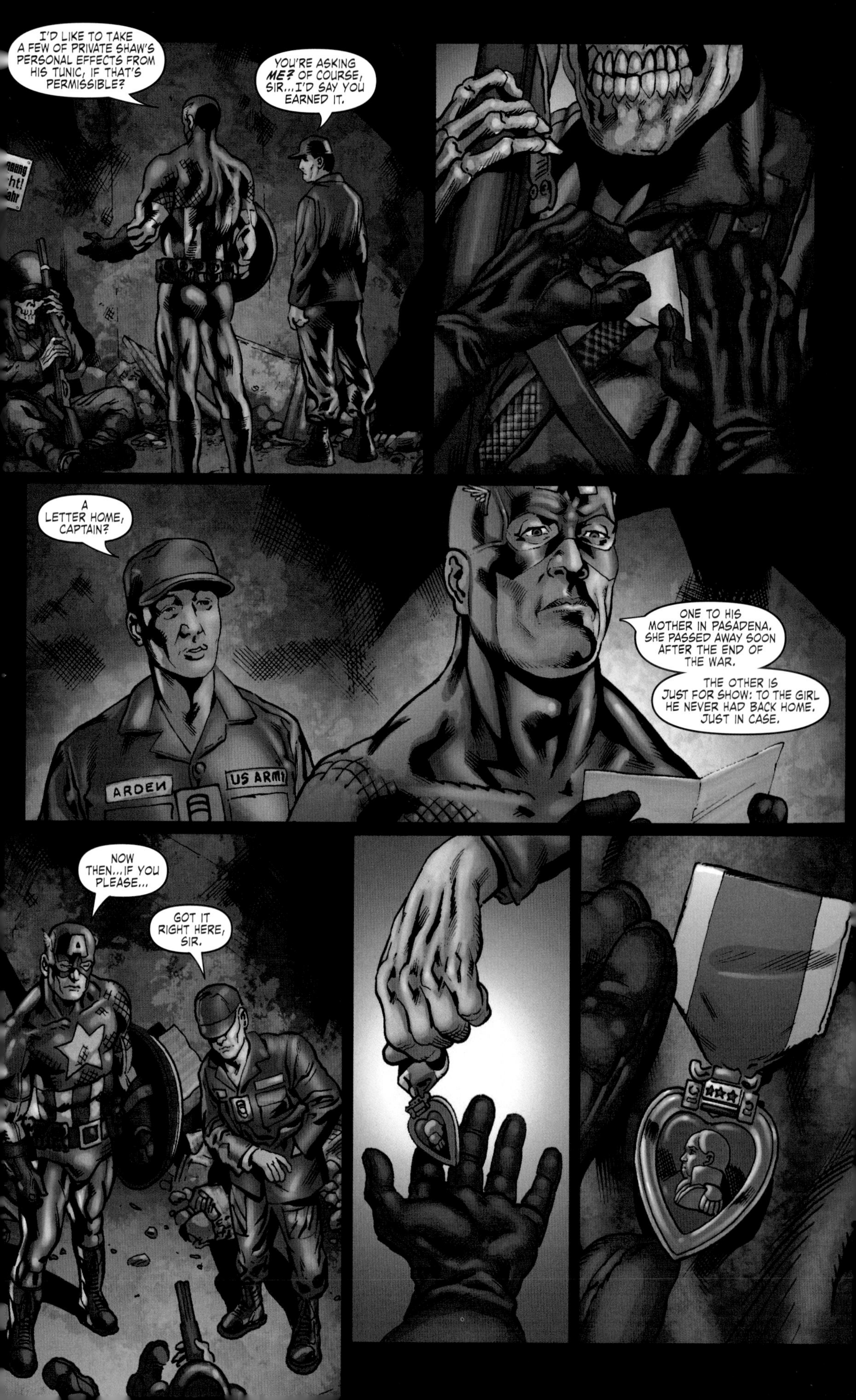
I'D LIKE TO TAKE A FEW OF PRIVATE SHAW'S PERSONAL EFFECTS FROM HIS TUNIC, IF THAT'S PERMISSIBLE?
YOU'RE ASKING ME? OF COURSE, SIR...I'D SAY YOU EARNED IT.
A LETTER HOME, CAPTAIN?
ONE TO HIS MOTHER IN PASADENA. SHE PASSED AWAY SOON AFTER THE END OF THE WAR.
THE OTHER IS JUST FOR SHOW: TO THE GIRL HE NEVER HAD BACK HOME. JUST IN CASE.
ARDEN
US ARMY
NOW THEN...IF YOU PLEASE...
GOT IT RIGHT HERE, SIR.

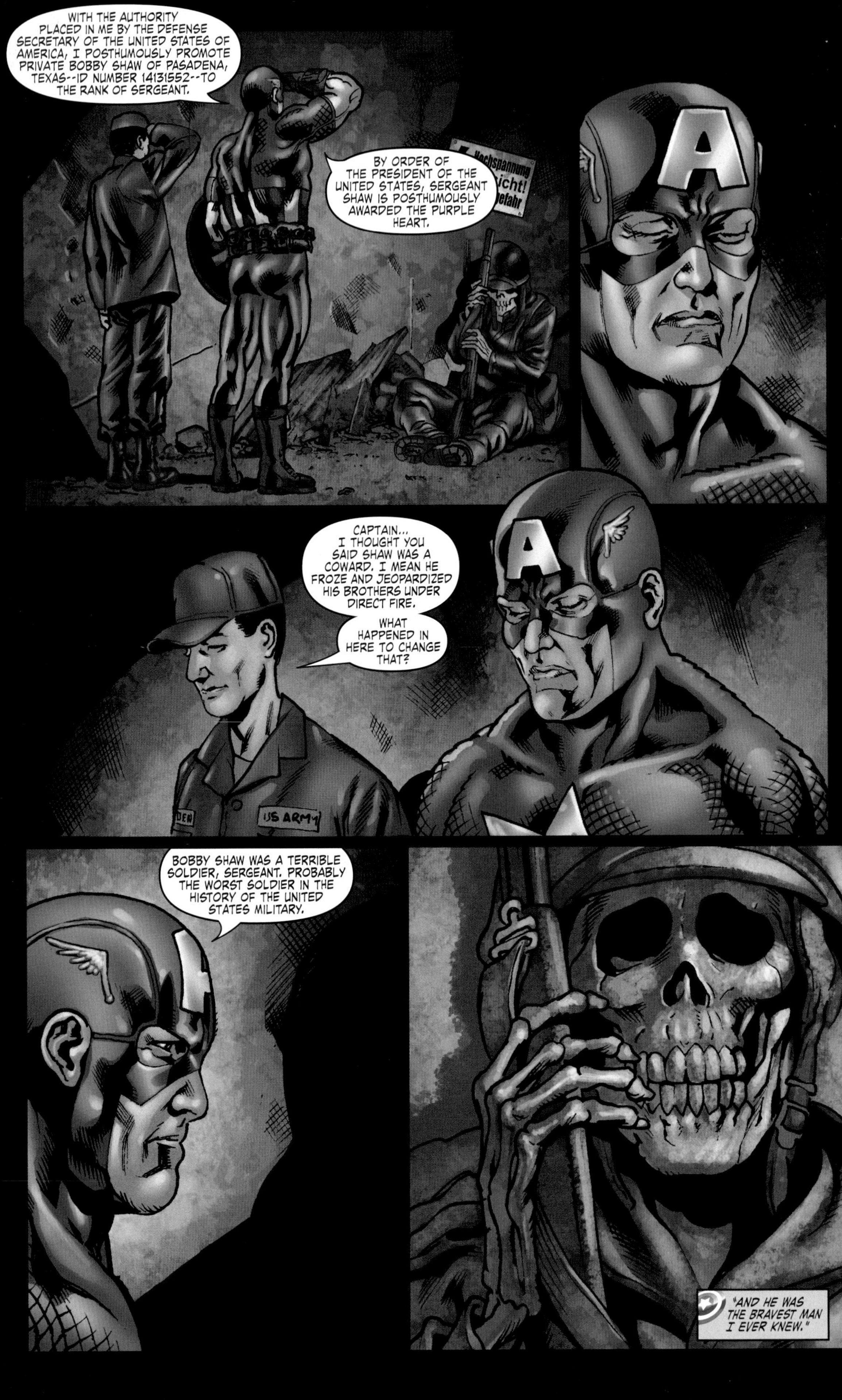
WITH THE AUTHORITY PLACED IN ME BY THE DEFENSE SECRETARY OF THE UNITED STATES OF AMERICA, I POSTHUMOUSLY PROMOTE PRIVATE BOBBY SHAW OF PASADENA, TEXAS--ID NUMBER 14131552--TO THE RANK OF SERGEANT.
BY ORDER OF THE PRESIDENT OF THE UNITED STATES, SERGEANT SHAW IS POSTHUMOUSLY AWARDED THE PURPLE HEART.
CAPTAIN... I THOUGHT YOU SAID SHAW WAS A COWARD. I MEAN HE FROZE AND JEOPARDIZED HIS BROTHERS UNDER DIRECT FIRE.
WHAT HAPPENED IN HERE TO CHANGE THAT?
US ARMY
BOBBY SHAW WAS A TERRIBLE SOLDIER, SERGEANT. PROBABLY THE WORST SOLDIER IN THE HISTORY OF THE UNITED STATES MILITARY.
"AND HE WAS THE BRAVEST MAN I EVER KNEW."

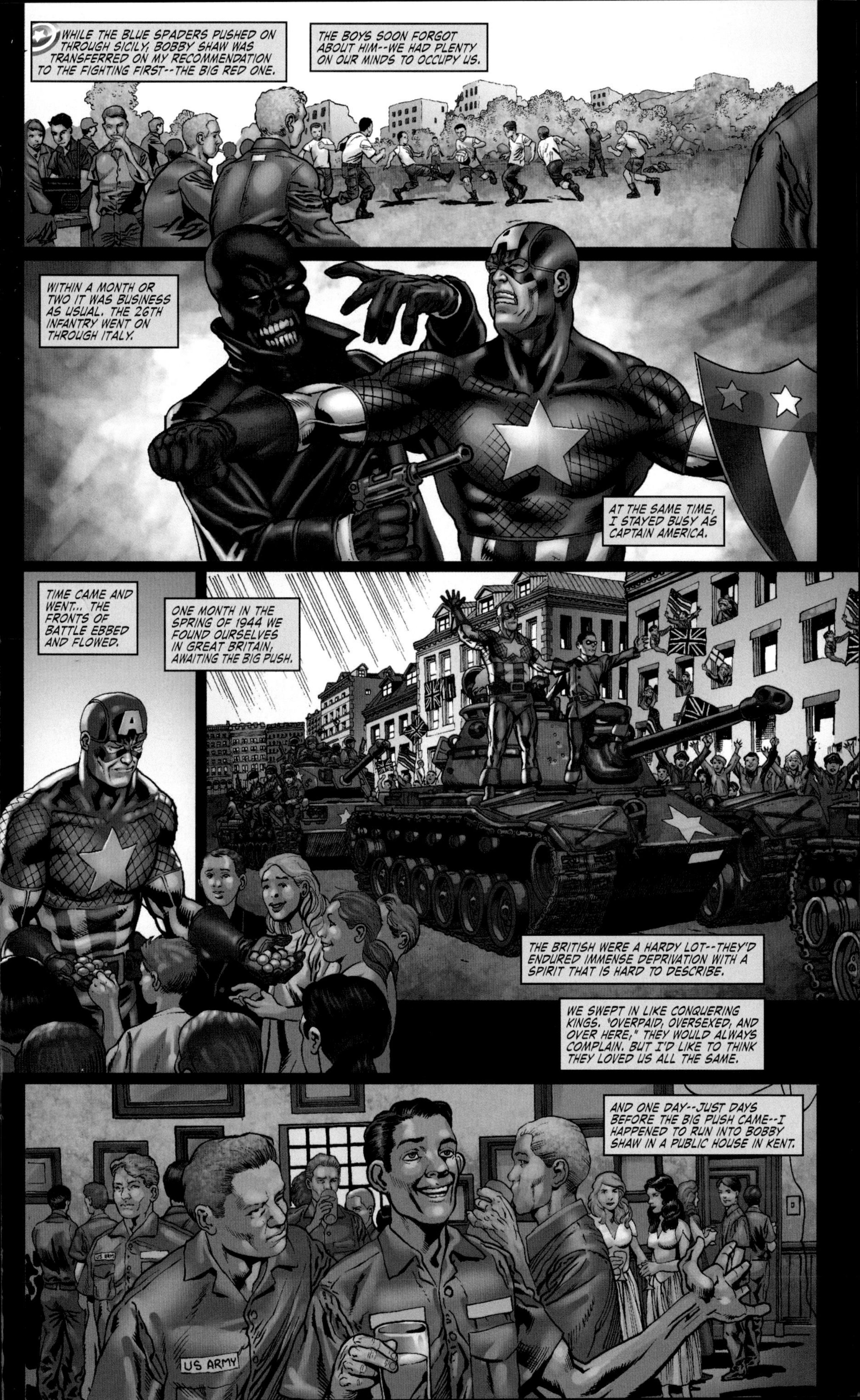
WHILE THE BLUE SPADERS PUSHED ON THROUGH SICILY, BOBBY SHAW WAS TRANSFERRED ON MY RECOMMENDATION TO THE FIGHTING FIRST--THE BIG RED ONE.
THE BOYS SOON FORGOT ABOUT HIM--WE HAD PLENTY ON OUR MINDS TO OCCUPY US.
WITHIN A MONTH OR TWO IT WAS BUSINESS AS USUAL. THE 26TH INFANTRY WENT ON THROUGH ITALY.
AT THE SAME TIME, I STAYED BUSY AS CAPTAIN AMERICA.
TIME CAME AND WENT... THE FRONTS OF BATTLE EBBED AND FLOWED.
ONE MONTH IN THE SPRING OF 1944 WE FOUND OURSELVES IN GREAT BRITAIN, AWAITING THE BIG PUSH.
THE BRITISH WERE A HARDY LOT--THEY'D ENDURED IMMENSE DEPRIVATION WITH A SPIRIT THAT IS HARD TO DESCRIBE.
WE SWEPT IN LIKE CONQUERING KINGS. "OVERPAID, OVERSEXED, AND OVER HERE," THEY WOULD ALWAYS COMPLAIN. BUT I'D LIKE TO THINK THEY LOVED US ALL THE SAME.
AND ONE DAY--JUST DAYS BEFORE THE BIG PUSH CAME--I HAPPENED TO RUN INTO BOBBY SHAW IN A PUBLIC HOUSE IN KENT.
US ARMY
US ARMY

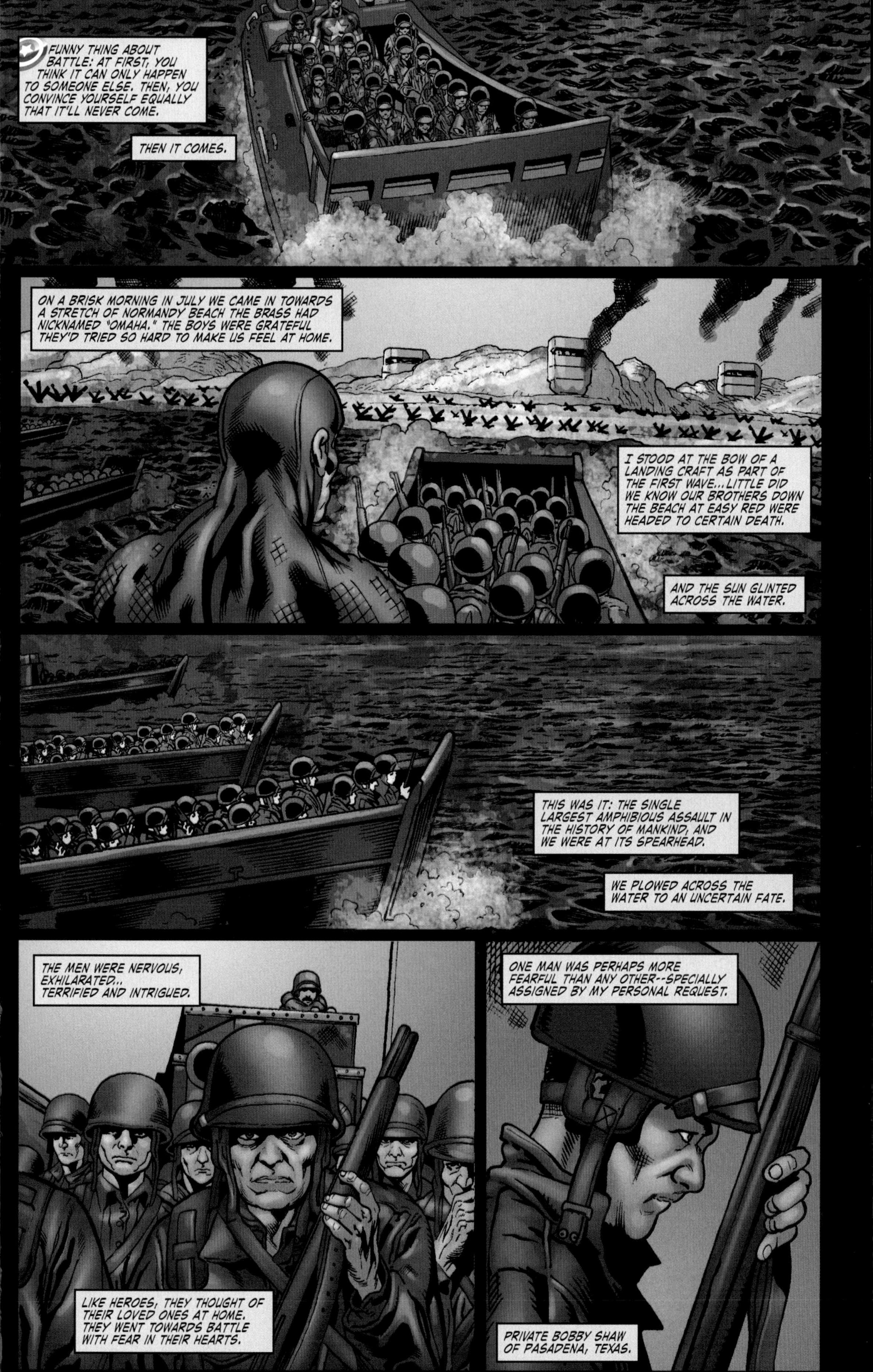
FUNNY THING ABOUT BATTLE: AT FIRST, YOU THINK IT CAN ONLY HAPPEN TO SOMEONE ELSE. THEN, YOU CONVINCE YOURSELF EQUALLY THAT IT'LL NEVER COME.
THEN IT COMES.
ON A BRISK MORNING IN JULY WE CAME IN TOWARDS A STRETCH OF NORMANDY BEACH THE BRASS HAD NICKNAMED "OMAHA." THE BOYS WERE GRATEFUL THEY'D TRIED SO HARD TO MAKE US FEEL AT HOME.
I STOOD AT THE BOW OF A LANDING CRAFT AS PART OF THE FIRST WAVE...LITTLE DID WE KNOW OUR BROTHERS DOWN THE BEACH AT EASY RED WERE HEADED TO CERTAIN DEATH.
AND THE SUN GLINTED ACROSS THE WATER.
THIS WAS IT: THE SINGLE LARGEST AMPHIBIOUS ASSAULT IN THE HISTORY OF MANKIND, AND WE WERE AT ITS SPEARHEAD.
WE PLOWED ACROSS THE WATER TO AN UNCERTAIN FATE.
THE MEN WERE NERVOUS, EXHILARATED... TERRIFIED AND INTRIGUED.
LIKE HEROES, THEY THOUGHT OF THEIR LOVED ONES AT HOME. THEY WENT TOWARDS BATTLE WITH FEAR IN THEIR HEARTS.
ONE MAN WAS PERHAPS MORE FEARFUL THAN ANY OTHER--SPECIALLY ASSIGNED BY MY PERSONAL REQUEST.
PRIVATE BOBBY SHAW OF PASADENA, TEXAS.

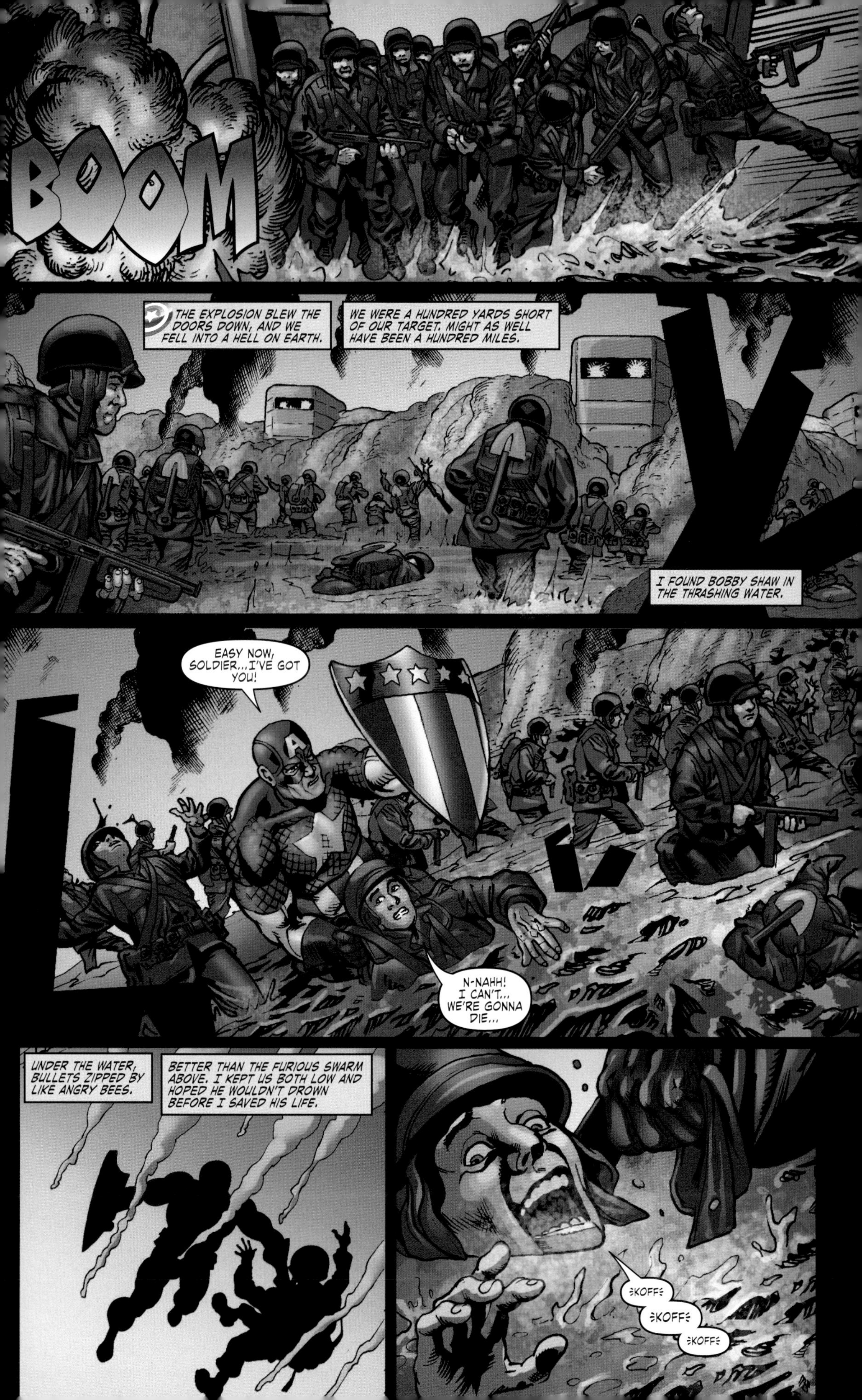
BOOM
THE EXPLOSION BLEW THE DOORS DOWN, AND WE FELL INTO A HELL ON EARTH.
WE WERE A HUNDRED YARDS SHORT OF OUR TARGET. MIGHT AS WELL HAVE BEEN A HUNDRED MILES.
I FOUND BOBBY SHAW IN THE THRASHING WATER.
EASY NOW, SOLDIER...I'VE GOT YOU!
N-NAHH! I CAN'T... WE'RE GONNA DIE...
UNDER THE WATER, BULLETS ZIPPED BY LIKE ANGRY BEES.
BETTER THAN THE FURIOUS SWARM ABOVE. I KEPT US BOTH LOW AND HOPED HE WOULDN'T DROWN BEFORE I SAVED HIS LIFE.
KOFF
KOFF
KOFF

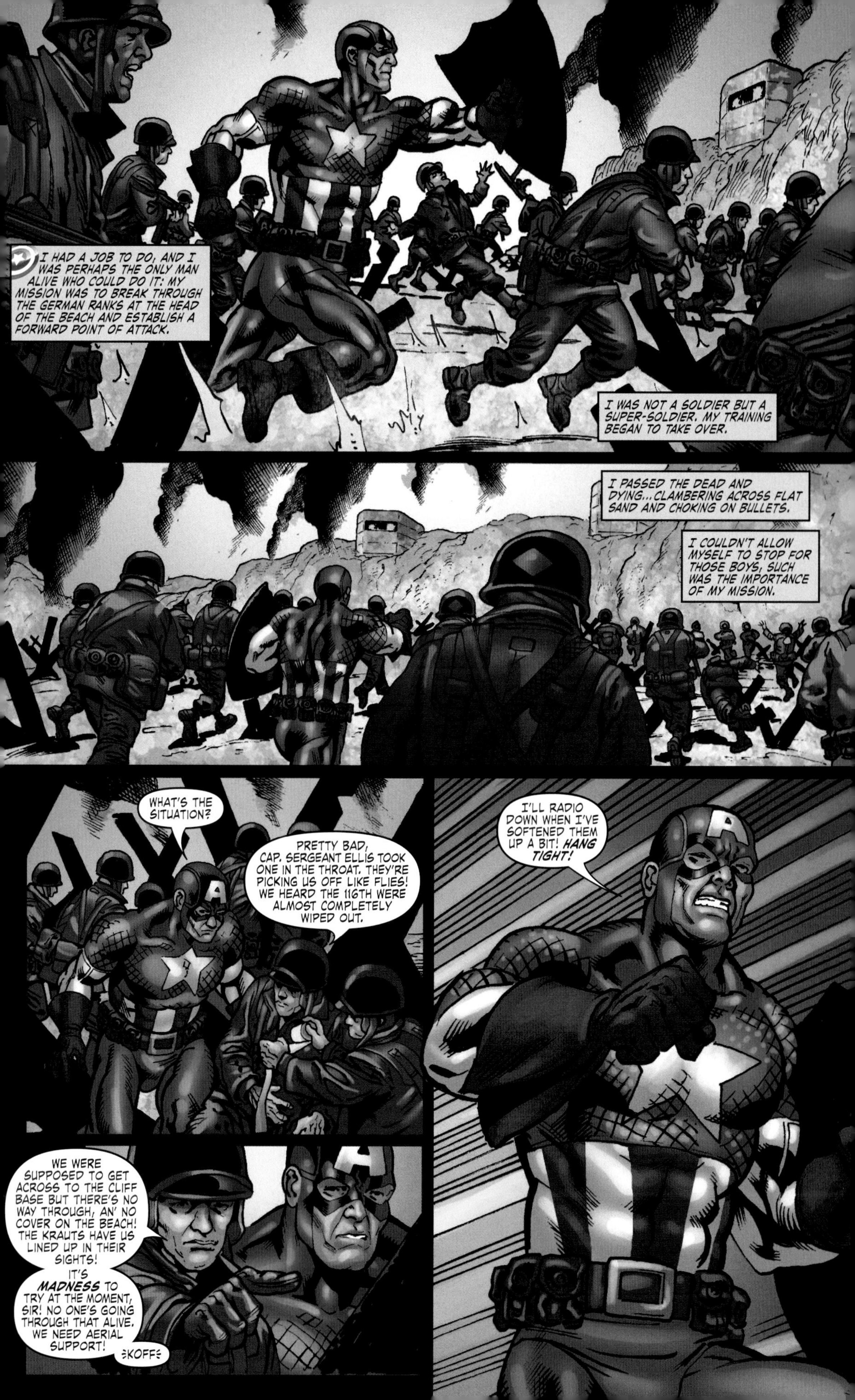
I HAD A JOB TO DO, AND I WAS PERHAPS THE ONLY MAN ALIVE WHO COULD DO IT: MY MISSION WAS TO BREAK THROUGH THE GERMAN RANKS AT THE HEAD OF THE BEACH AND ESTABLISH A FORWARD POINT OF ATTACK.
I WAS NOT A SOLDIER BUT A SUPER-SOLDIER. MY TRAINING BEGAN TO TAKE OVER.
I PASSED THE DEAD AND DYING...CLAMBERING ACROSS FLAT SAND AND CHOKING ON BULLETS.
I COULDN'T ALLOW MYSELF TO STOP FOR THOSE BOYS, SUCH WAS THE IMPORTANCE OF MY MISSION.
WHAT'S THE SITUATION?
PRETTY BAD, CAP. SERGEANT ELLIS TOOK ONE IN THE THROAT. THEY'RE PICKING US OFF LIKE FLIES! WE HEARD THE 116TH WERE ALMOST COMPLETELY WIPED OUT.
WE WERE SUPPOSED TO GET ACROSS TO THE CLIFF BASE BUT THERE'S NO WAY THROUGH, AN' NO COVER ON THE BEACH! THE KRAUTS HAVE US LINED UP IN THEIR SIGHTS!
IT'S MADNESS TO TRY AT THE MOMENT, SIR! NO ONE'S GOING THROUGH THAT ALIVE. WE NEED AERIAL SUPPORT!
KOFF
I'LL RADIO DOWN WHEN I'VE SOFTENED THEM UP A BIT! HANG TIGHT!

I RAN THAT MORNING THROUGH A MAELSTROM OF LEAD AND SHRAPNEL. BUT I KNEW MY PURPOSE, AND I NEVER QUESTIONED THAT THIS WAS WHERE I WAS ALWAYS DESTINED TO BE.

FOR ME IT WAS EASY-- NOT SO FOR THE BOYS OF THE BIG RED ONE.

I COMPETED AGAINST A THOUSAND BULLETS WITH A CURIOUS SENSE OF CALM.

PING PANG

PANG

sping
ping
pang
ping

DAMMIT.

FOXTROT COMPANY, THIS IS *CAPTAIN AMERICA:* I'VE SPOTTED AN ACCESS TUNNEL JUST TO THE WEST-SOUTH-WEST! IT'S PROBABLY A MAINTENANCE PARTITION THAT LEADS DIRECTLY UP INTO THE GERMAN DEFENSIVE POSITIONS.

FOXTROT, DO YOU COPY? OVER.

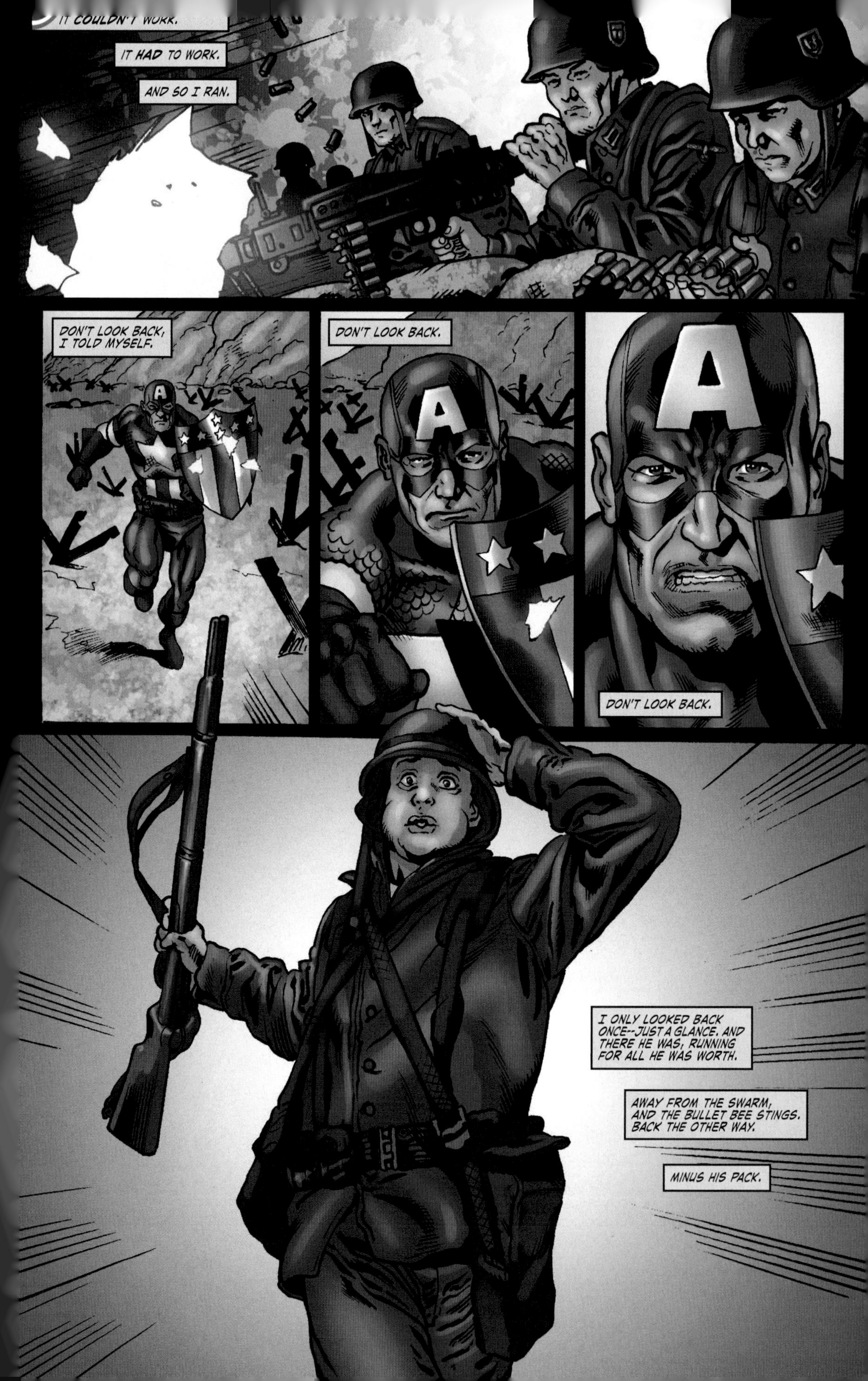
IT COULDN'T WORK.
IT HAD TO WORK.
AND SO I RAN.
DON'T LOOK BACK, I TOLD MYSELF.
DON'T LOOK BACK.
DON'T LOOK BACK.
I ONLY LOOKED BACK ONCE--JUST A GLANCE. AND THERE HE WAS, RUNNING FOR ALL HE WAS WORTH.
AWAY FROM THE SWARM, AND THE BULLET BEE STINGS. BACK THE OTHER WAY.
MINUS HIS PACK.

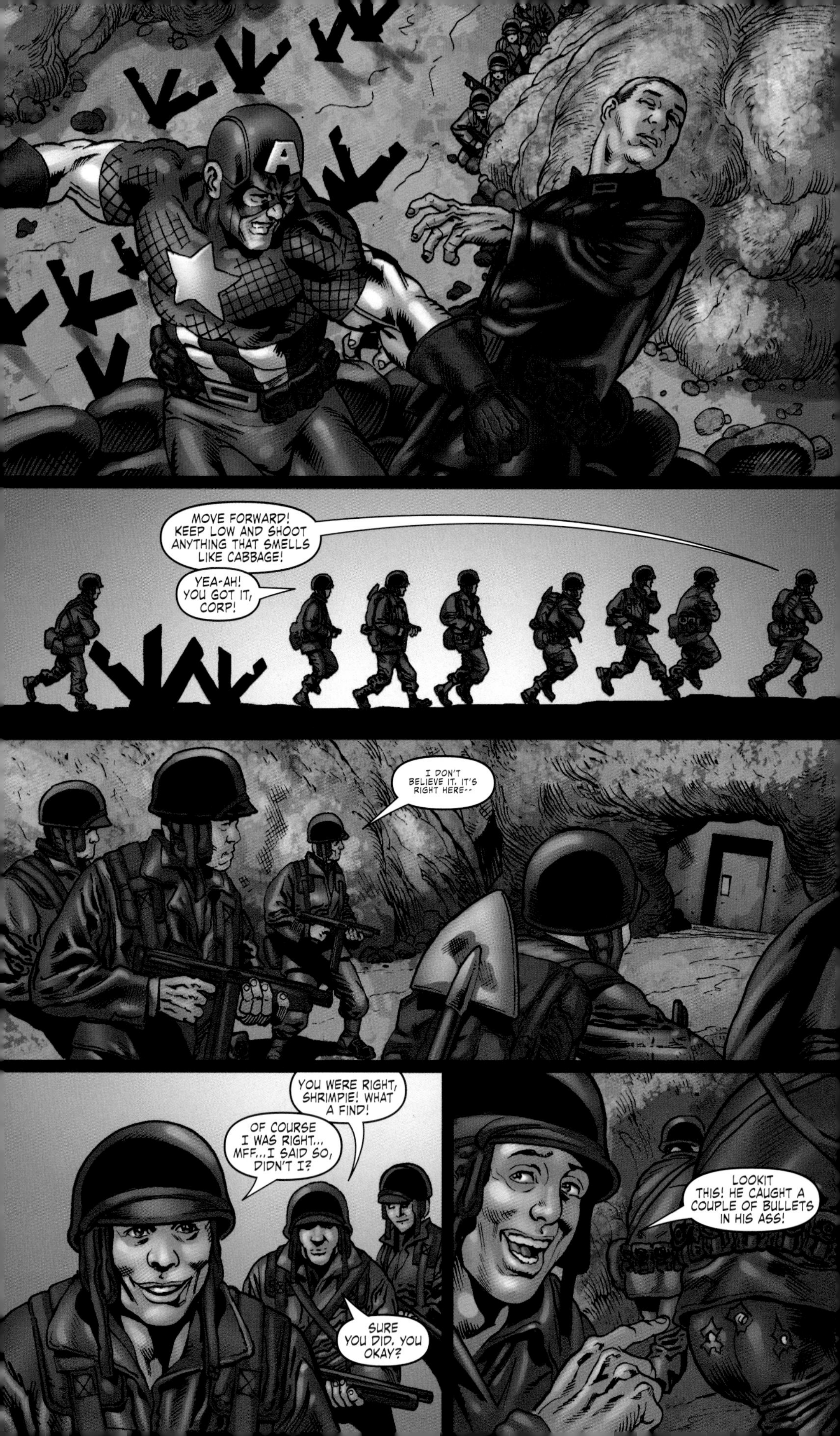
MOVE FORWARD! KEEP LOW AND SHOOT ANYTHING THAT SMELLS LIKE CABBAGE!
YEA-AH! YOU GOT IT, CORP!
I DON'T BELIEVE IT. IT'S RIGHT HERE--
YOU WERE RIGHT, SHRIMPIE! WHAT A FIND!
OF COURSE I WAS RIGHT... MFF...I SAID SO, DIDN'T I?
SURE YOU DID. YOU OKAY?
LOOKIT THIS! HE CAUGHT A COUPLE OF BULLETS IN HIS ASS!

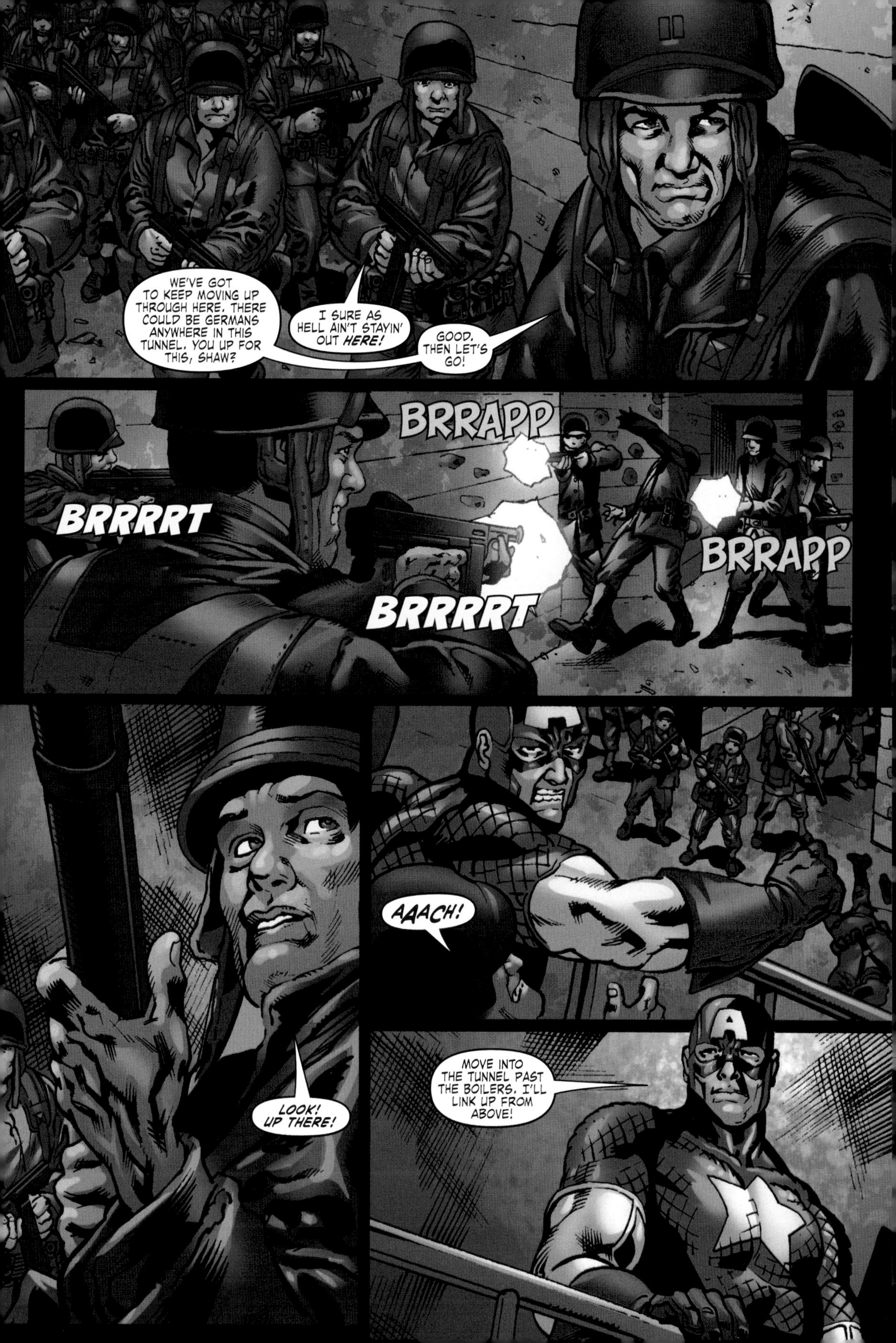
WE'VE GOT TO KEEP MOVING UP THROUGH HERE. THERE COULD BE GERMANS ANYWHERE IN THIS TUNNEL. YOU UP FOR THIS, SHAW?
I SURE AS HELL AIN'T STAYIN' OUT *HERE!*
GOOD. THEN LET'S GO!
BRRAPP
BRRRRT
BRRAPP
BRRRRT
LOOK! UP THERE!
AAACH!
MOVE INTO THE TUNNEL PAST THE BOILERS. I'LL LINK UP FROM ABOVE!

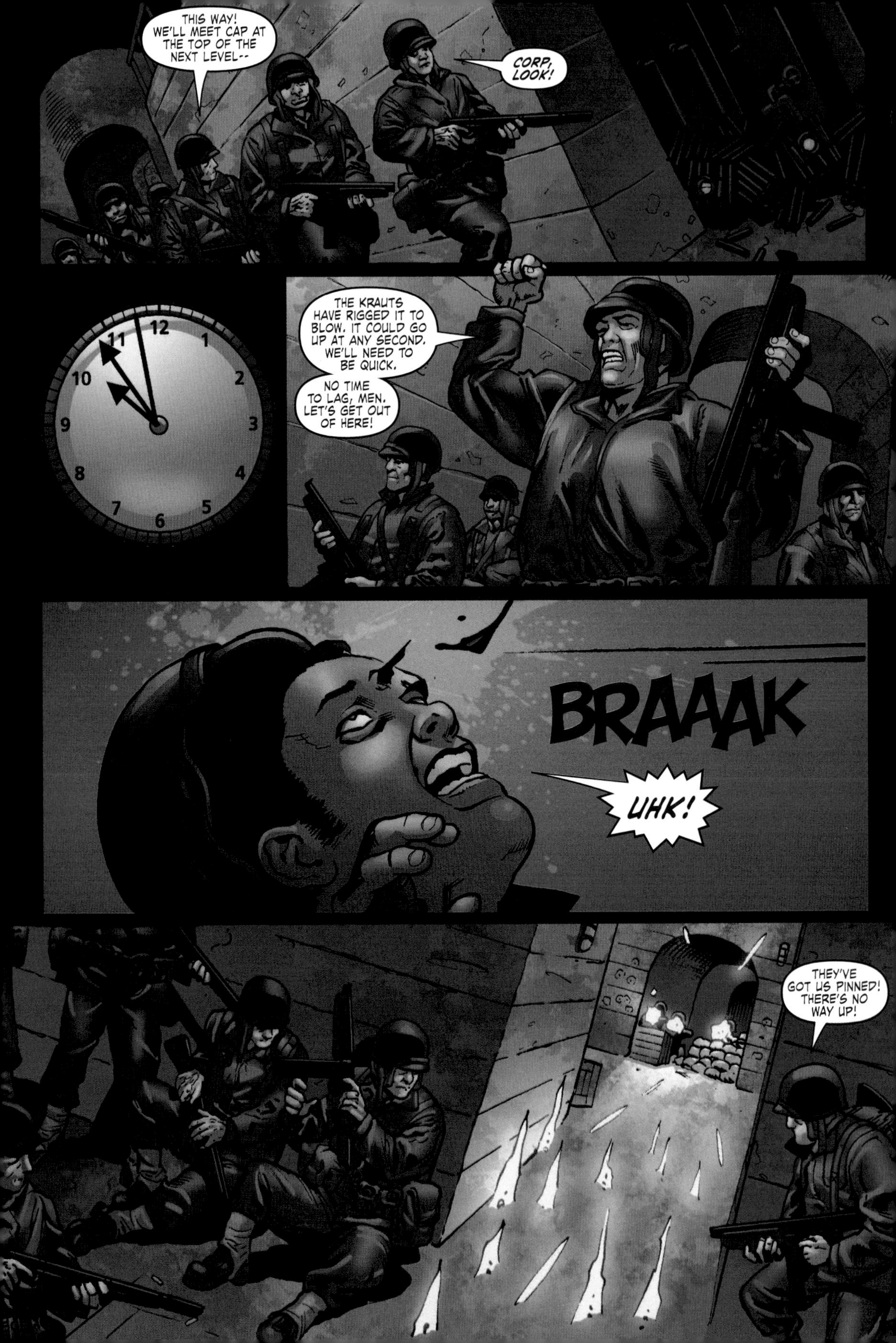
THIS WAY! WE'LL MEET CAP AT THE TOP OF THE NEXT LEVEL--
CORP, LOOK!
THE KRAUTS HAVE RIGGED IT TO BLOW. IT COULD GO UP AT ANY SECOND. WE'LL NEED TO BE QUICK.
NO TIME TO LAG, MEN. LET'S GET OUT OF HERE!
BRAAAK
UHK!
THEY'VE GOT US PINNED! THERE'S NO WAY UP!

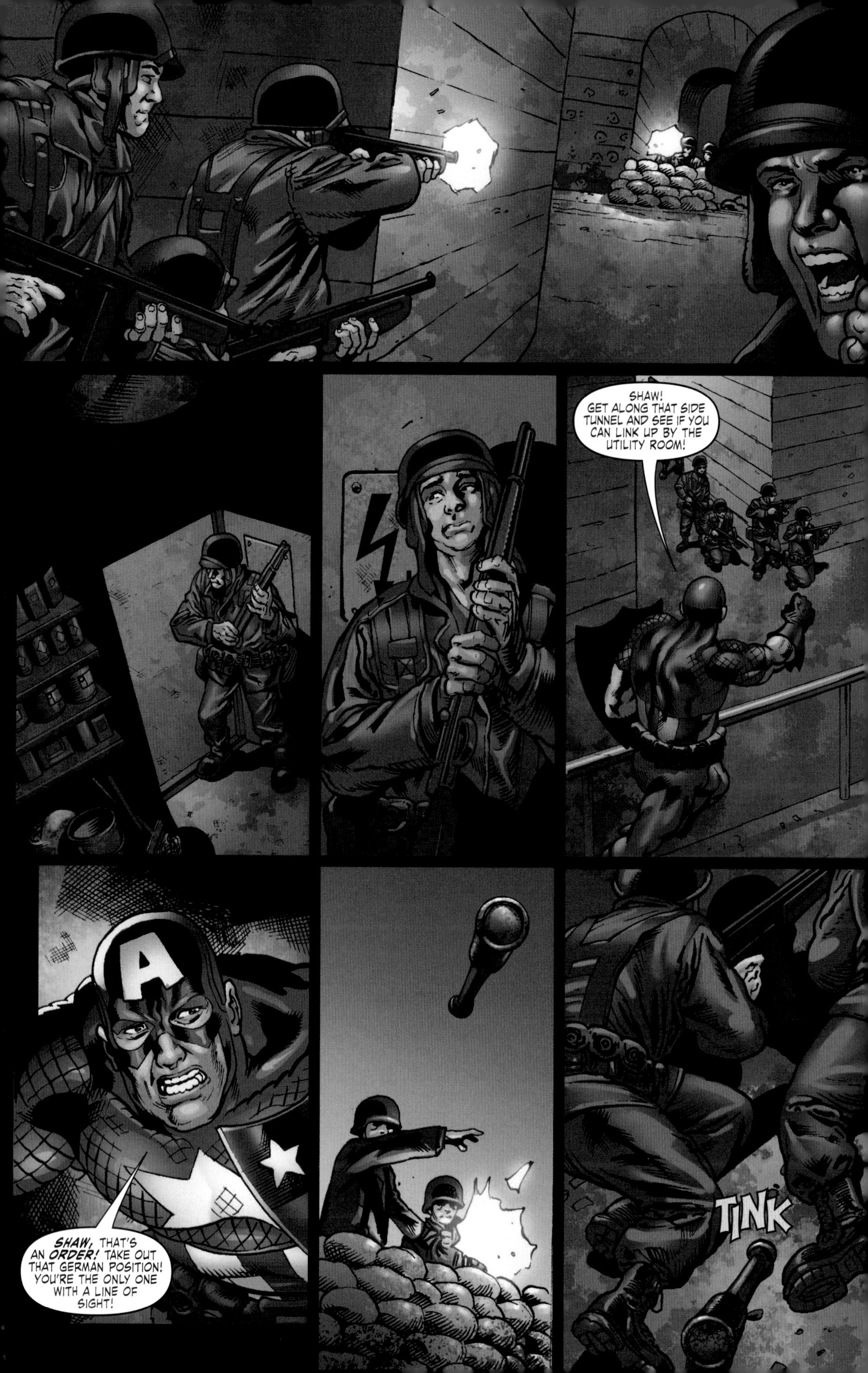
SHAW! GET ALONG THAT SIDE TUNNEL AND SEE IF YOU CAN LINK UP BY THE UTILITY ROOM!
SHAW, THAT'S AN ORDER! TAKE OUT THAT GERMAN POSITION! YOU'RE THE ONLY ONE WITH A LINE OF SIGHT!
TINK

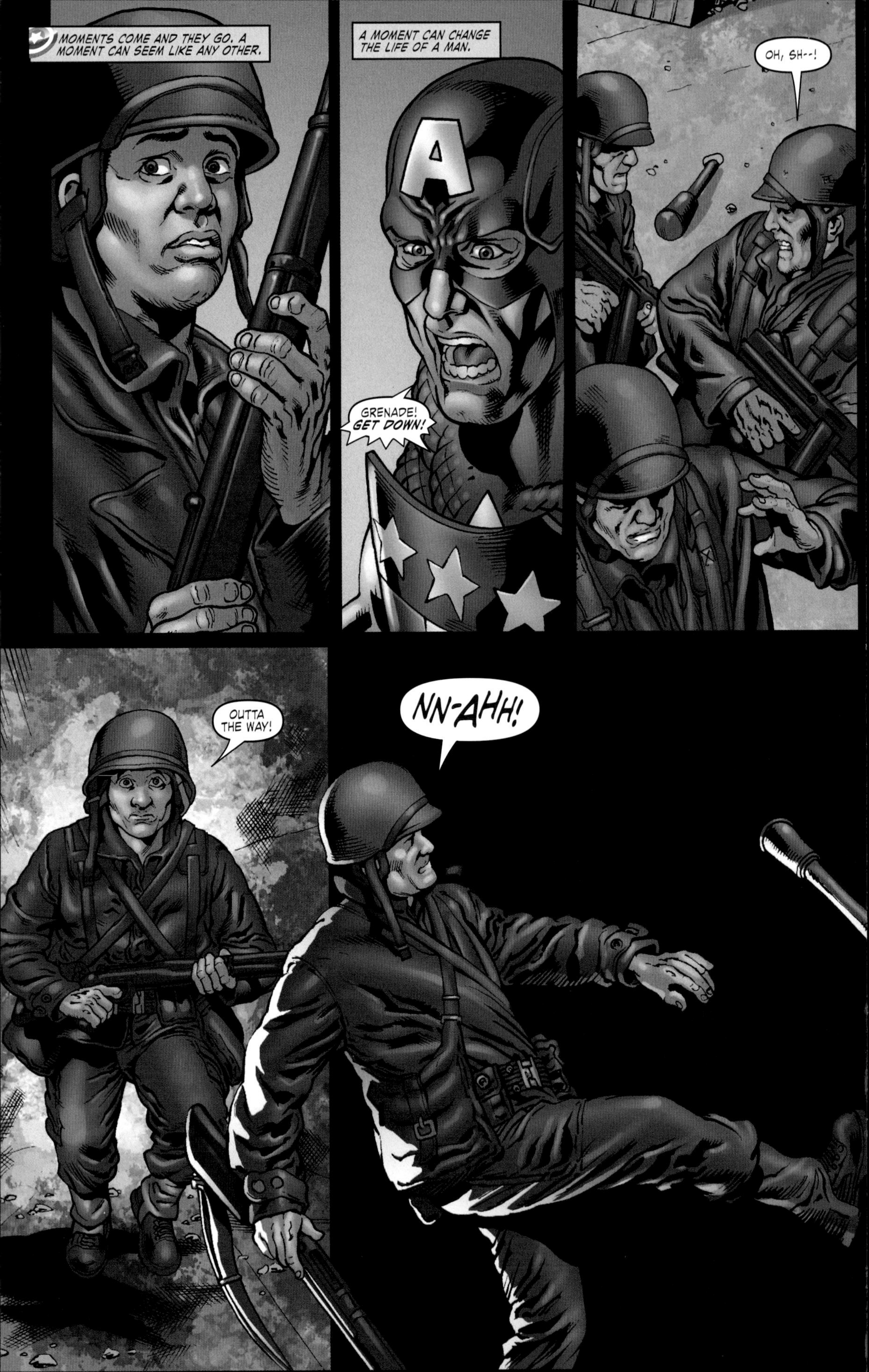
MOMENTS COME AND THEY GO. A MOMENT CAN SEEM LIKE ANY OTHER.
A MOMENT CAN CHANGE THE LIFE OF A MAN.
GRENADE! GET DOWN!
OH, SH--!
OUTTA THE WAY!
NN-AHH!

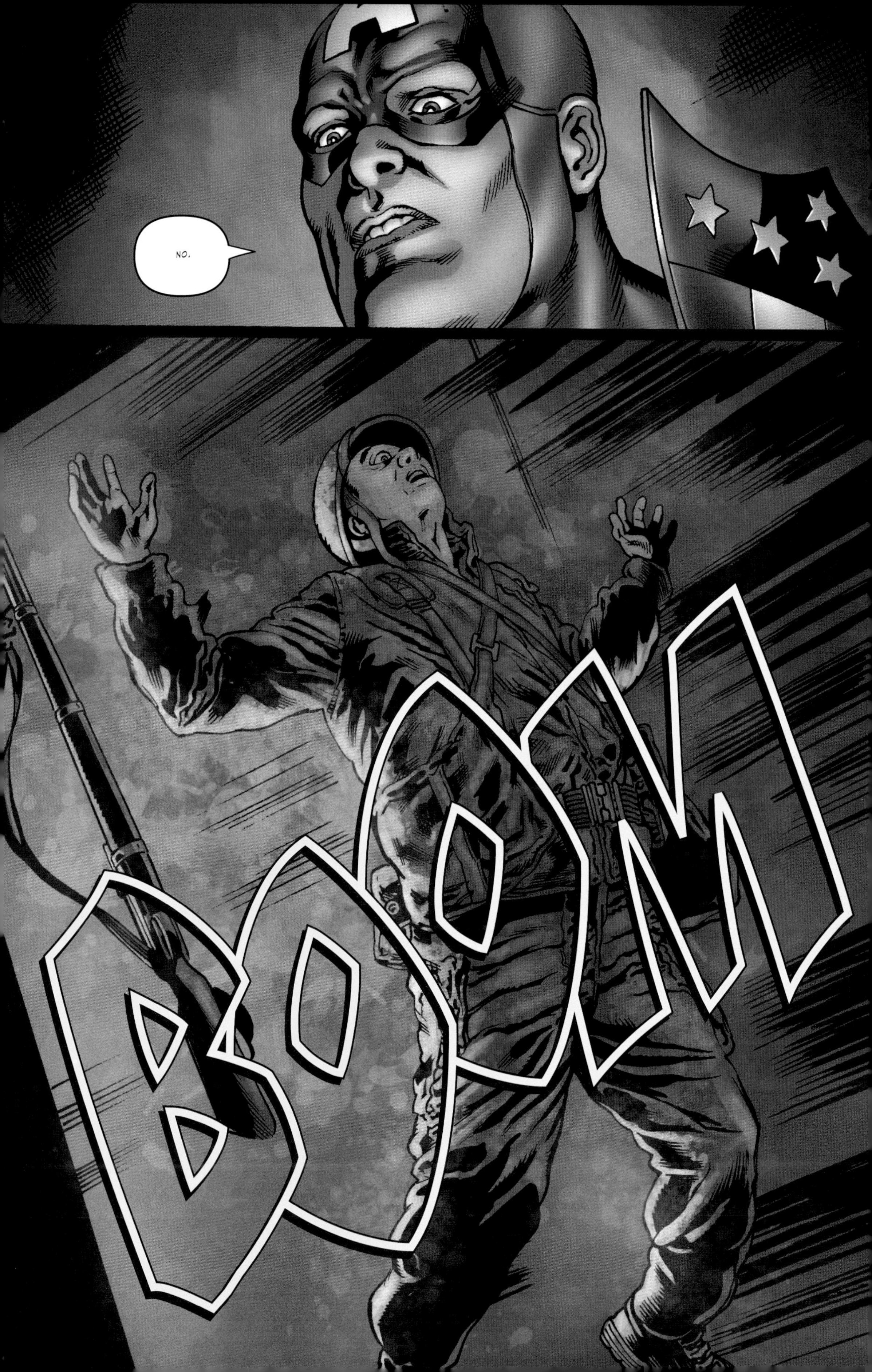
NO.
BOOM

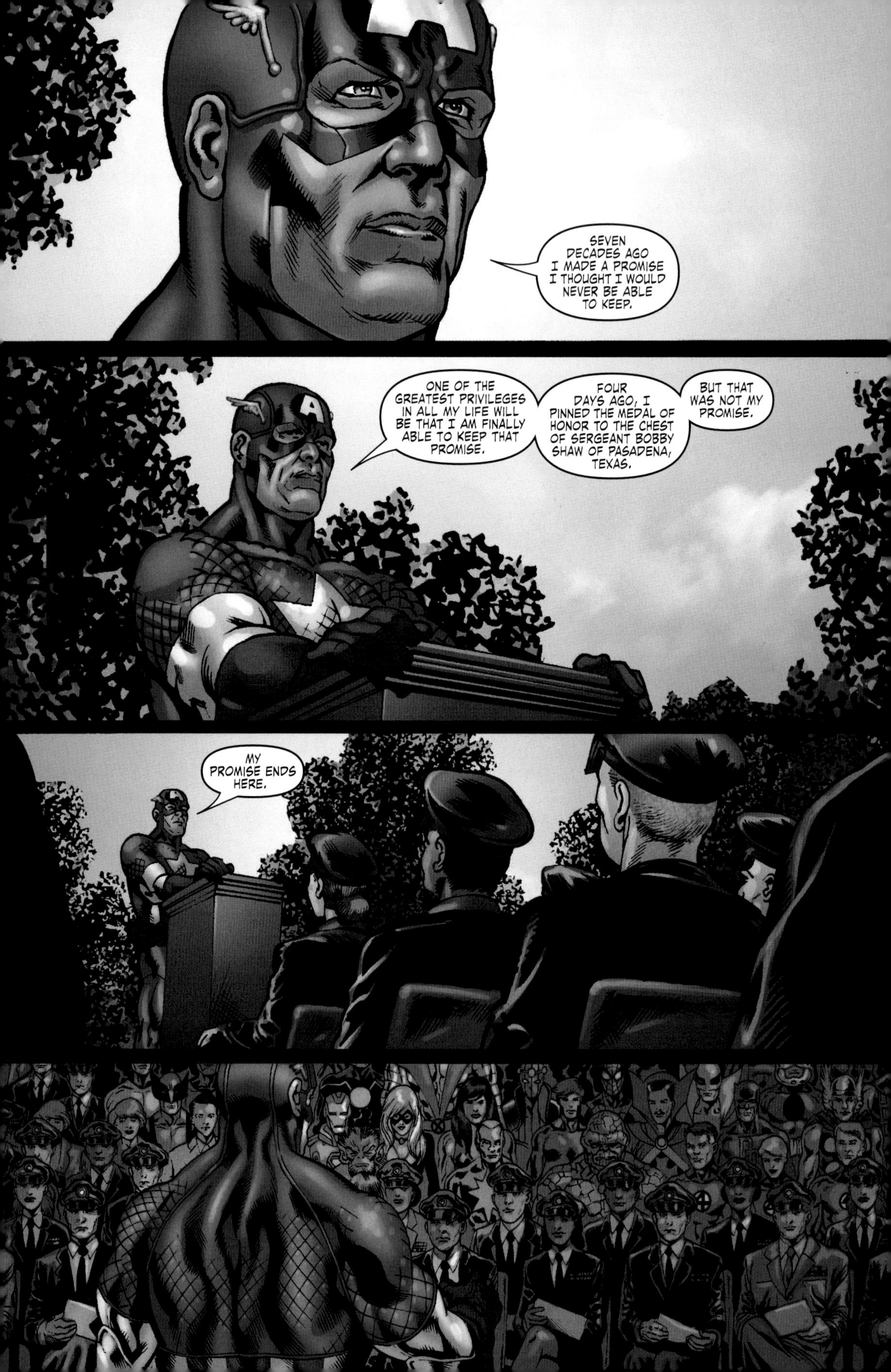
SEVEN DECADES AGO I MADE A PROMISE I THOUGHT I WOULD NEVER BE ABLE TO KEEP.
ONE OF THE GREATEST PRIVILEGES IN ALL MY LIFE WILL BE THAT I AM FINALLY ABLE TO KEEP THAT PROMISE.
FOUR DAYS AGO, I PINNED THE MEDAL OF HONOR TO THE CHEST OF SERGEANT BOBBY SHAW OF PASADENA, TEXAS.
BUT THAT WAS NOT MY PROMISE.
MY PROMISE ENDS HERE.

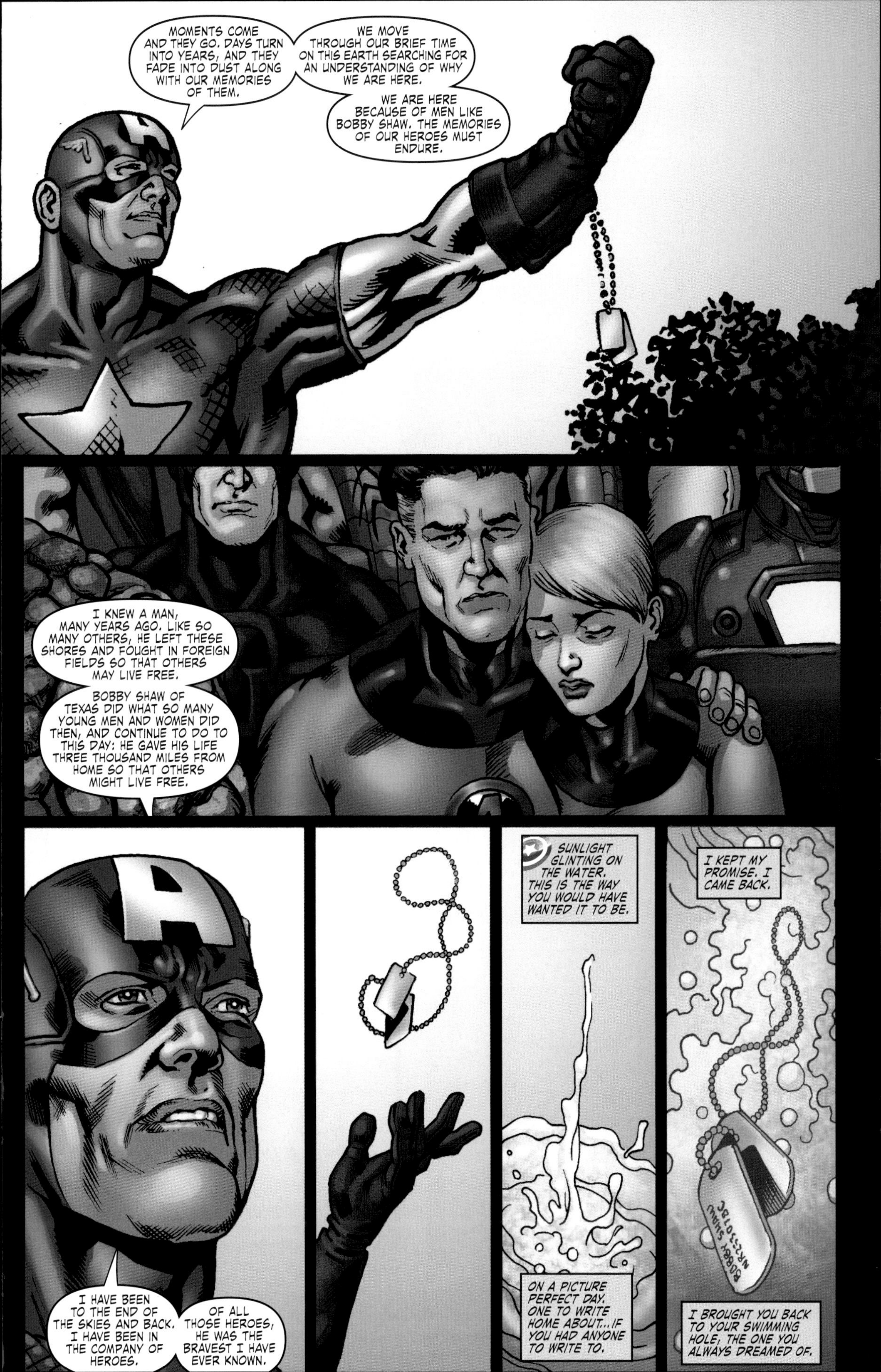
MOMENTS COME AND THEY GO. DAYS TURN INTO YEARS, AND THEY FADE INTO DUST ALONG WITH OUR MEMORIES OF THEM.
WE MOVE THROUGH OUR BRIEF TIME ON THIS EARTH SEARCHING FOR AN UNDERSTANDING OF WHY WE ARE HERE.
WE ARE HERE BECAUSE OF MEN LIKE BOBBY SHAW. THE MEMORIES OF OUR HEROES MUST ENDURE.
I KNEW A MAN, MANY YEARS AGO. LIKE SO MANY OTHERS, HE LEFT THESE SHORES AND FOUGHT IN FOREIGN FIELDS SO THAT OTHERS MAY LIVE FREE.
BOBBY SHAW OF TEXAS DID WHAT SO MANY YOUNG MEN AND WOMEN DID THEN, AND CONTINUE TO DO TO THIS DAY: HE GAVE HIS LIFE THREE THOUSAND MILES FROM HOME SO THAT OTHERS MIGHT LIVE FREE.
I HAVE BEEN TO THE END OF THE SKIES AND BACK. I HAVE BEEN IN THE COMPANY OF HEROES.
OF ALL THOSE HEROES, HE WAS THE BRAVEST I HAVE EVER KNOWN.
SUNLIGHT GLINTING ON THE WATER. THIS IS THE WAY YOU WOULD HAVE WANTED IT TO BE.
ON A PICTURE PERFECT DAY. ONE TO WRITE HOME ABOUT...IF YOU HAD ANYONE TO WRITE TO.
I KEPT MY PROMISE. I CAME BACK.
I BROUGHT YOU BACK TO YOUR SWIMMING HOLE, THE ONE YOU ALWAYS DREAMED OF.

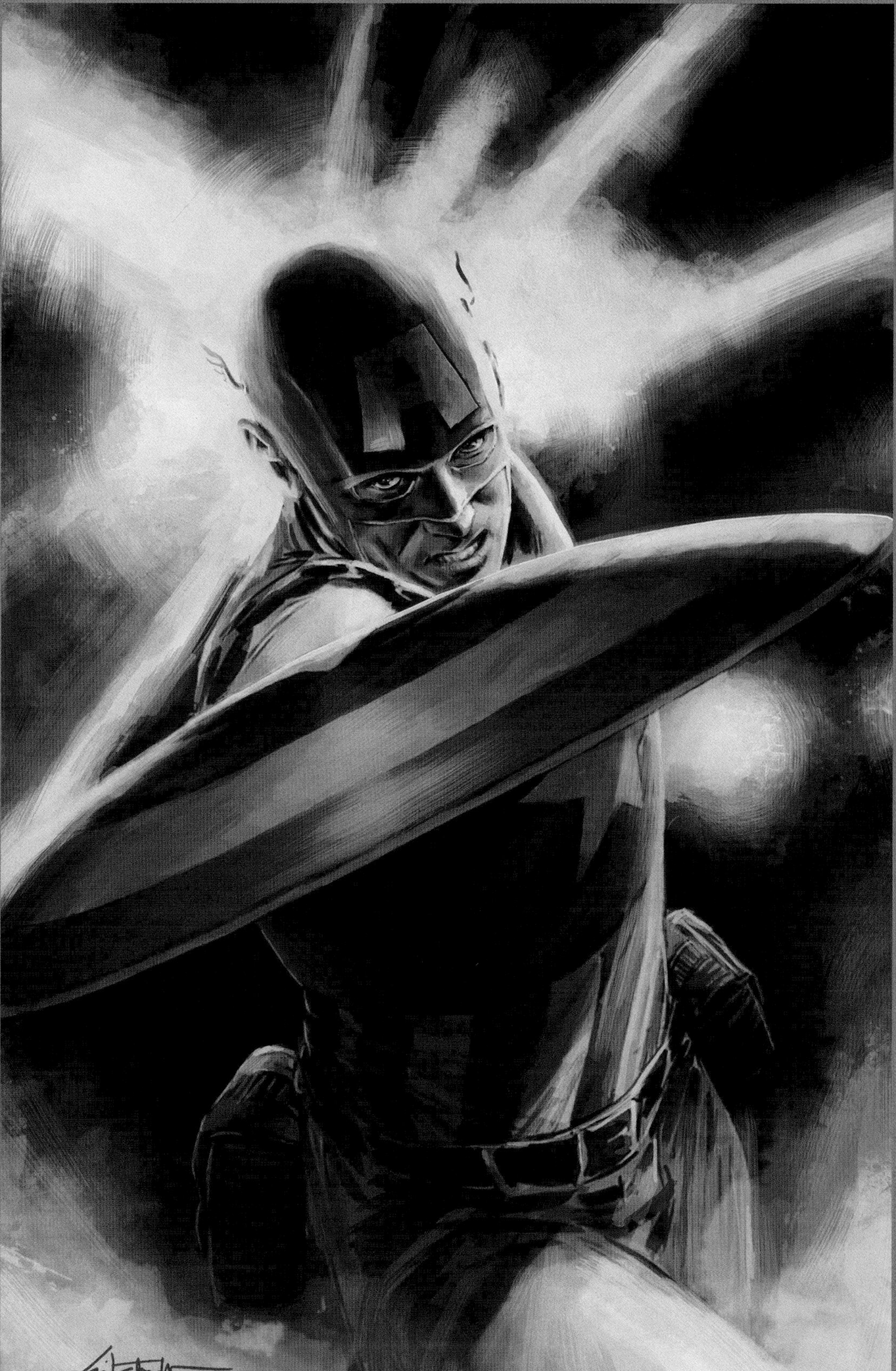

A BROTHER IN ARMS

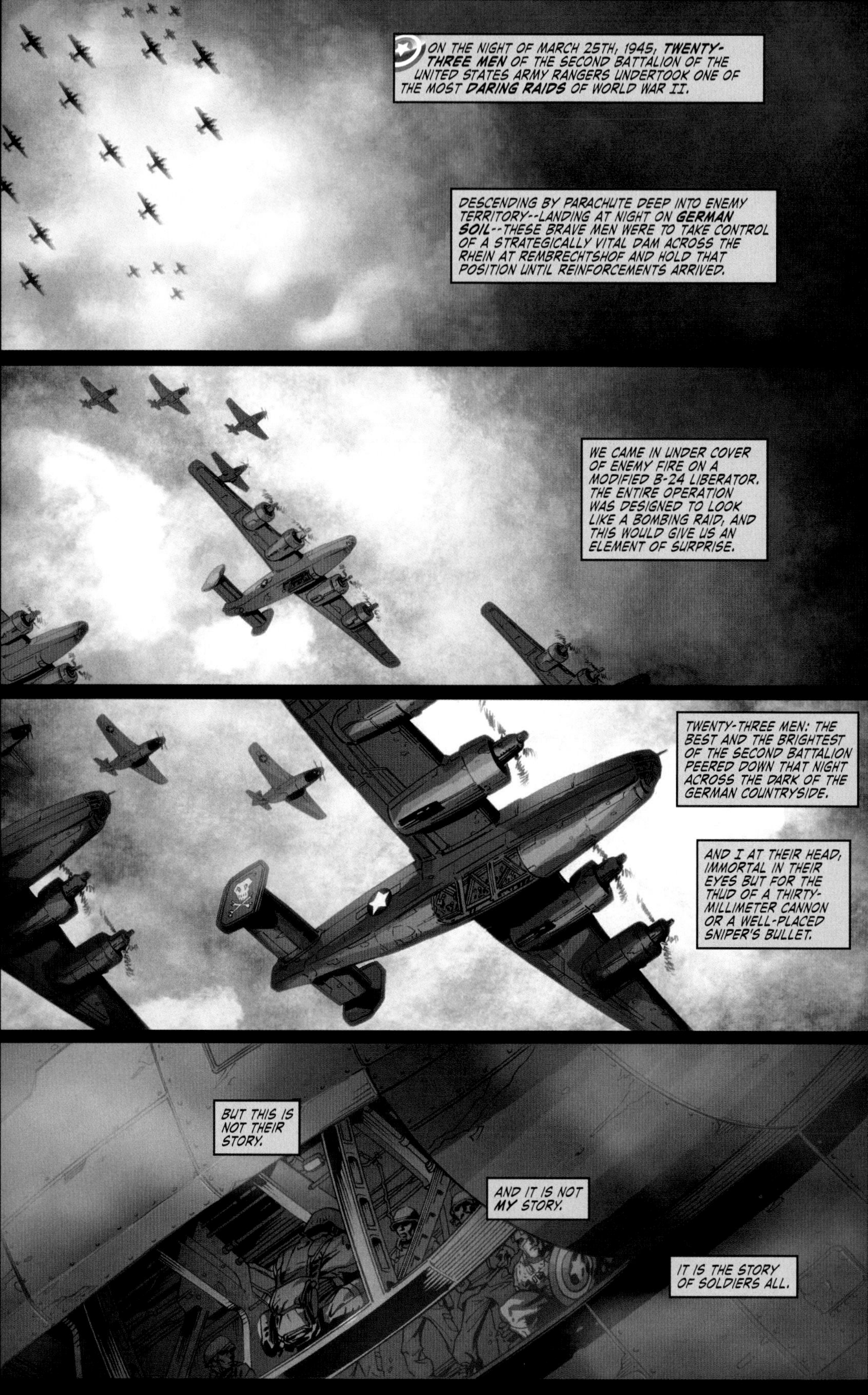
ON THE NIGHT OF MARCH 25TH, 1945, TWENTY-THREE MEN OF THE SECOND BATTALION OF THE UNITED STATES ARMY RANGERS UNDERTOOK ONE OF THE MOST DARING RAIDS OF WORLD WAR II.
DESCENDING BY PARACHUTE DEEP INTO ENEMY TERRITORY--LANDING AT NIGHT ON GERMAN SOIL--THESE BRAVE MEN WERE TO TAKE CONTROL OF A STRATEGICALLY VITAL DAM ACROSS THE RHEIN AT REMBRECHTSHOF AND HOLD THAT POSITION UNTIL REINFORCEMENTS ARRIVED.
WE CAME IN UNDER COVER OF ENEMY FIRE ON A MODIFIED B-24 LIBERATOR. THE ENTIRE OPERATION WAS DESIGNED TO LOOK LIKE A BOMBING RAID, AND THIS WOULD GIVE US AN ELEMENT OF SURPRISE.
TWENTY-THREE MEN: THE BEST AND THE BRIGHTEST OF THE SECOND BATTALION PEERED DOWN THAT NIGHT ACROSS THE DARK OF THE GERMAN COUNTRYSIDE.
AND I AT THEIR HEAD, IMMORTAL IN THEIR EYES BUT FOR THE THUD OF A THIRTY-MILLIMETER CANNON OR A WELL-PLACED SNIPER'S BULLET.
BUT THIS IS NOT THEIR STORY.
AND IT IS NOT MY STORY.
IT IS THE STORY OF SOLDIERS ALL.

A BROTHER IN ARMS

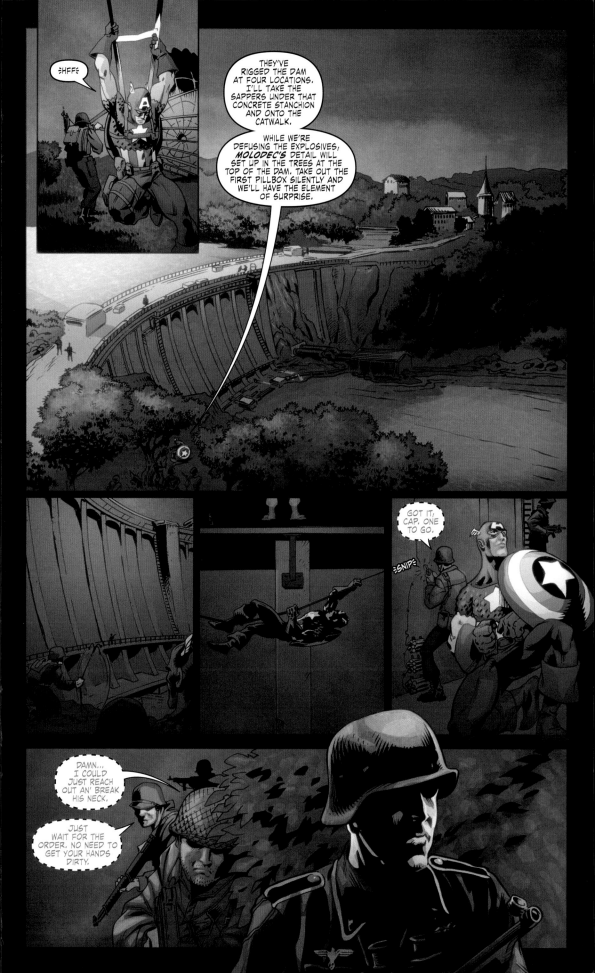

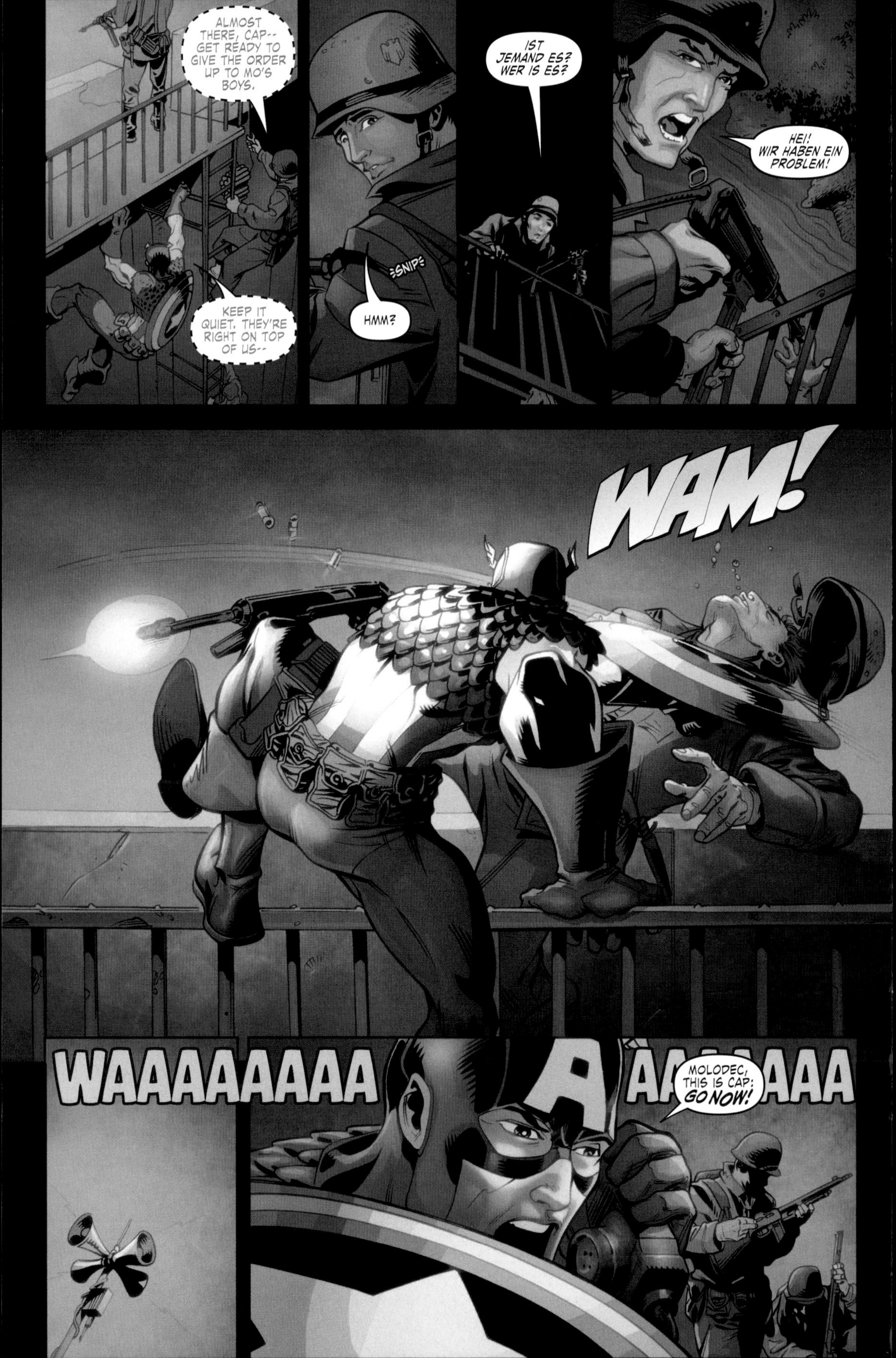
ALMOST THERE, CAP-- GET READY TO GIVE THE ORDER UP TO MO'S BOYS.
KEEP IT QUIET. THEY'RE RIGHT ON TOP OF US--
SNIP
HMM?
IST JEMAND ES? WER IS ES?
HEI! WIR HABEN EIN PROBLEM!
WAM!
WAAAAAAAAA
AAAAAAA
MOLODEC, THIS IS CAP: GO NOW!

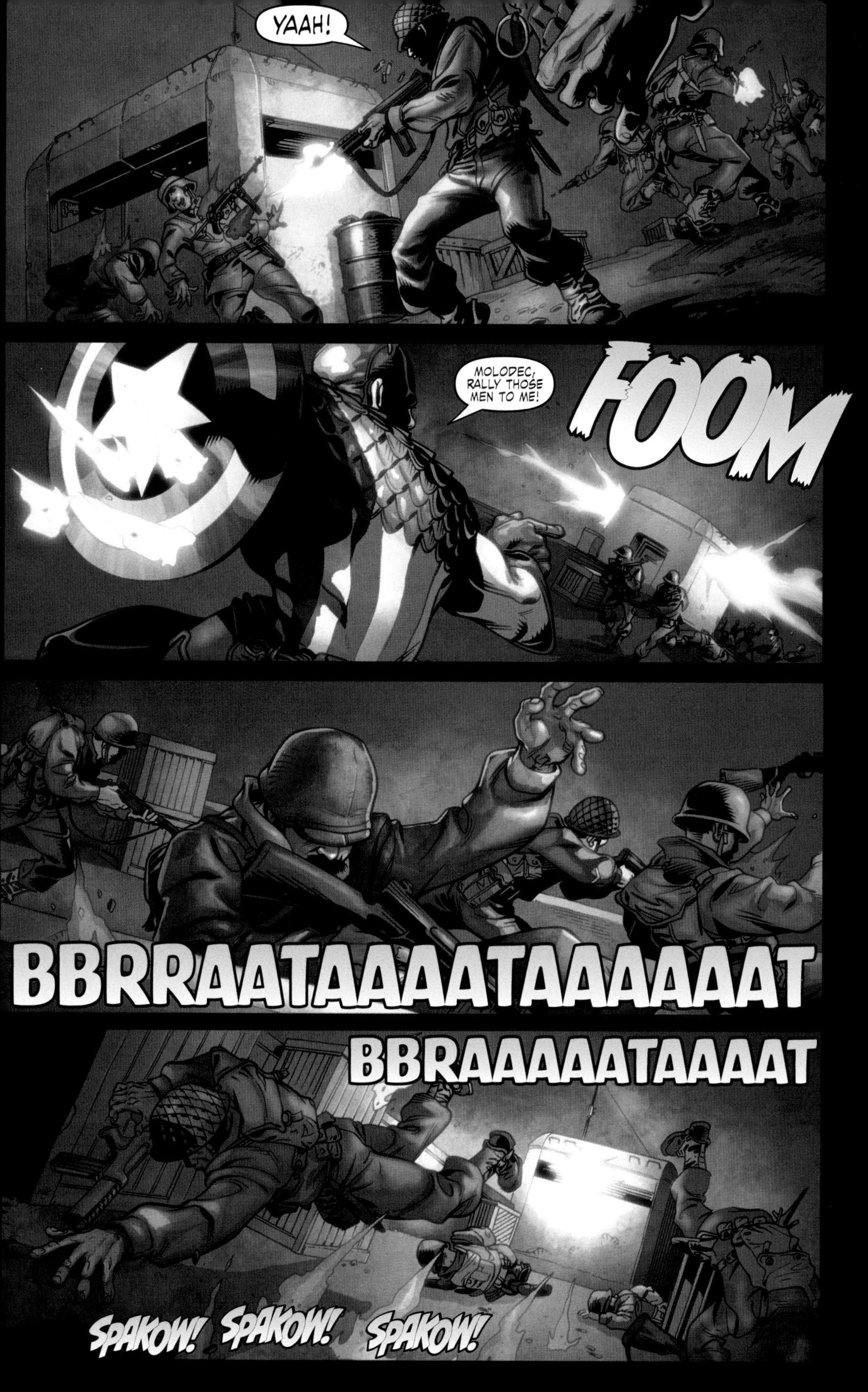
YAAH!
MOLODEC, RALLY THOSE MEN TO ME!
FOOM
BBRRAATAAAATAAAAAAT
BBRAAAAATAAAAT
SPAKOW! SPAKOW! SPAKOW!

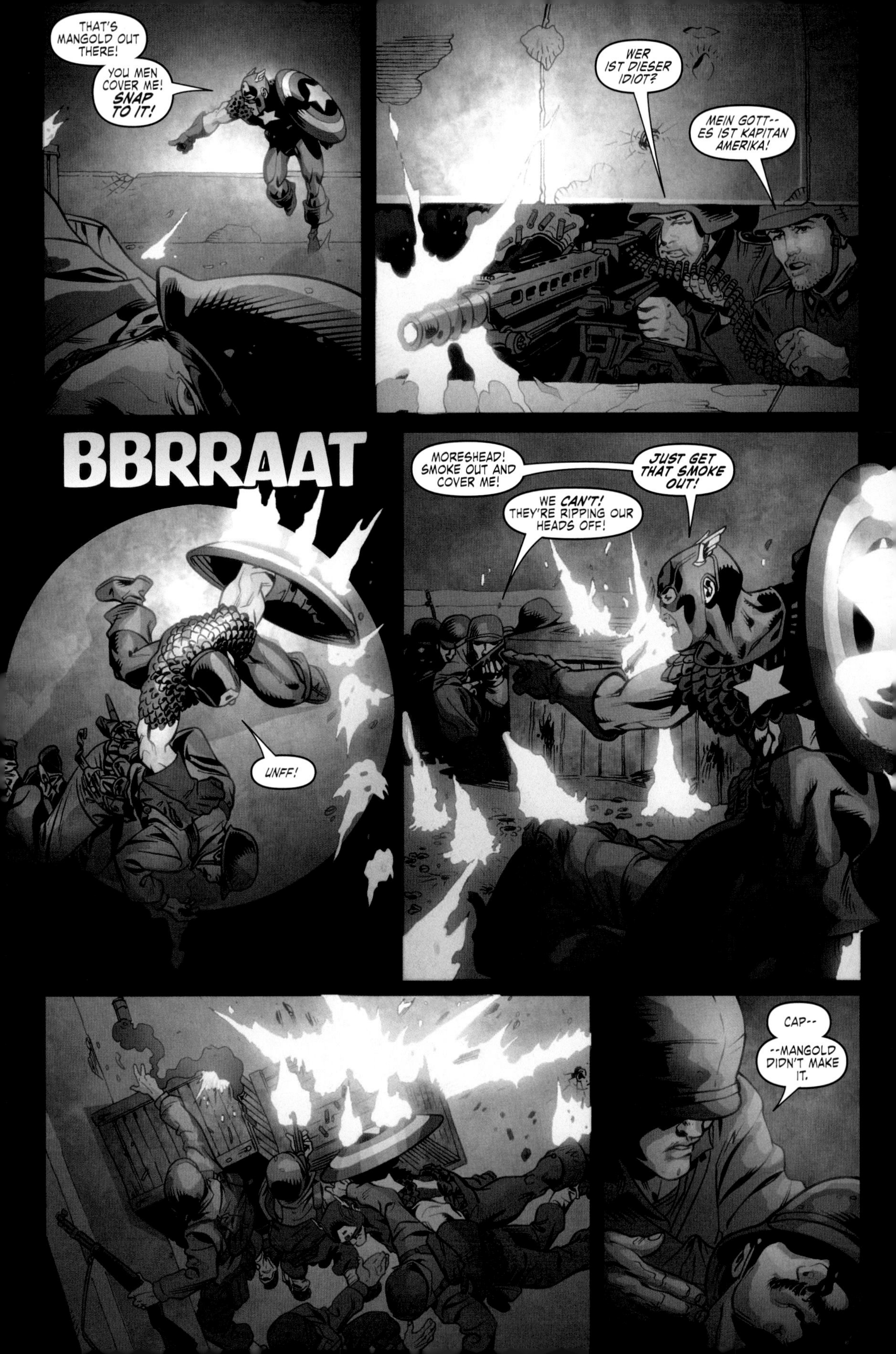
THAT'S MANGOLD OUT THERE!
YOU MEN COVER ME! SNAP TO IT!
WER IST DIESER IDIOT?
MEIN GOTT-- ES IST KAPITAN AMERIKA!
BBRRAAT
UNFF!
MORESHEAD! SMOKE OUT AND COVER ME!
WE CAN'T! THEY'RE RIPPING OUR HEADS OFF!
JUST GET THAT SMOKE OUT!
CAP--
--MANGOLD DIDN'T MAKE IT.

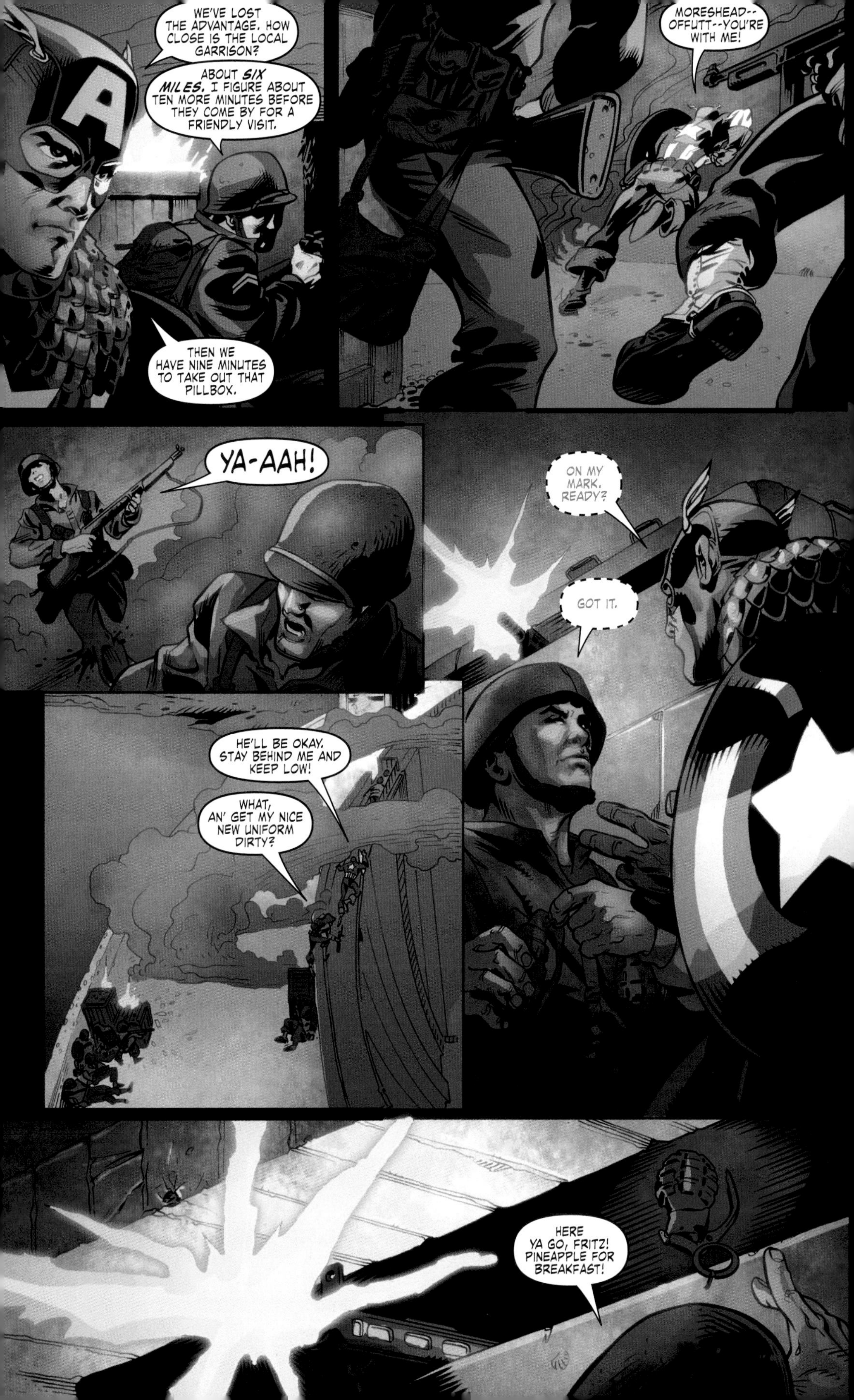
WE'VE LOST THE ADVANTAGE. HOW CLOSE IS THE LOCAL GARRISON?
ABOUT SIX MILES. I FIGURE ABOUT TEN MORE MINUTES BEFORE THEY COME BY FOR A FRIENDLY VISIT.
THEN WE HAVE NINE MINUTES TO TAKE OUT THAT PILLBOX.
MORESHEAD-- OFFUTT--YOU'RE WITH ME!
YA-AAH!
HE'LL BE OKAY. STAY BEHIND ME AND KEEP LOW!
WHAT, AN' GET MY NICE NEW UNIFORM DIRTY?
ON MY MARK. READY?
GOT IT.
HERE YA GO, FRITZ! PINEAPPLE FOR BREAKFAST!

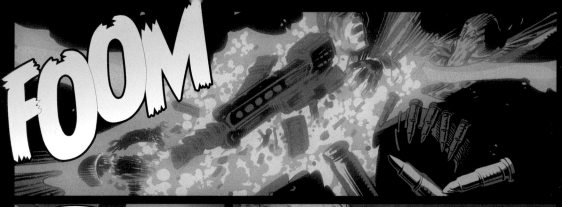

FOOM

WE'VE GOT TO GET IN THERE BEFORE THEY CAN RECOVER. THE TOWN GARRISON WILL BE HERE WITHIN MINUTES.

⇟KOFF⇟ ⇟HKK⇟

SPANG

BAM!

MOLODEC, FLUSH ME OUT SOME RATS!

ON IT, CAP!

BBRRAATAAAAT

KAMERAD! KAMERAD!

YOU DIRTY NAZI!

NEIN--

MOLODEC, DO NOT FIRE YOUR WEAPON! CEASE FIRE!

ARE YOU SERIOUS, CAP? THAT KRAUT BANDIT KILLED TWO OF OUR BOYS.

THAT MAN IS A COMPLIANT PRISONER OF WAR. CLOSE COMBAT RULES DO NOT APPLY.

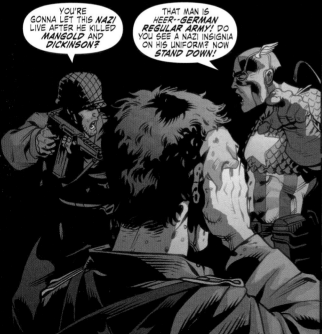

YOU'RE GONNA LET THIS NAZI LIVE AFTER HE KILLED MANGOLD AND DICKINSON?

THAT MAN IS HEER--GERMAN REGULAR ARMY! DO YOU SEE A NAZI INSIGNIA ON HIS UNIFORM? NOW STAND DOWN!

OH, DANKE-- DANKE SEHR--

KRAK

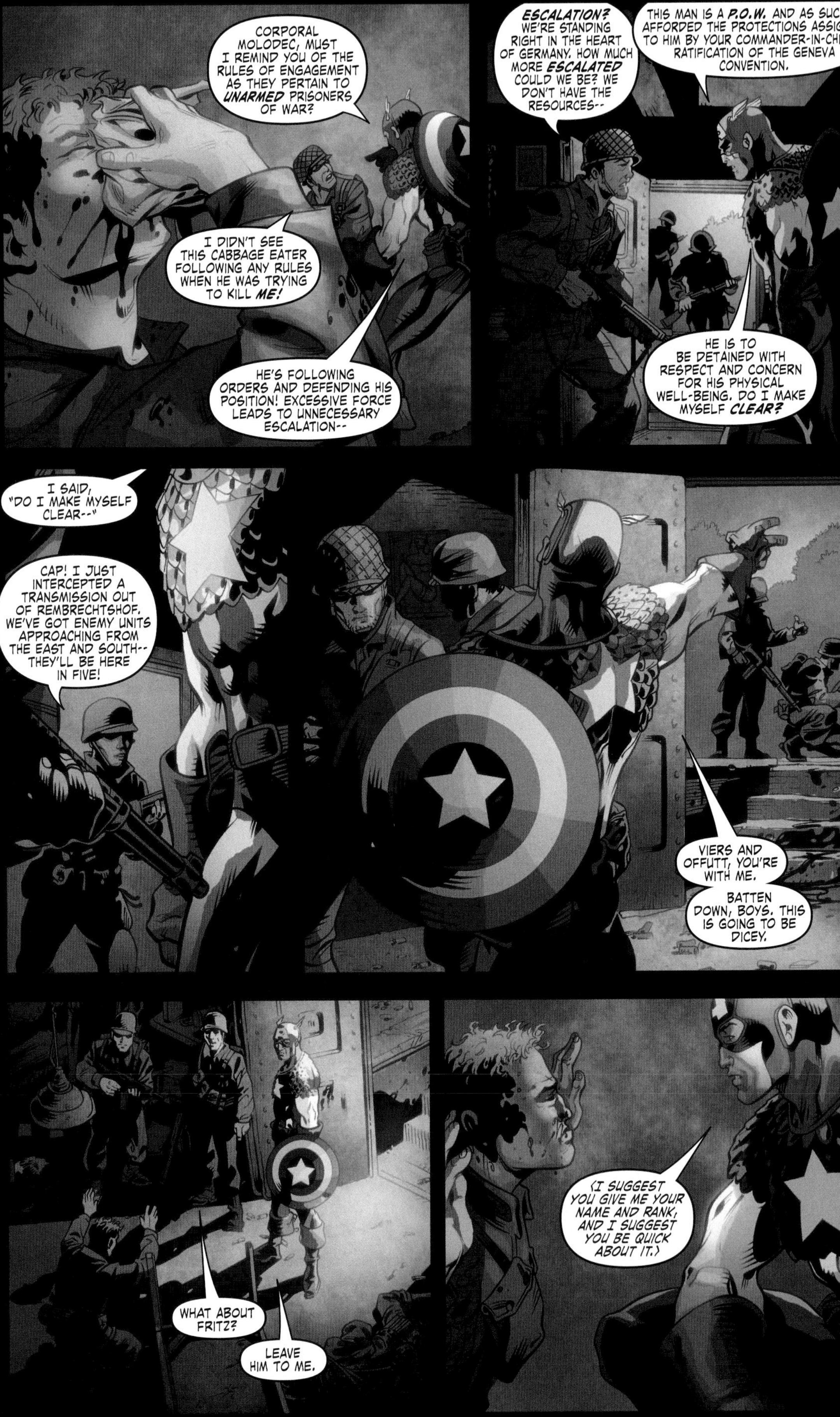
CORPORAL MOLODEC, MUST I REMIND YOU OF THE RULES OF ENGAGEMENT AS THEY PERTAIN TO UNARMED PRISONERS OF WAR?
I DIDN'T SEE THIS CABBAGE EATER FOLLOWING ANY RULES WHEN HE WAS TRYING TO KILL ME!
HE'S FOLLOWING ORDERS AND DEFENDING HIS POSITION! EXCESSIVE FORCE LEADS TO UNNECESSARY ESCALATION--
ESCALATION? WE'RE STANDING RIGHT IN THE HEART OF GERMANY. HOW MUCH MORE ESCALATED COULD WE BE? WE DON'T HAVE THE RESOURCES--
THIS MAN IS A P.O.W. AND AS SUCH IS AFFORDED THE PROTECTIONS ASSIGNED TO HIM BY YOUR COMMANDER-IN-CHIEF'S RATIFICATION OF THE GENEVA CONVENTION.
HE IS TO BE DETAINED WITH RESPECT AND CONCERN FOR HIS PHYSICAL WELL-BEING. DO I MAKE MYSELF CLEAR?
I SAID, "DO I MAKE MYSELF CLEAR--"
CAP! I JUST INTERCEPTED A TRANSMISSION OUT OF REMBRECHTSHOF. WE'VE GOT ENEMY UNITS APPROACHING FROM THE EAST AND SOUTH-- THEY'LL BE HERE IN FIVE!
VIERS AND OFFUTT, YOU'RE WITH ME.
BATTEN DOWN, BOYS. THIS IS GOING TO BE DICEY.
WHAT ABOUT FRITZ?
LEAVE HIM TO ME.
<I SUGGEST YOU GIVE ME YOUR NAME AND RANK, AND I SUGGEST YOU BE QUICK ABOUT IT.>

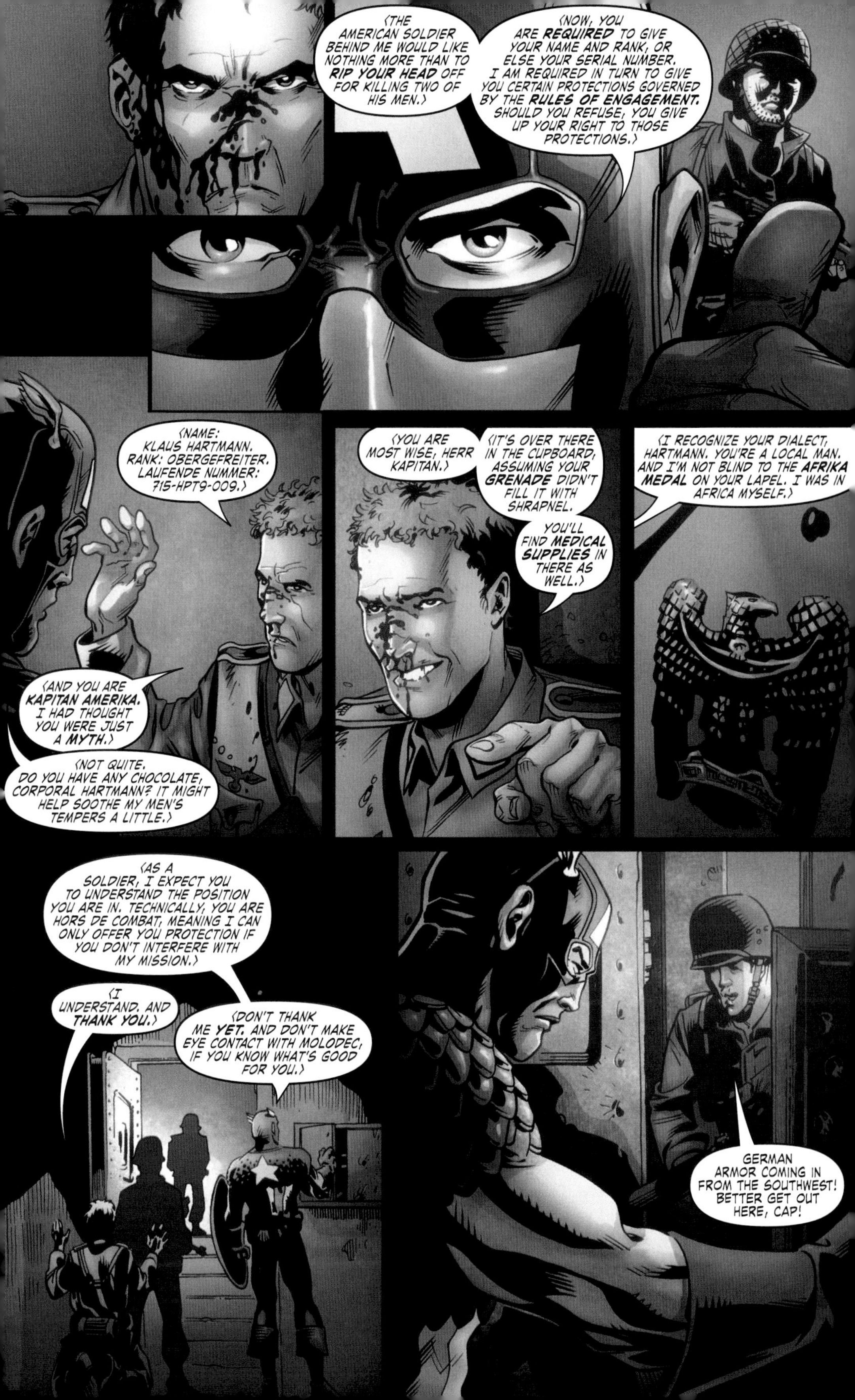
‹THE AMERICAN SOLDIER BEHIND ME WOULD LIKE NOTHING MORE THAN TO **RIP YOUR HEAD** OFF FOR KILLING TWO OF HIS MEN.›
‹NOW, YOU ARE **REQUIRED** TO GIVE YOUR NAME AND RANK, OR ELSE YOUR SERIAL NUMBER. I AM REQUIRED IN TURN TO GIVE YOU CERTAIN PROTECTIONS GOVERNED BY THE **RULES OF ENGAGEMENT.** SHOULD YOU REFUSE, YOU GIVE UP YOUR RIGHT TO THOSE PROTECTIONS.›
‹NAME: KLAUS HARTMANN. RANK: OBERGEFREITER. LAUFENDE NUMMER: 715-HPT9-009.›
‹AND YOU ARE **KAPITAN AMERIKA.** I HAD THOUGHT YOU WERE JUST A **MYTH.**›
‹NOT QUITE. DO YOU HAVE ANY CHOCOLATE, CORPORAL HARTMANN? IT MIGHT HELP SOOTHE MY MEN'S TEMPERS A LITTLE.›
‹YOU ARE MOST WISE, HERR KAPITAN.›
‹IT'S OVER THERE IN THE CUPBOARD, ASSUMING YOUR **GRENADE** DIDN'T FILL IT WITH SHRAPNEL.
YOU'LL FIND **MEDICAL SUPPLIES** IN THERE AS WELL.›
‹I RECOGNIZE YOUR DIALECT, HARTMANN. YOU'RE A LOCAL MAN. AND I'M NOT BLIND TO THE **AFRIKA MEDAL** ON YOUR LAPEL. I WAS IN AFRICA MYSELF.›
‹AS A SOLDIER, I EXPECT YOU TO UNDERSTAND THE POSITION YOU ARE IN. TECHNICALLY, YOU ARE HORS DE COMBAT, MEANING I CAN ONLY OFFER YOU PROTECTION IF YOU DON'T INTERFERE WITH MY MISSION.›
‹I UNDERSTAND. AND **THANK YOU.**›
‹DON'T THANK ME **YET.** AND DON'T MAKE EYE CONTACT WITH MOLODEC, IF YOU KNOW WHAT'S GOOD FOR YOU.›
GERMAN ARMOR COMING IN FROM THE SOUTHWEST! BETTER GET OUT HERE, CAP!

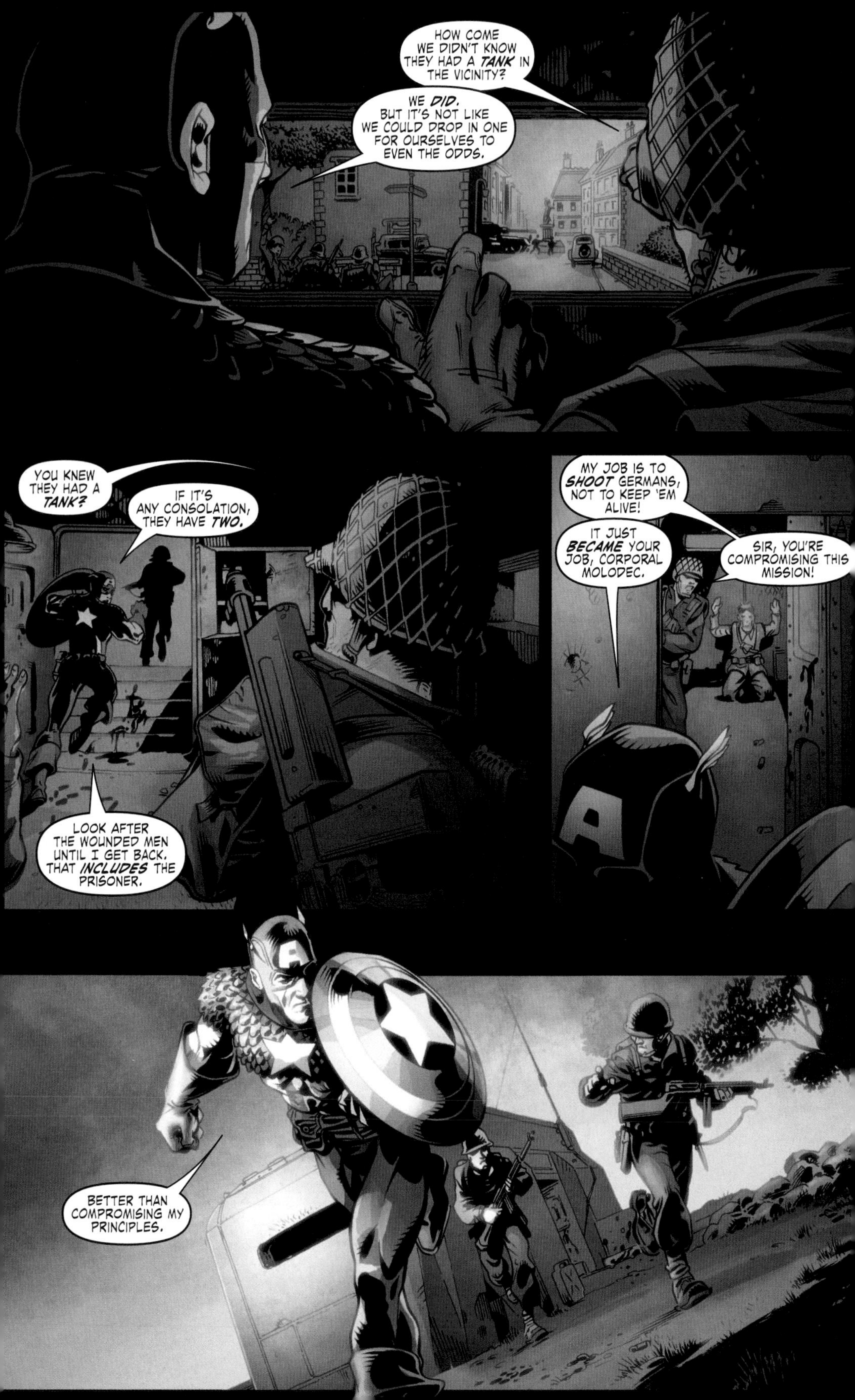
HOW COME WE DIDN'T KNOW THEY HAD A *TANK* IN THE VICINITY?
WE *DID*. BUT IT'S NOT LIKE WE COULD DROP IN ONE FOR OURSELVES TO EVEN THE ODDS.
YOU KNEW THEY HAD A *TANK?*
IF IT'S ANY CONSOLATION, THEY HAVE *TWO.*
LOOK AFTER THE WOUNDED MEN UNTIL I GET BACK. THAT *INCLUDES* THE PRISONER.
MY JOB IS TO *SHOOT* GERMANS, NOT TO KEEP 'EM ALIVE!
IT JUST *BECAME* YOUR JOB, CORPORAL MOLODEC.
SIR, YOU'RE COMPROMISING THIS MISSION!
BETTER THAN COMPROMISING MY PRINCIPLES.

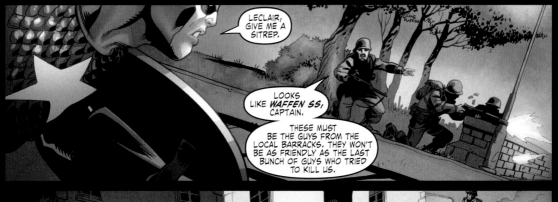

LECLAIR, GIVE ME A SITREP.

LOOKS LIKE *WAFFEN SS*, CAPTAIN.

THESE MUST BE THE GUYS FROM THE LOCAL BARRACKS. THEY WON'T BE AS FRIENDLY AS THE LAST BUNCH OF GUYS WHO TRIED TO KILL US.

CAP--THIS IS *NUTS!* WHY DIDN'T WE COME IN WITH BAZOOKAS?

TOO BULKY. BESIDES, WE HAVE A SECRET WEAPON.

WEAPON? WHAT WEAPON?

ME.

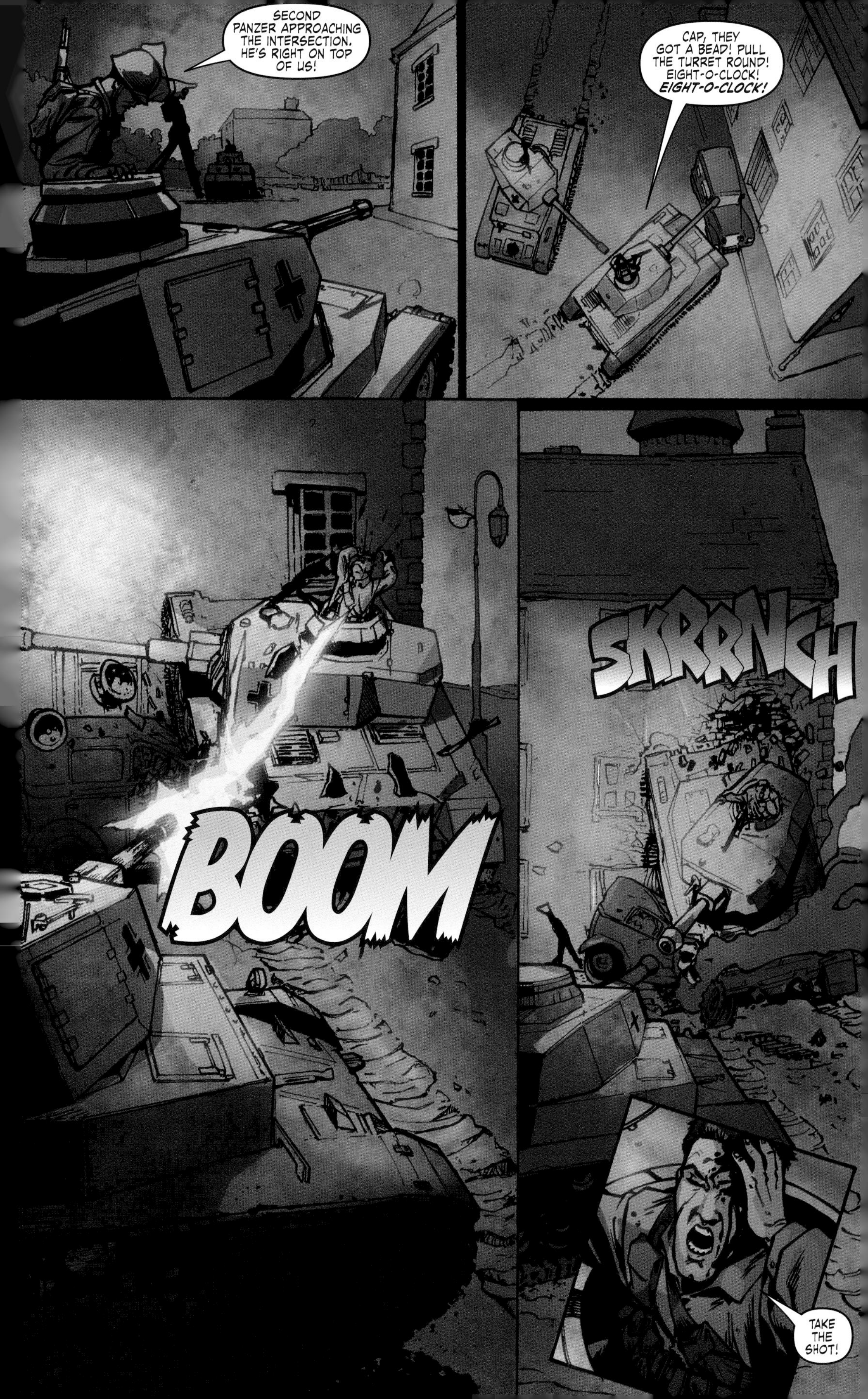
SECOND PANZER APPROACHING THE INTERSECTION. HE'S RIGHT ON TOP OF US!
CAP, THEY GOT A BEAD! PULL THE TURRET ROUND! EIGHT-O-CLOCK! *EIGHT-O-CLOCK!*
BOOM
SKRRNCH
TAKE THE SHOT!

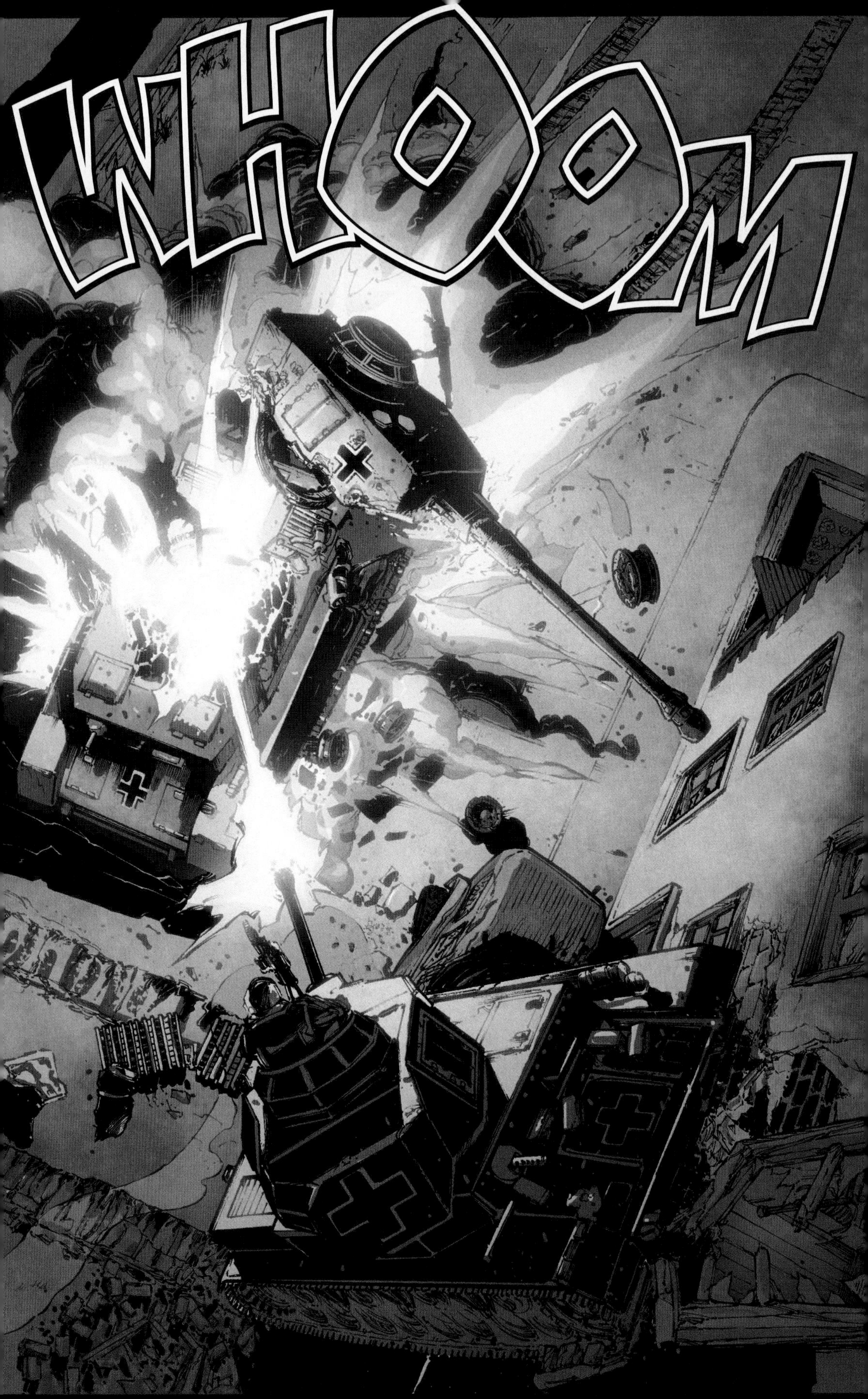
WHOOM

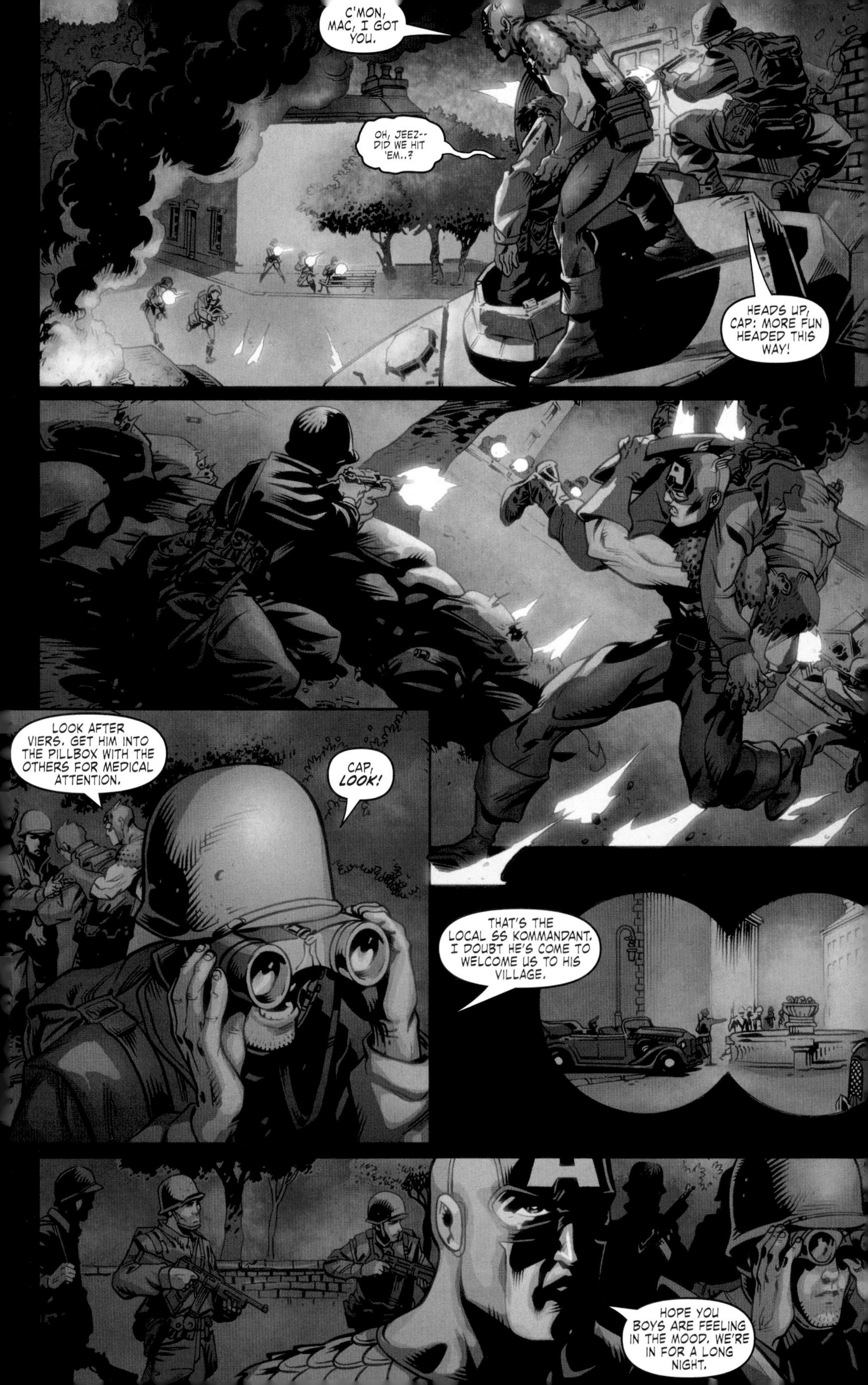
C'MON, MAC, I GOT YOU.
OH, JEEZ-- DID WE HIT 'EM..?
HEADS UP, CAP: MORE FUN HEADED THIS WAY!
LOOK AFTER VIERS. GET HIM INTO THE PILLBOX WITH THE OTHERS FOR MEDICAL ATTENTION.
CAP, LOOK!
THAT'S THE LOCAL SS KOMMANDANT. I DOUBT HE'S COME TO WELCOME US TO HIS VILLAGE.
HOPE YOU BOYS ARE FEELING IN THE MOOD. WE'RE IN FOR A LONG NIGHT.

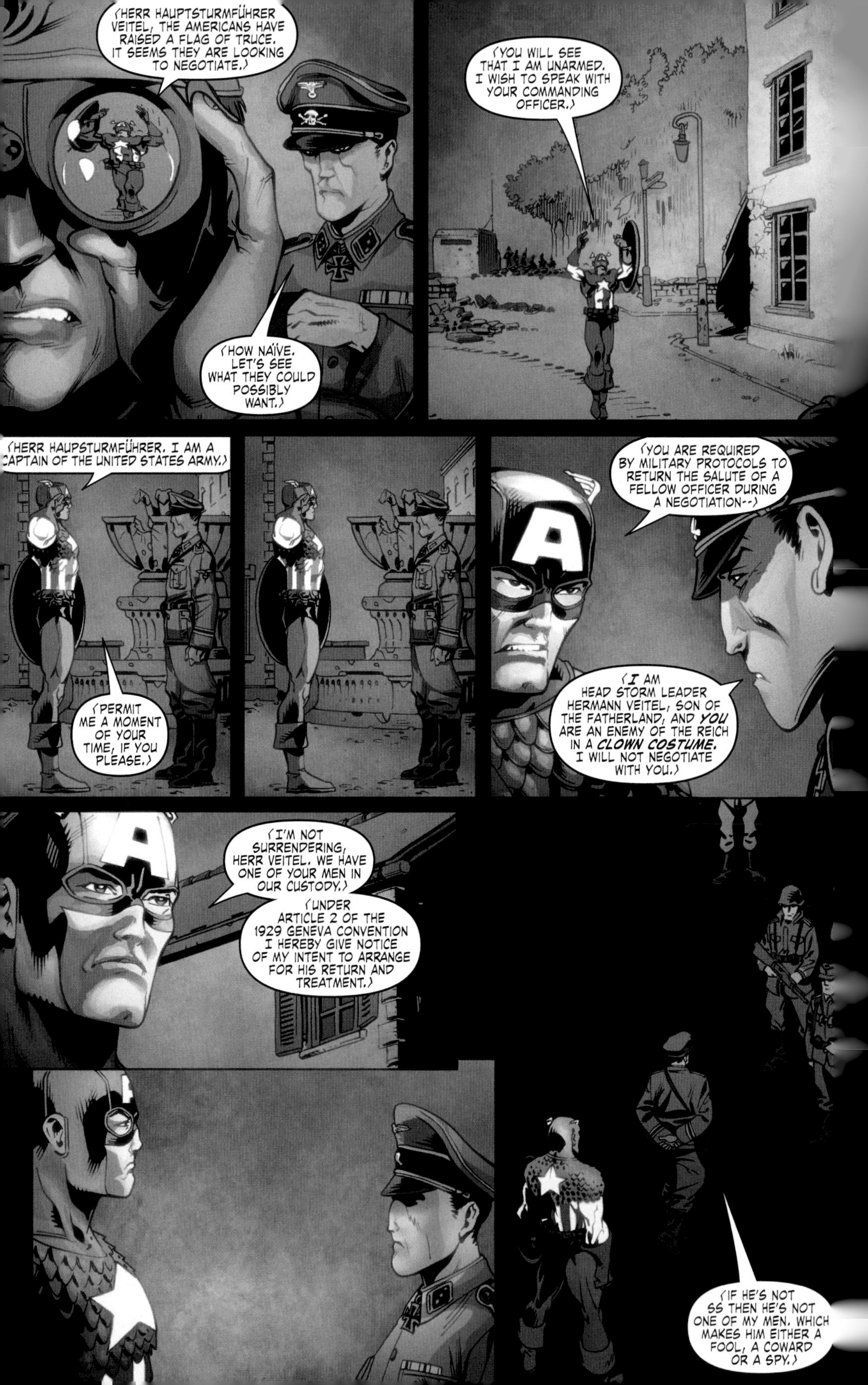
‹HERR HAUPTSTURMFÜHRER VEITEL, THE AMERICANS HAVE RAISED A FLAG OF TRUCE. IT SEEMS THEY ARE LOOKING TO NEGOTIATE.›
‹HOW NAÏVE. LET'S SEE WHAT THEY COULD POSSIBLY WANT.›
‹YOU WILL SEE THAT I AM UNARMED. I WISH TO SPEAK WITH YOUR COMMANDING OFFICER.›
‹HERR HAUPSTURMFÜHRER. I AM A CAPTAIN OF THE UNITED STATES ARMY.›
‹PERMIT ME A MOMENT OF YOUR TIME, IF YOU PLEASE.›
‹YOU ARE REQUIRED BY MILITARY PROTOCOLS TO RETURN THE SALUTE OF A FELLOW OFFICER DURING A NEGOTIATION--›
‹I AM HEAD STORM LEADER HERMANN VEITEL, SON OF THE FATHERLAND, AND YOU ARE AN ENEMY OF THE REICH IN A CLOWN COSTUME. I WILL NOT NEGOTIATE WITH YOU.›
‹I'M NOT SURRENDERING, HERR VEITEL. WE HAVE ONE OF YOUR MEN IN OUR CUSTODY.›
‹UNDER ARTICLE 2 OF THE 1929 GENEVA CONVENTION I HEREBY GIVE NOTICE OF MY INTENT TO ARRANGE FOR HIS RETURN AND TREATMENT.›
‹IF HE'S NOT SS THEN HE'S NOT ONE OF MY MEN. WHICH MAKES HIM EITHER A FOOL, A COWARD OR A SPY.›

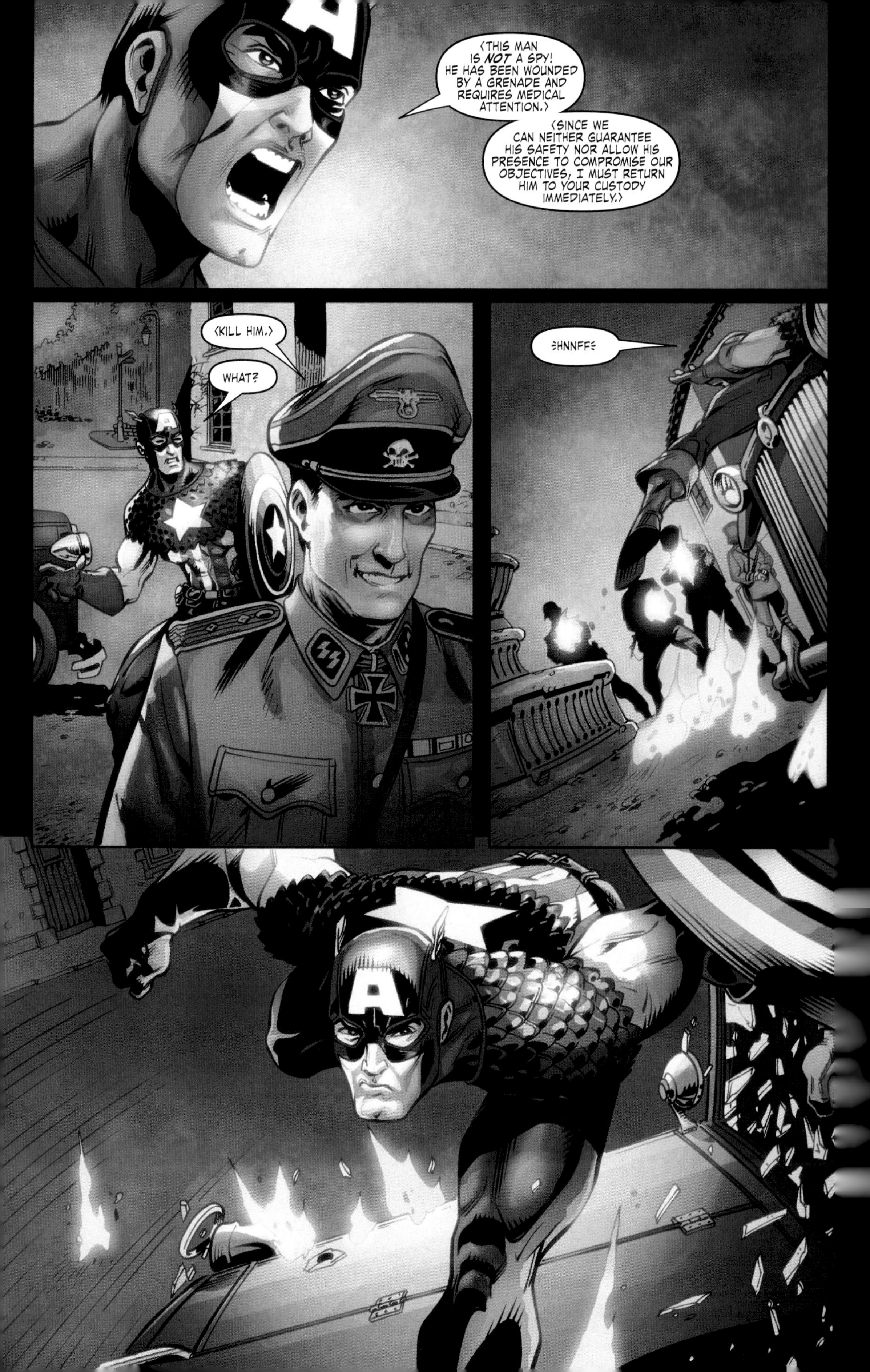

‹THIS MAN IS NOT A SPY! HE HAS BEEN WOUNDED BY A GRENADE AND REQUIRES MEDICAL ATTENTION.›
‹SINCE WE CAN NEITHER GUARANTEE HIS SAFETY NOR ALLOW HIS PRESENCE TO COMPROMISE OUR OBJECTIVES, I MUST RETURN HIM TO YOUR CUSTODY IMMEDIATELY.›
‹KILL HIM.›
WHAT?
HNNFF

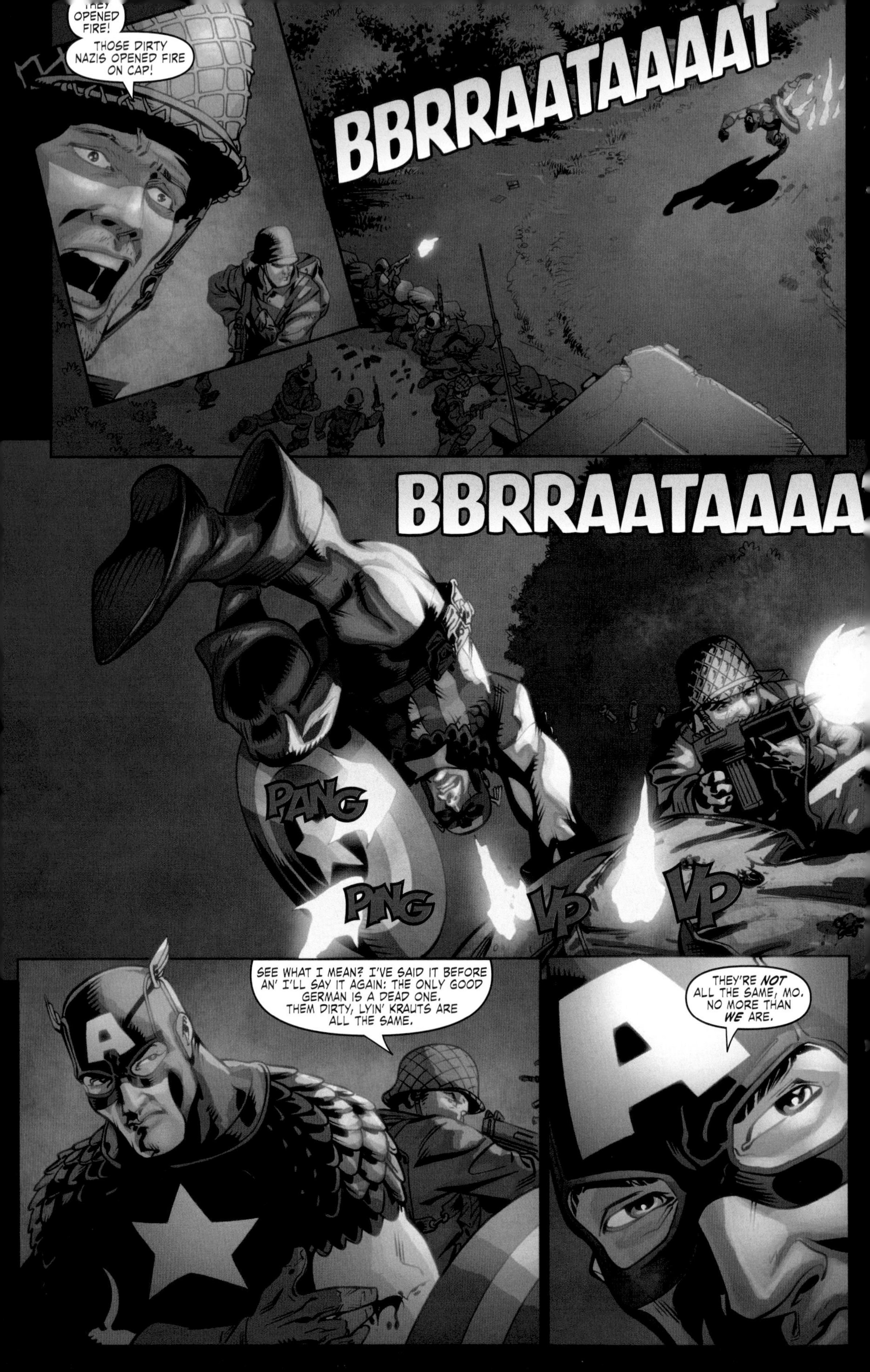
THEY OPENED FIRE!
THOSE DIRTY NAZIS OPENED FIRE ON CAP!
BBRRAATAAAAT
BBRRAATAAAA
PANG
PING
VIP
VIP
SEE WHAT I MEAN? I'VE SAID IT BEFORE AN' I'LL SAY IT AGAIN: THE ONLY GOOD GERMAN IS A DEAD ONE. THEM DIRTY, LYIN' KRAUTS ARE ALL THE SAME.
THEY'RE NOT ALL THE SAME, MO. NO MORE THAN WE ARE.

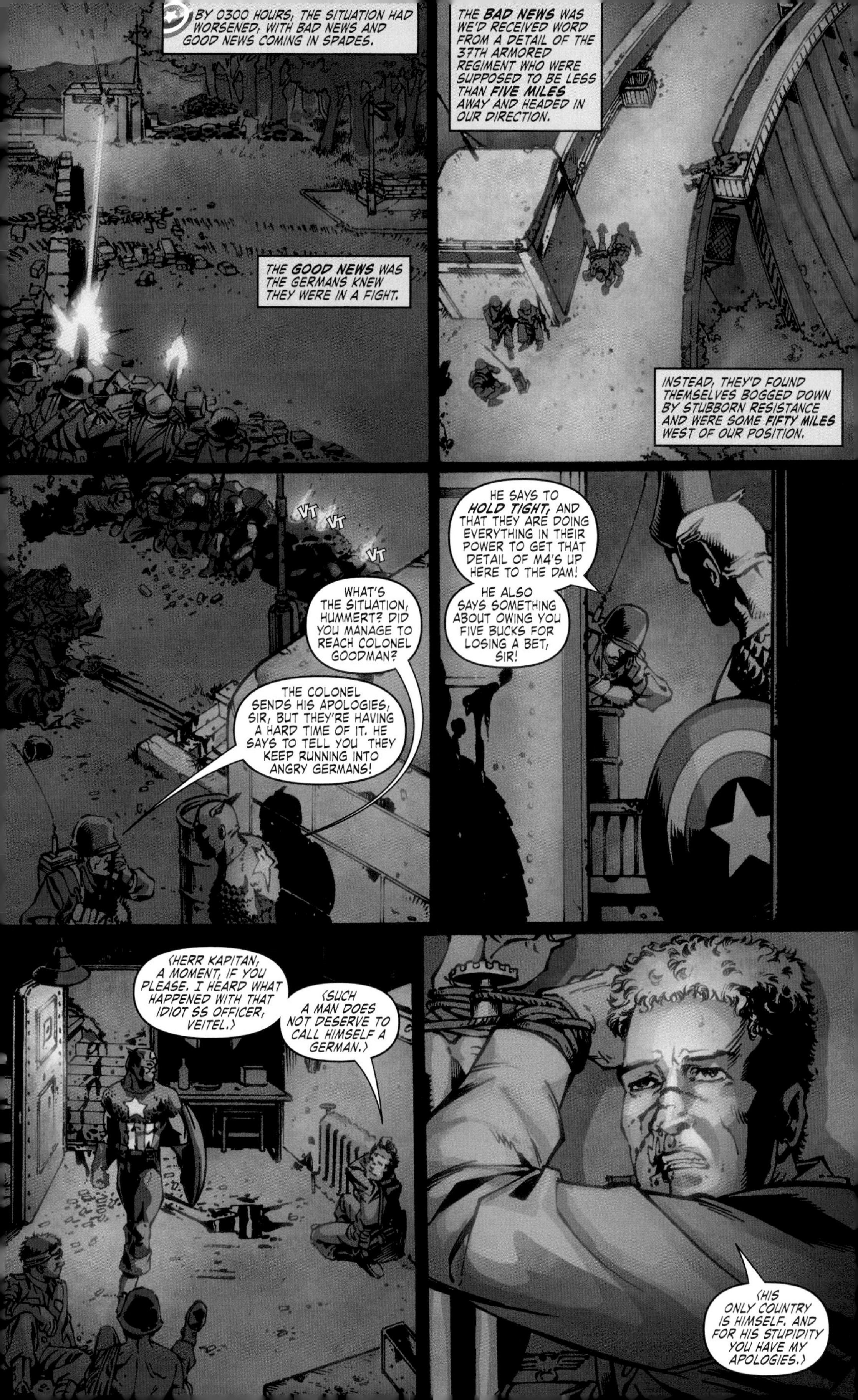
BY 0300 HOURS, THE SITUATION HAD WORSENED, WITH BAD NEWS AND GOOD NEWS COMING IN SPADES.
THE GOOD NEWS WAS THE GERMANS KNEW THEY WERE IN A FIGHT.
THE BAD NEWS WAS WE'D RECEIVED WORD FROM A DETAIL OF THE 37TH ARMORED REGIMENT WHO WERE SUPPOSED TO BE LESS THAN FIVE MILES AWAY AND HEADED IN OUR DIRECTION.
INSTEAD, THEY'D FOUND THEMSELVES BOGGED DOWN BY STUBBORN RESISTANCE AND WERE SOME FIFTY MILES WEST OF OUR POSITION.
VT
VT
VT
WHAT'S THE SITUATION, HUMMERT? DID YOU MANAGE TO REACH COLONEL GOODMAN?
THE COLONEL SENDS HIS APOLOGIES, SIR, BUT THEY'RE HAVING A HARD TIME OF IT. HE SAYS TO TELL YOU THEY KEEP RUNNING INTO ANGRY GERMANS!
HE SAYS TO HOLD TIGHT, AND THAT THEY ARE DOING EVERYTHING IN THEIR POWER TO GET THAT DETAIL OF M4'S UP HERE TO THE DAM!
HE ALSO SAYS SOMETHING ABOUT OWING YOU FIVE BUCKS FOR LOSING A BET, SIR!
<HERR KAPITAN, A MOMENT, IF YOU PLEASE. I HEARD WHAT HAPPENED WITH THAT IDIOT SS OFFICER, VEITEL.>
<SUCH A MAN DOES NOT DESERVE TO CALL HIMSELF A GERMAN.>
<HIS ONLY COUNTRY IS HIMSELF. AND FOR HIS STUPIDITY YOU HAVE MY APOLOGIES.>

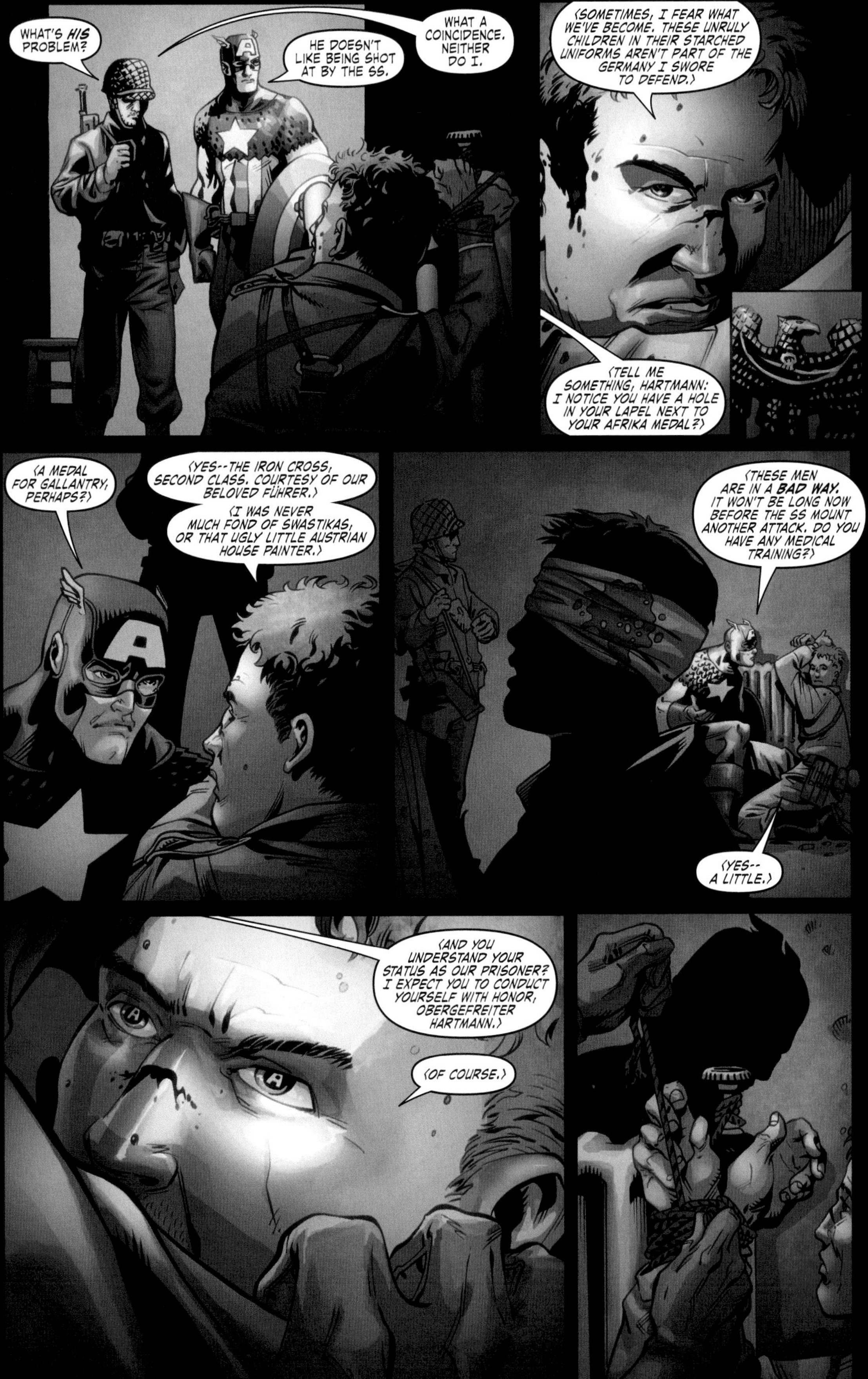
WHAT'S HIS PROBLEM?
HE DOESN'T LIKE BEING SHOT AT BY THE SS.
WHAT A COINCIDENCE. NEITHER DO I.
⟨SOMETIMES, I FEAR WHAT WE'VE BECOME. THESE UNRULY CHILDREN IN THEIR STARCHED UNIFORMS AREN'T PART OF THE GERMANY I SWORE TO DEFEND.⟩
⟨TELL ME SOMETHING, HARTMANN: I NOTICE YOU HAVE A HOLE IN YOUR LAPEL NEXT TO YOUR AFRIKA MEDAL?⟩
⟨A MEDAL FOR GALLANTRY, PERHAPS?⟩
⟨YES--THE IRON CROSS, SECOND CLASS. COURTESY OF OUR BELOVED FÜHRER.⟩
⟨I WAS NEVER MUCH FOND OF SWASTIKAS, OR THAT UGLY LITTLE AUSTRIAN HOUSE PAINTER.⟩
⟨THESE MEN ARE IN A BAD WAY. IT WON'T BE LONG NOW BEFORE THE SS MOUNT ANOTHER ATTACK. DO YOU HAVE ANY MEDICAL TRAINING?⟩
⟨YES-- A LITTLE.⟩
⟨AND YOU UNDERSTAND YOUR STATUS AS OUR PRISONER? I EXPECT YOU TO CONDUCT YOURSELF WITH HONOR, OBERGEFREITER HARTMANN.⟩
⟨OF COURSE.⟩

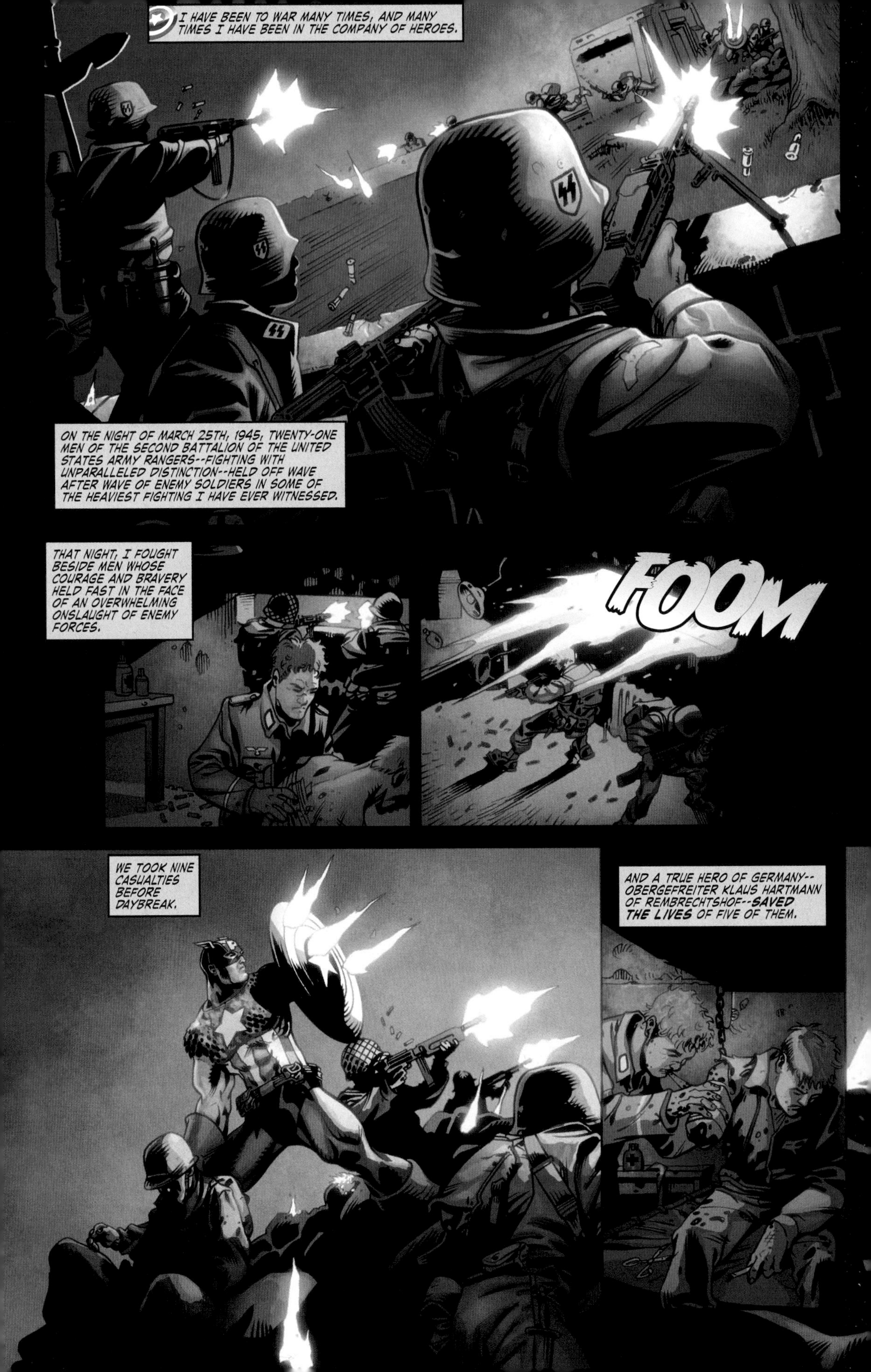

I HAVE BEEN TO WAR MANY TIMES, AND MANY TIMES I HAVE BEEN IN THE COMPANY OF HEROES.
ON THE NIGHT OF MARCH 25TH, 1945, TWENTY-ONE MEN OF THE SECOND BATTALION OF THE UNITED STATES ARMY RANGERS--FIGHTING WITH UNPARALLELED DISTINCTION--HELD OFF WAVE AFTER WAVE OF ENEMY SOLDIERS IN SOME OF THE HEAVIEST FIGHTING I HAVE EVER WITNESSED.
THAT NIGHT, I FOUGHT BESIDE MEN WHOSE COURAGE AND BRAVERY HELD FAST IN THE FACE OF AN OVERWHELMING ONSLAUGHT OF ENEMY FORCES.
FOOM
WE TOOK NINE CASUALTIES BEFORE DAYBREAK.
AND A TRUE HERO OF GERMANY--OBERGEFREITER KLAUS HARTMANN OF REMBRECHTSHOF--**SAVED THE LIVES** OF FIVE OF THEM.

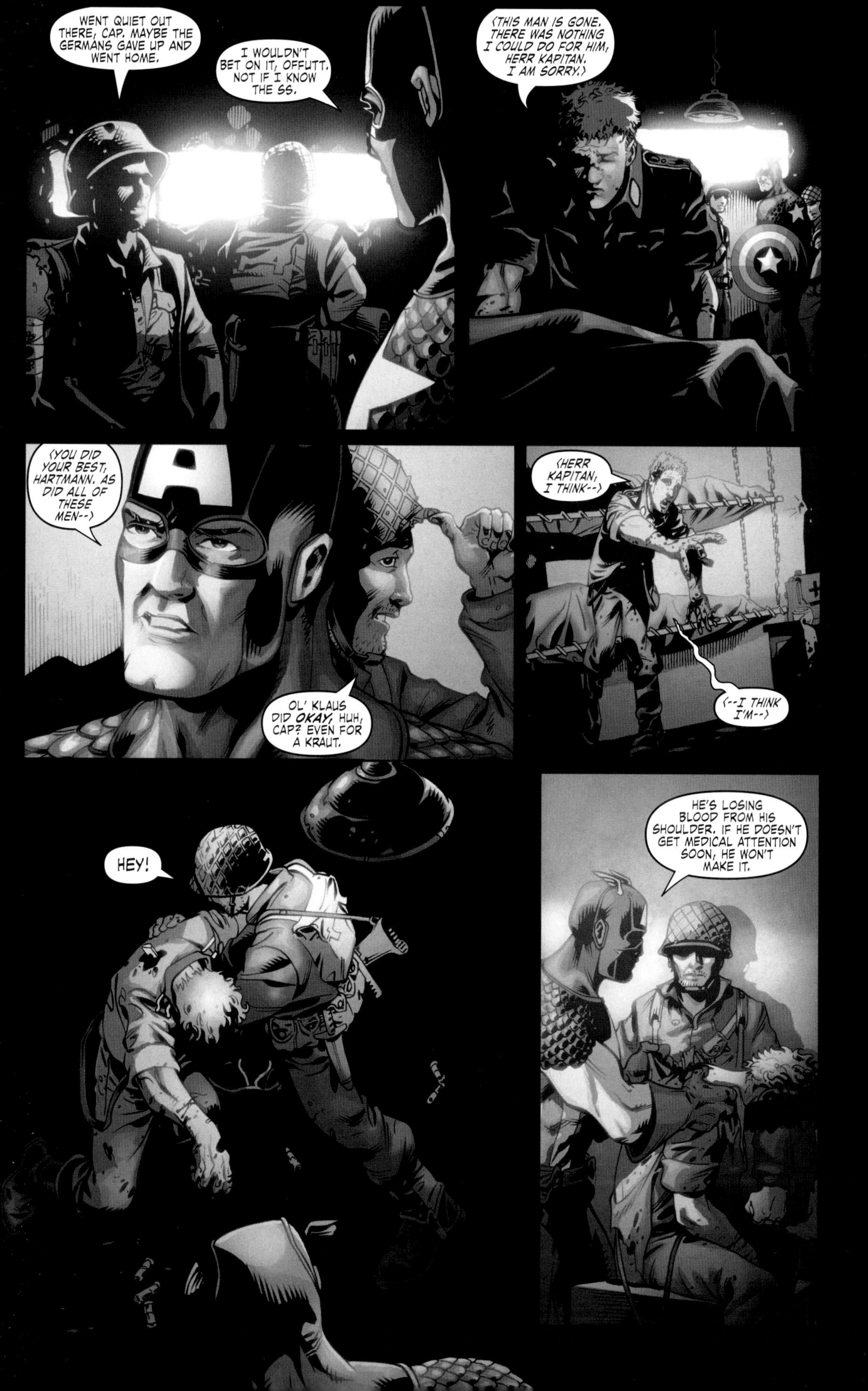
WENT QUIET OUT THERE, CAP. MAYBE THE GERMANS GAVE UP AND WENT HOME.
I WOULDN'T BET ON IT, OFFUTT. NOT IF I KNOW THE SS.
‹THIS MAN IS GONE. THERE WAS NOTHING I COULD DO FOR HIM, HERR KAPITAN. I AM SORRY.›
‹YOU DID YOUR BEST, HARTMANN. AS DID ALL OF THESE MEN--›
OL' KLAUS DID OKAY, HUH, CAP? EVEN FOR A KRAUT.
‹HERR KAPITAN, I THINK--›
‹--I THINK I'M--›
HEY!
HE'S LOSING BLOOD FROM HIS SHOULDER. IF HE DOESN'T GET MEDICAL ATTENTION SOON, HE WON'T MAKE IT.

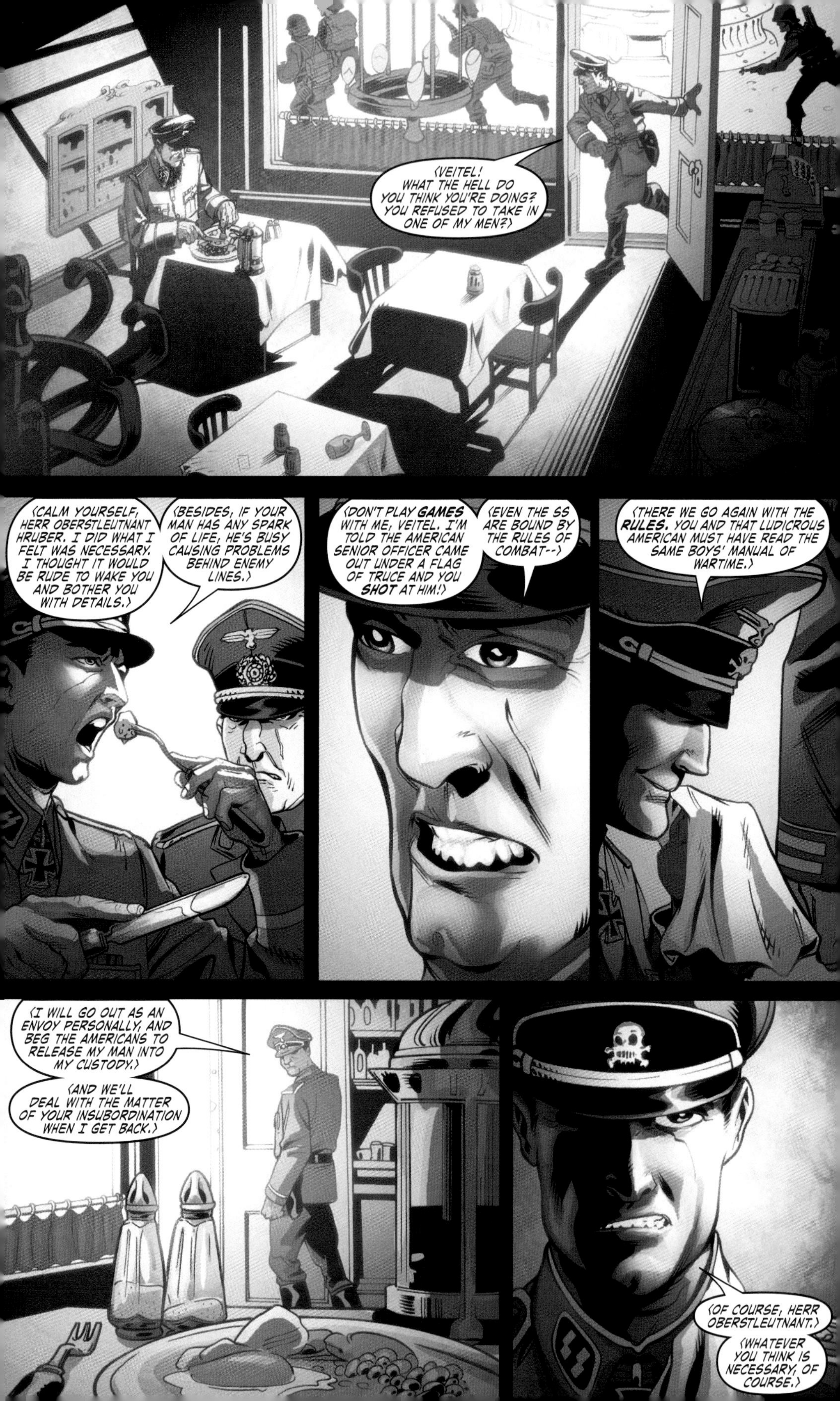
‹VEITEL! WHAT THE HELL DO YOU THINK YOU'RE DOING? YOU REFUSED TO TAKE IN ONE OF MY MEN?›
‹CALM YOURSELF, HERR OBERSTLEUTNANT HRUBER. I DID WHAT I FELT WAS NECESSARY. I THOUGHT IT WOULD BE RUDE TO WAKE YOU AND BOTHER YOU WITH DETAILS.›
‹BESIDES, IF YOUR MAN HAS ANY SPARK OF LIFE, HE'S BUSY CAUSING PROBLEMS BEHIND ENEMY LINES.›
‹DON'T PLAY GAMES WITH ME, VEITEL. I'M TOLD THE AMERICAN SENIOR OFFICER CAME OUT UNDER A FLAG OF TRUCE AND YOU SHOT AT HIM!›
‹EVEN THE SS ARE BOUND BY THE RULES OF COMBAT--›
‹THERE WE GO AGAIN WITH THE RULES. YOU AND THAT LUDICROUS AMERICAN MUST HAVE READ THE SAME BOYS' MANUAL OF WARTIME.›
‹I WILL GO OUT AS AN ENVOY PERSONALLY, AND BEG THE AMERICANS TO RELEASE MY MAN INTO MY CUSTODY.›
‹AND WE'LL DEAL WITH THE MATTER OF YOUR INSUBORDINATION WHEN I GET BACK.›
‹OF COURSE, HERR OBERSTLEUTNANT.›
‹WHATEVER YOU THINK IS NECESSARY, OF COURSE.›

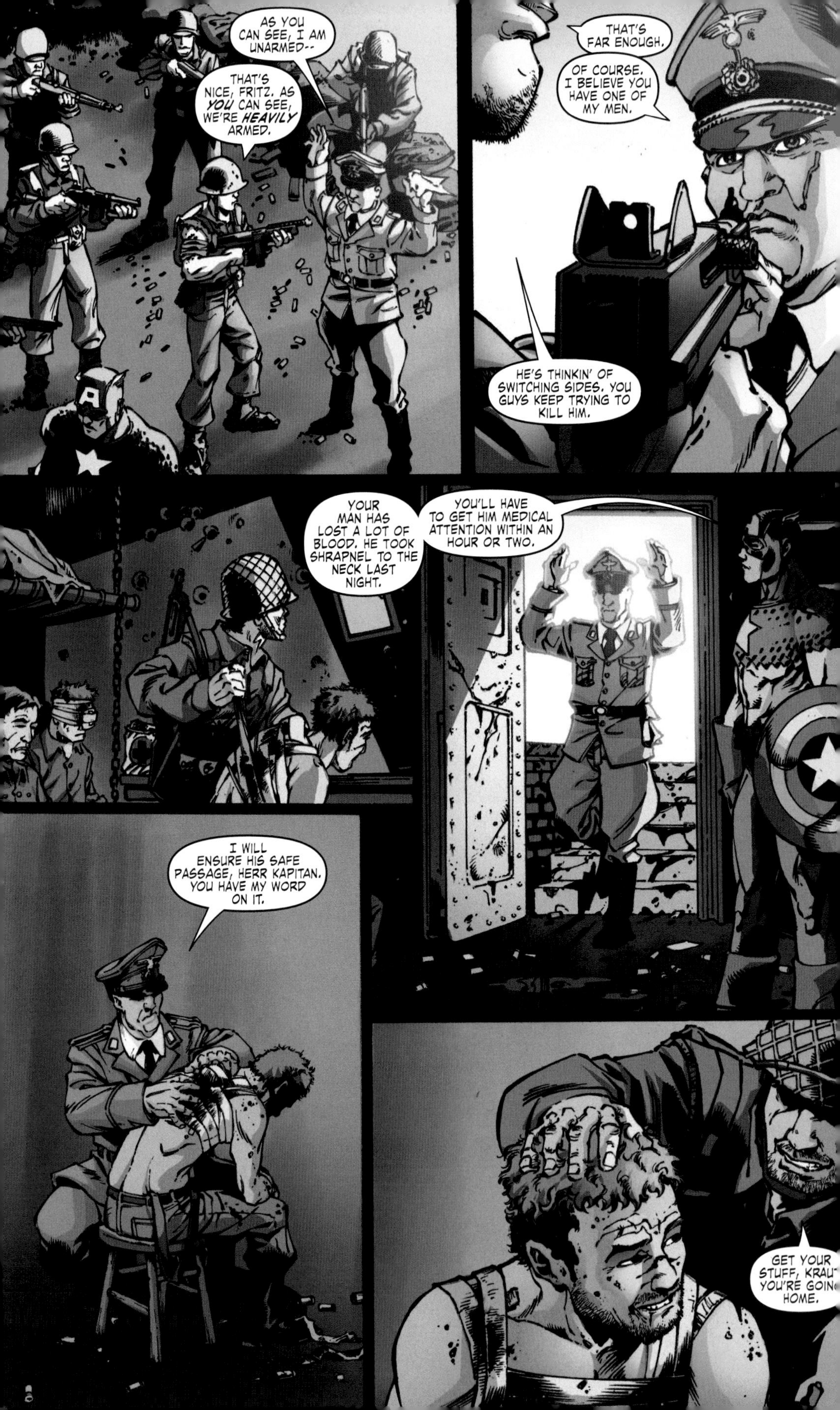

AS YOU CAN SEE, I AM UNARMED--
THAT'S NICE, FRITZ. AS *YOU* CAN SEE, WE'RE ***HEAVILY*** ARMED.
THAT'S FAR ENOUGH.
OF COURSE, I BELIEVE YOU HAVE ONE OF MY MEN.
HE'S THINKIN' OF SWITCHING SIDES. YOU GUYS KEEP TRYING TO KILL HIM.
YOUR MAN HAS LOST A LOT OF BLOOD. HE TOOK SHRAPNEL TO THE NECK LAST NIGHT.
YOU'LL HAVE TO GET HIM MEDICAL ATTENTION WITHIN AN HOUR OR TWO.
I WILL ENSURE HIS SAFE PASSAGE, HERR KAPITAN. YOU HAVE MY WORD ON IT.
GET YOUR STUFF, KRAU YOU'RE GOIN HOME.

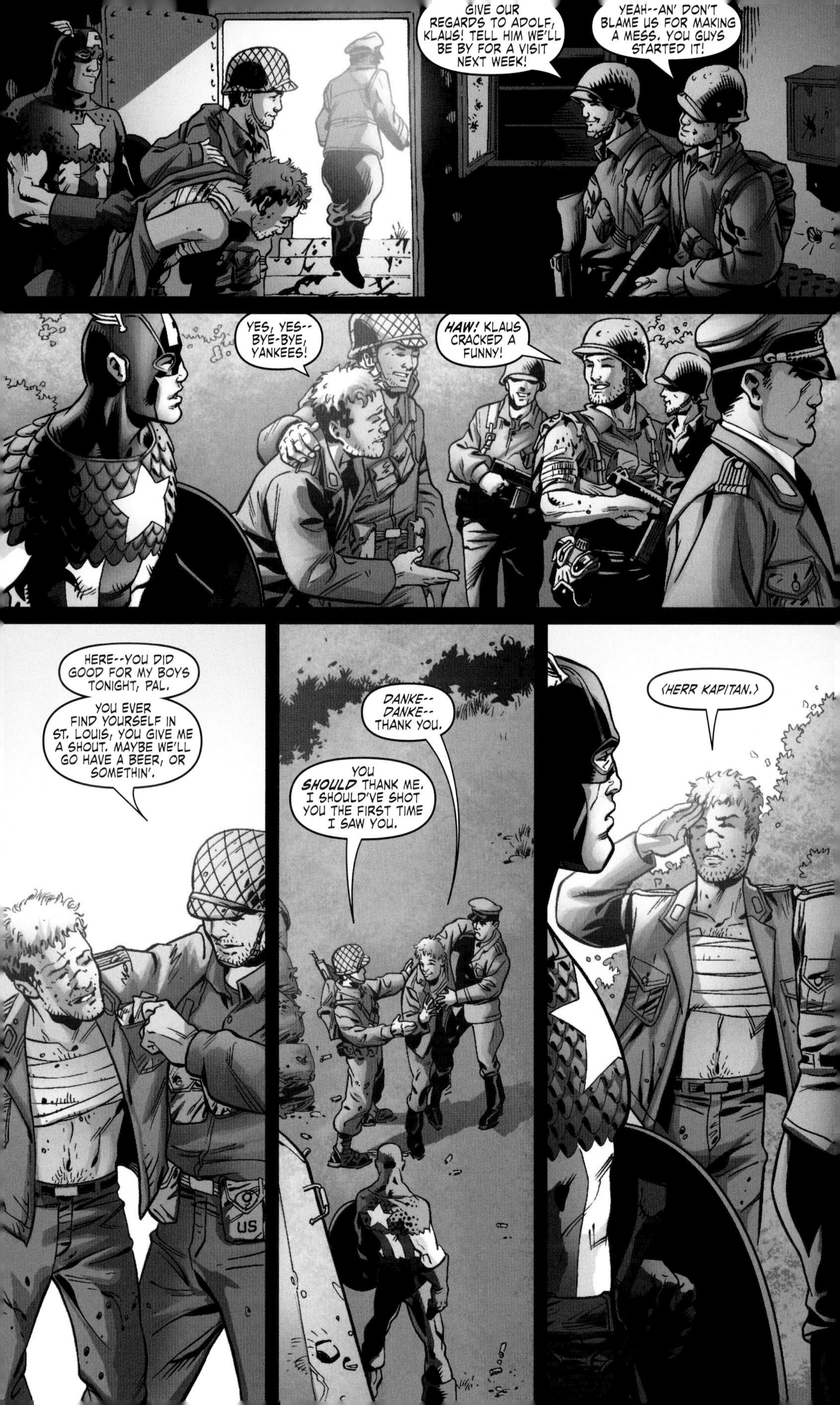
GIVE OUR REGARDS TO ADOLF, KLAUS! TELL HIM WE'LL BE BY FOR A VISIT NEXT WEEK!
YEAH--AN' DON'T BLAME US FOR MAKING A MESS. YOU GUYS STARTED IT!
YES, YES--BYE-BYE, YANKEES!
HAW! KLAUS CRACKED A FUNNY!
HERE--YOU DID GOOD FOR MY BOYS TONIGHT, PAL.
YOU EVER FIND YOURSELF IN ST. LOUIS, YOU GIVE ME A SHOUT. MAYBE WE'LL GO HAVE A BEER, OR SOMETHIN'.
DANKE--DANKE--THANK YOU.
YOU SHOULD THANK ME. I SHOULD'VE SHOT YOU THE FIRST TIME I SAW YOU.
<HERR KAPITAN.>
US

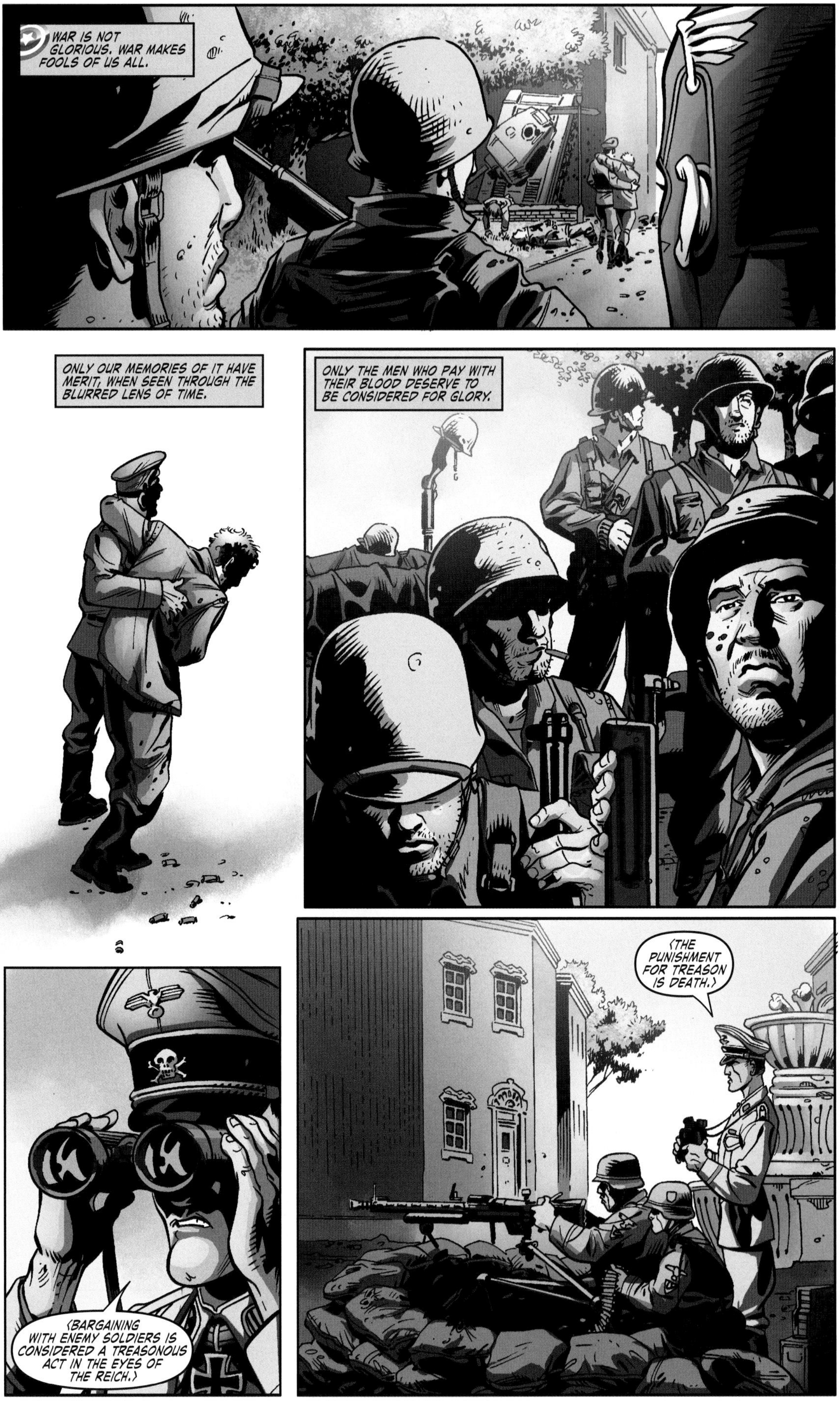
WAR IS NOT GLORIOUS. WAR MAKES FOOLS OF US ALL.
ONLY OUR MEMORIES OF IT HAVE MERIT, WHEN SEEN THROUGH THE BLURRED LENS OF TIME.
ONLY THE MEN WHO PAY WITH THEIR BLOOD DESERVE TO BE CONSIDERED FOR GLORY.
‹BARGAINING WITH ENEMY SOLDIERS IS CONSIDERED A TREASONOUS ACT IN THE EYES OF THE REICH.›
‹THE PUNISHMENT FOR TREASON IS DEATH.›

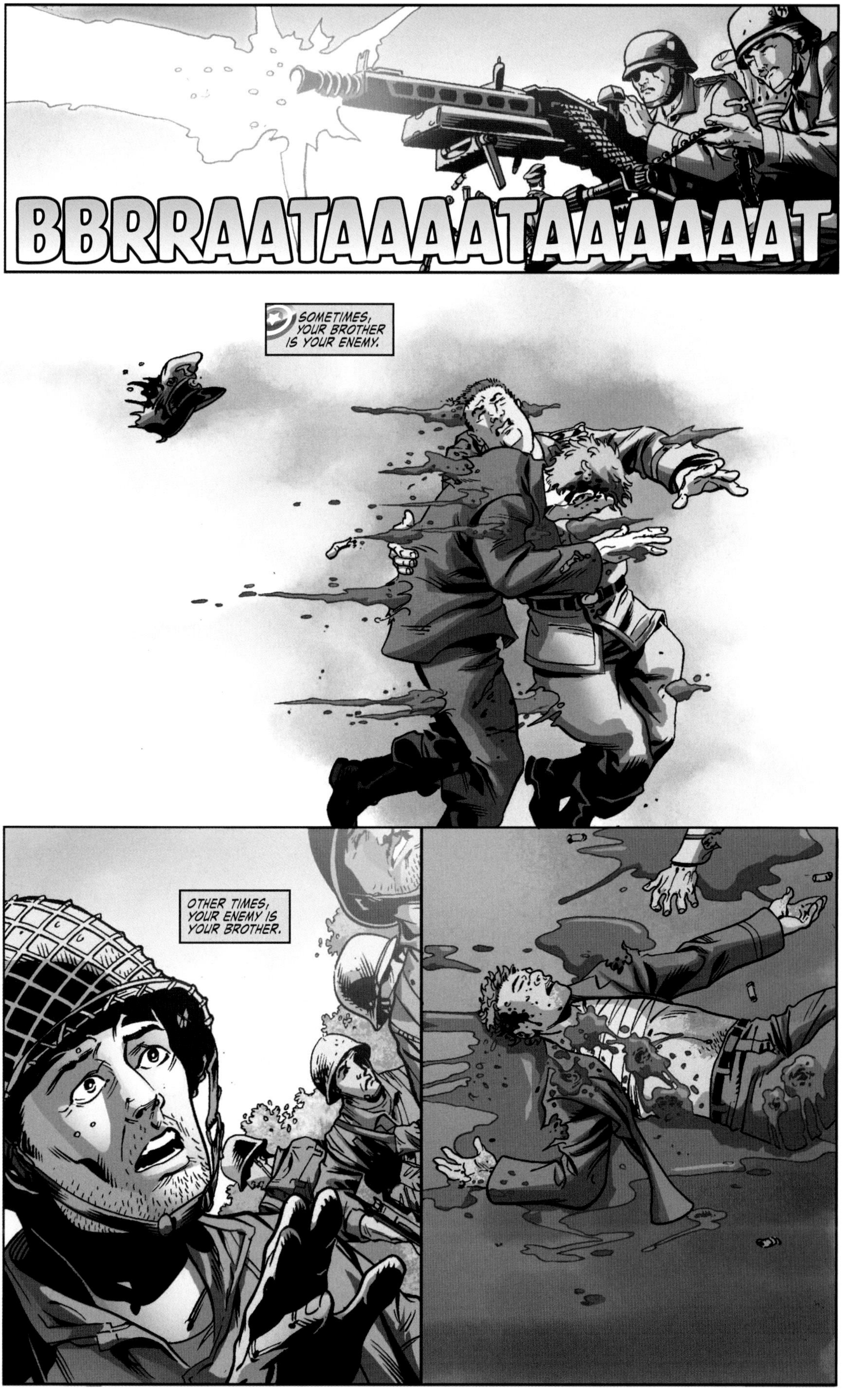
BBRRAATAAAATAAAAAAT
SOMETIMES, YOUR BROTHER IS YOUR ENEMY.
OTHER TIMES, YOUR ENEMY IS YOUR BROTHER.

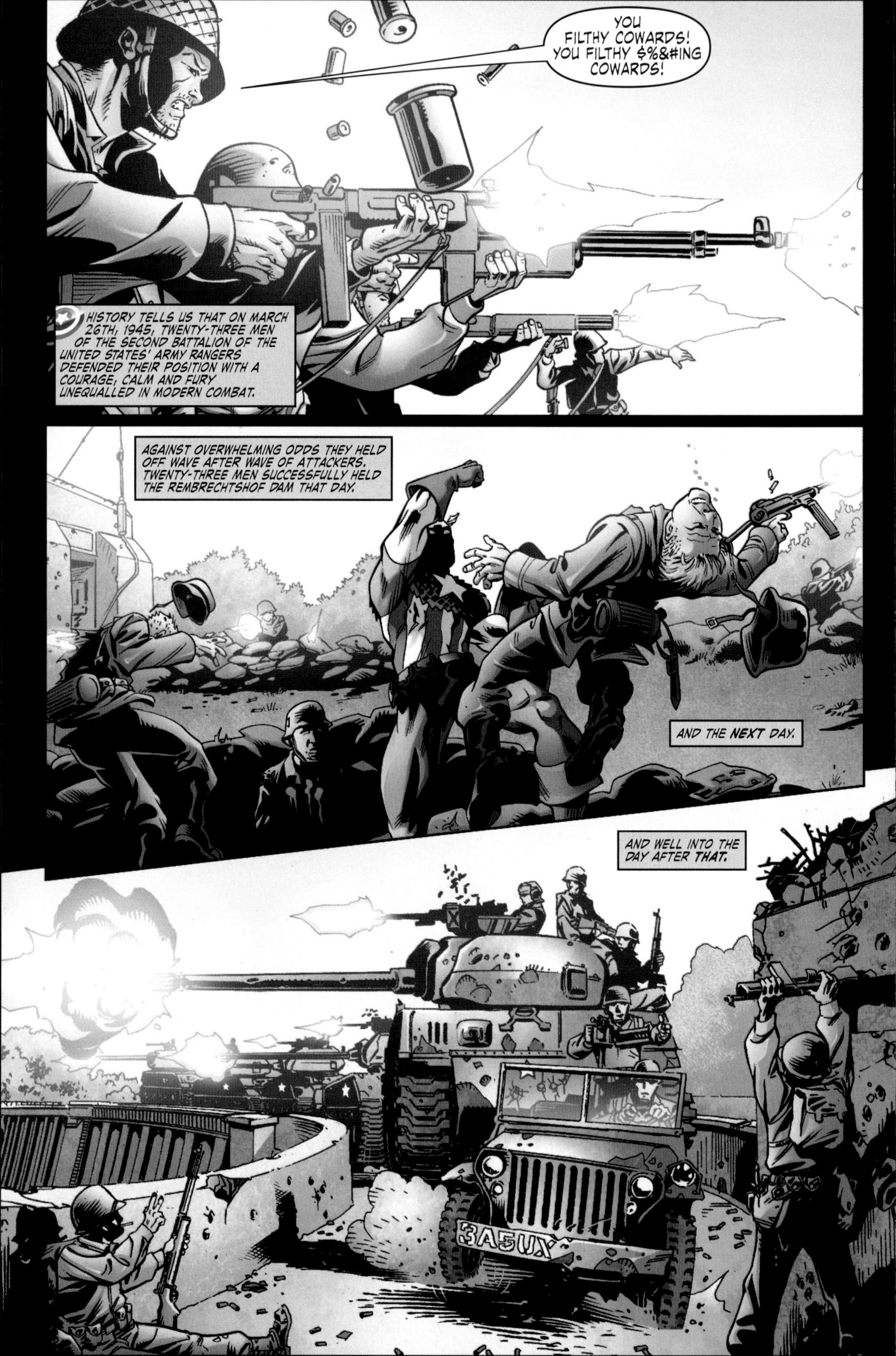
YOU FILTHY COWARDS! YOU FILTHY $%&#ING COWARDS!
HISTORY TELLS US THAT ON MARCH 26TH, 1945, TWENTY-THREE MEN OF THE SECOND BATTALION OF THE UNITED STATES' ARMY RANGERS DEFENDED THEIR POSITION WITH A COURAGE, CALM AND FURY UNEQUALLED IN MODERN COMBAT.
AGAINST OVERWHELMING ODDS THEY HELD OFF WAVE AFTER WAVE OF ATTACKERS. TWENTY-THREE MEN SUCCESSFULLY HELD THE REMBRECHTSHOF DAM THAT DAY.
AND THE NEXT DAY.
AND WELL INTO THE DAY AFTER THAT.
3A5UX

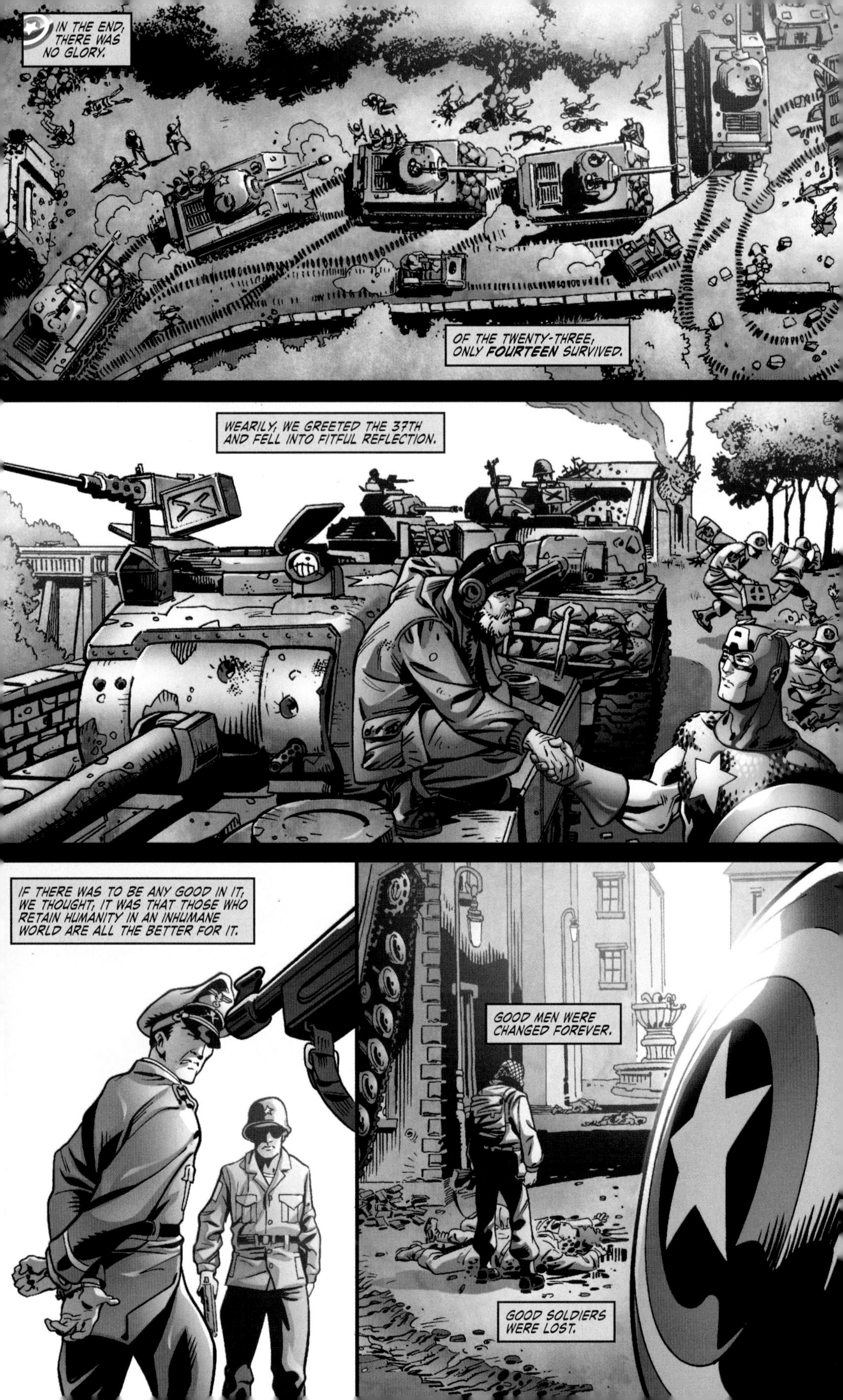
IN THE END, THERE WAS NO GLORY.
OF THE TWENTY-THREE, ONLY FOURTEEN SURVIVED.
WEARILY, WE GREETED THE 37TH AND FELL INTO FITFUL REFLECTION.
IF THERE WAS TO BE ANY GOOD IN IT, WE THOUGHT, IT WAS THAT THOSE WHO RETAIN HUMANITY IN AN INHUMANE WORLD ARE ALL THE BETTER FOR IT.
GOOD MEN WERE CHANGED FOREVER.
GOOD SOLDIERS WERE LOST.

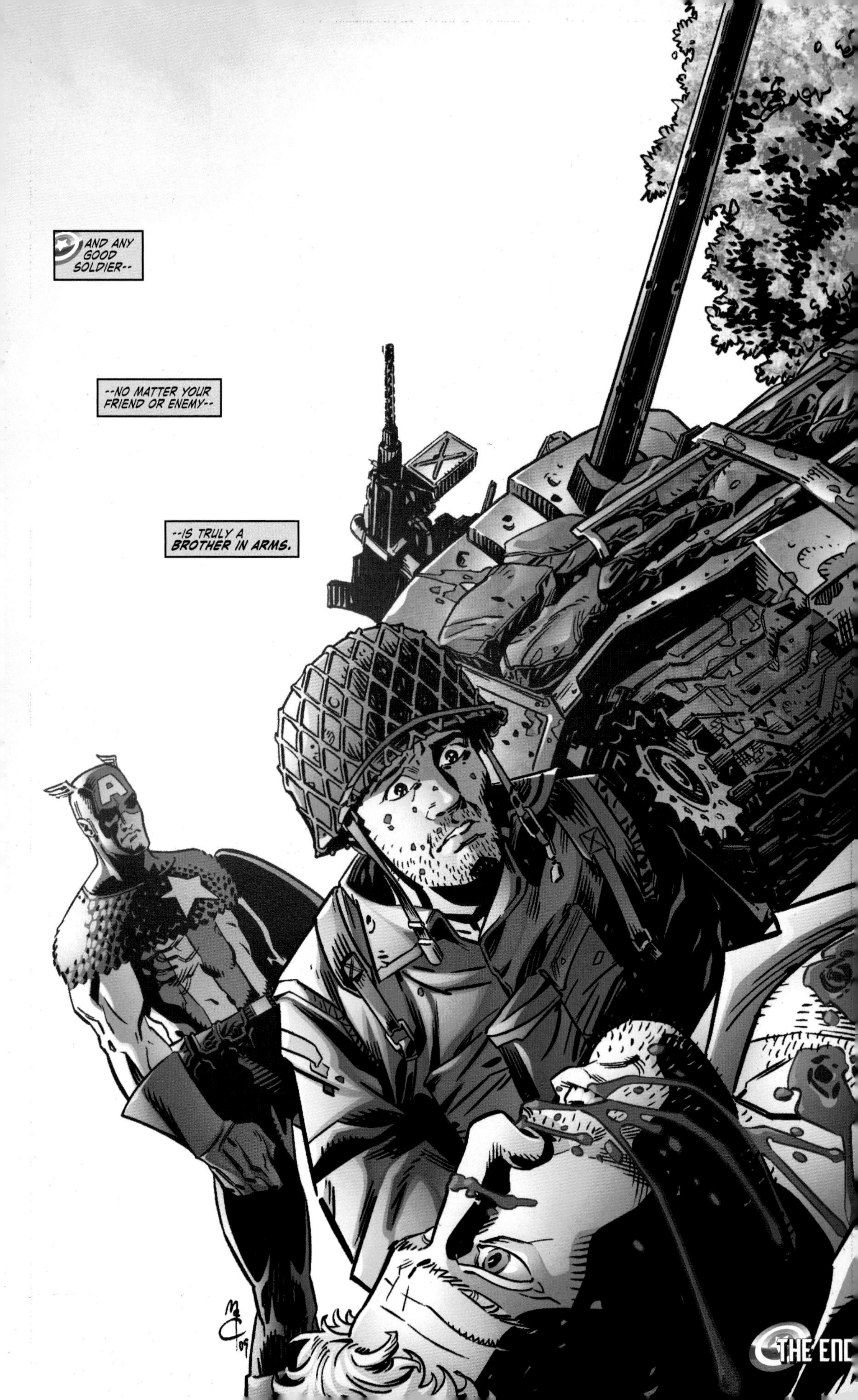
AND ANY GOOD SOLDIER--
--NO MATTER YOUR FRIEND OR ENEMY--
--IS TRULY A BROTHER IN ARMS.
THE END

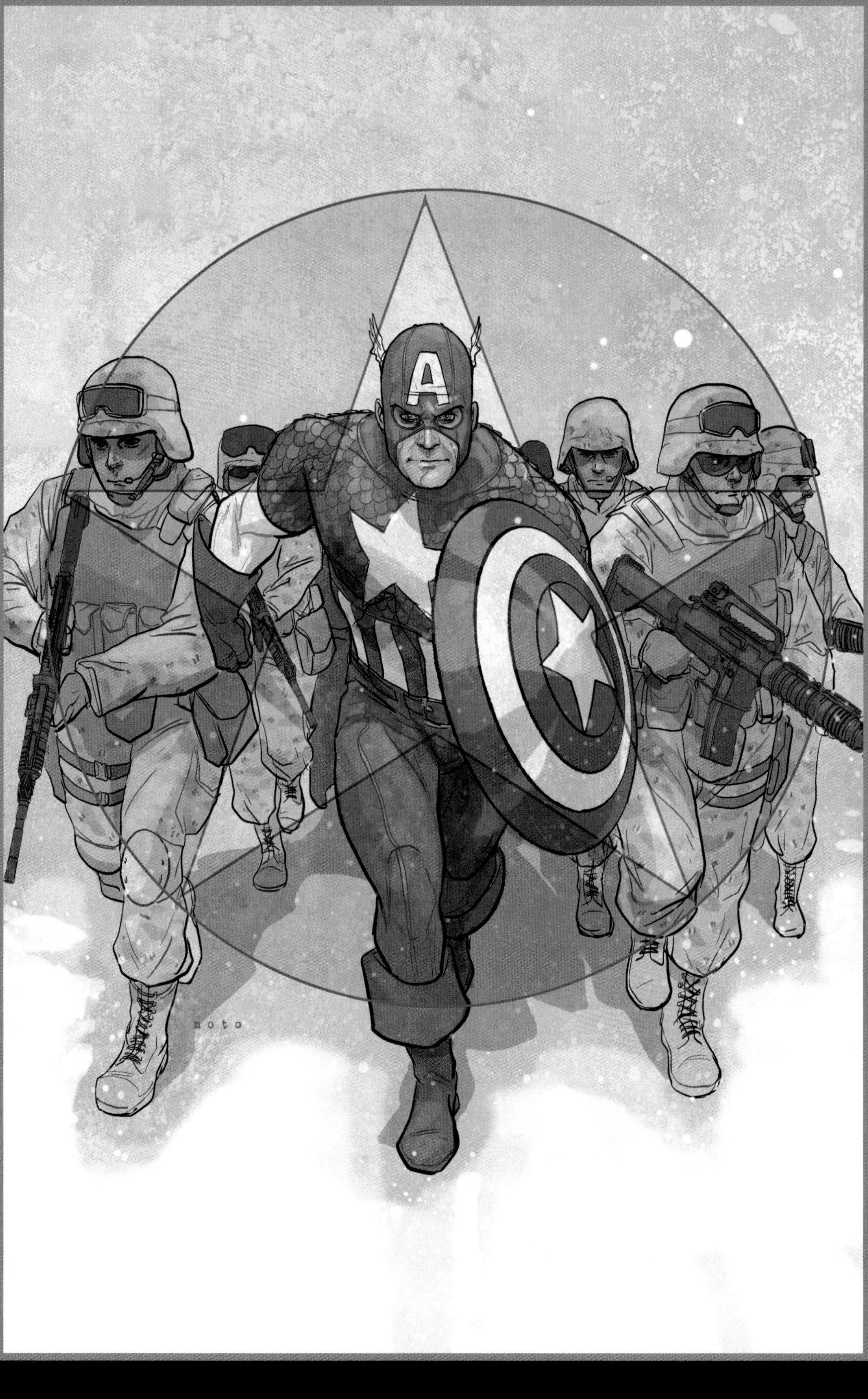
noto

TO SOLDIER ON

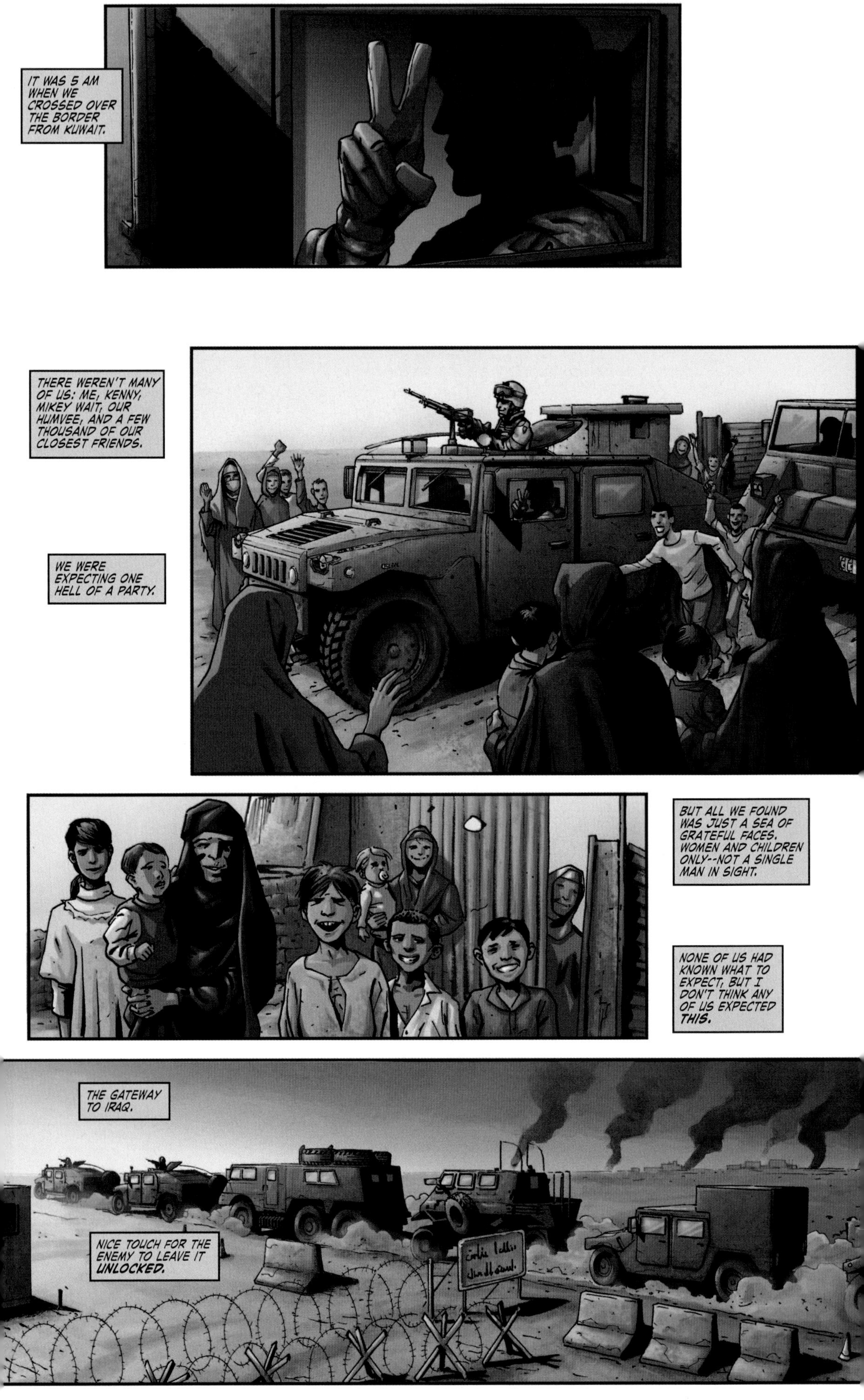
IT WAS 5 AM WHEN WE CROSSED OVER THE BORDER FROM KUWAIT.
THERE WEREN'T MANY OF US: ME, KENNY, MIKEY WAIT, OUR HUMVEE, AND A FEW THOUSAND OF OUR CLOSEST FRIENDS.
WE WERE EXPECTING ONE HELL OF A PARTY.
BUT ALL WE FOUND WAS JUST A SEA OF GRATEFUL FACES. WOMEN AND CHILDREN ONLY--NOT A SINGLE MAN IN SIGHT.
NONE OF US HAD KNOWN WHAT TO EXPECT, BUT I DON'T THINK ANY OF US EXPECTED THIS.
THE GATEWAY TO IRAQ.
NICE TOUCH FOR THE ENEMY TO LEAVE IT UNLOCKED.

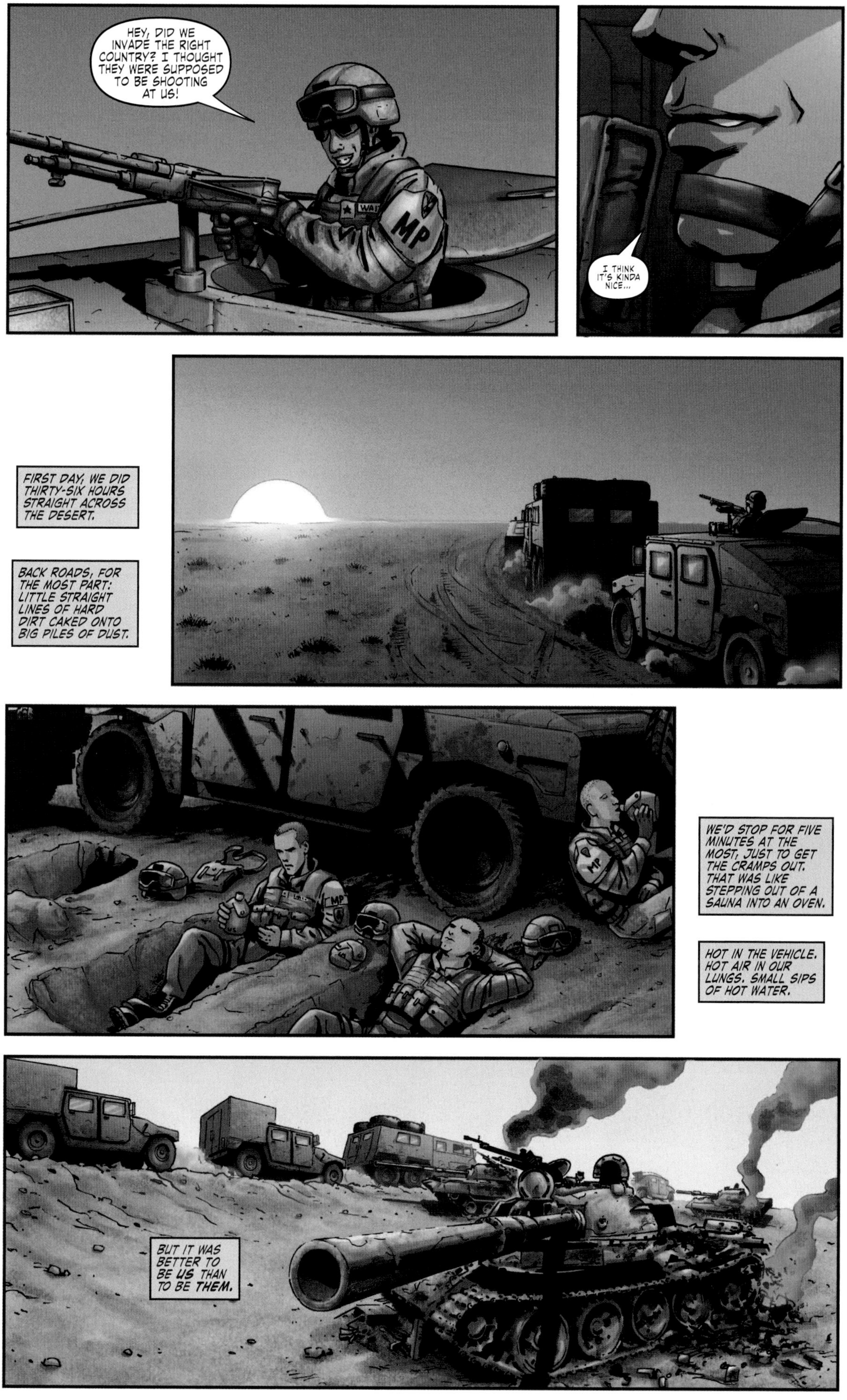
HEY, DID WE INVADE THE RIGHT COUNTRY? I THOUGHT THEY WERE SUPPOSED TO BE SHOOTING AT US!
I THINK IT'S KINDA NICE...
FIRST DAY, WE DID THIRTY-SIX HOURS STRAIGHT ACROSS THE DESERT.
BACK ROADS, FOR THE MOST PART: LITTLE STRAIGHT LINES OF HARD DIRT CAKED ONTO BIG PILES OF DUST.
WE'D STOP FOR FIVE MINUTES AT THE MOST, JUST TO GET THE CRAMPS OUT. THAT WAS LIKE STEPPING OUT OF A SAUNA INTO AN OVEN.
HOT IN THE VEHICLE. HOT AIR IN OUR LUNGS. SMALL SIPS OF HOT WATER.
BUT IT WAS BETTER TO BE US THAN TO BE THEM.

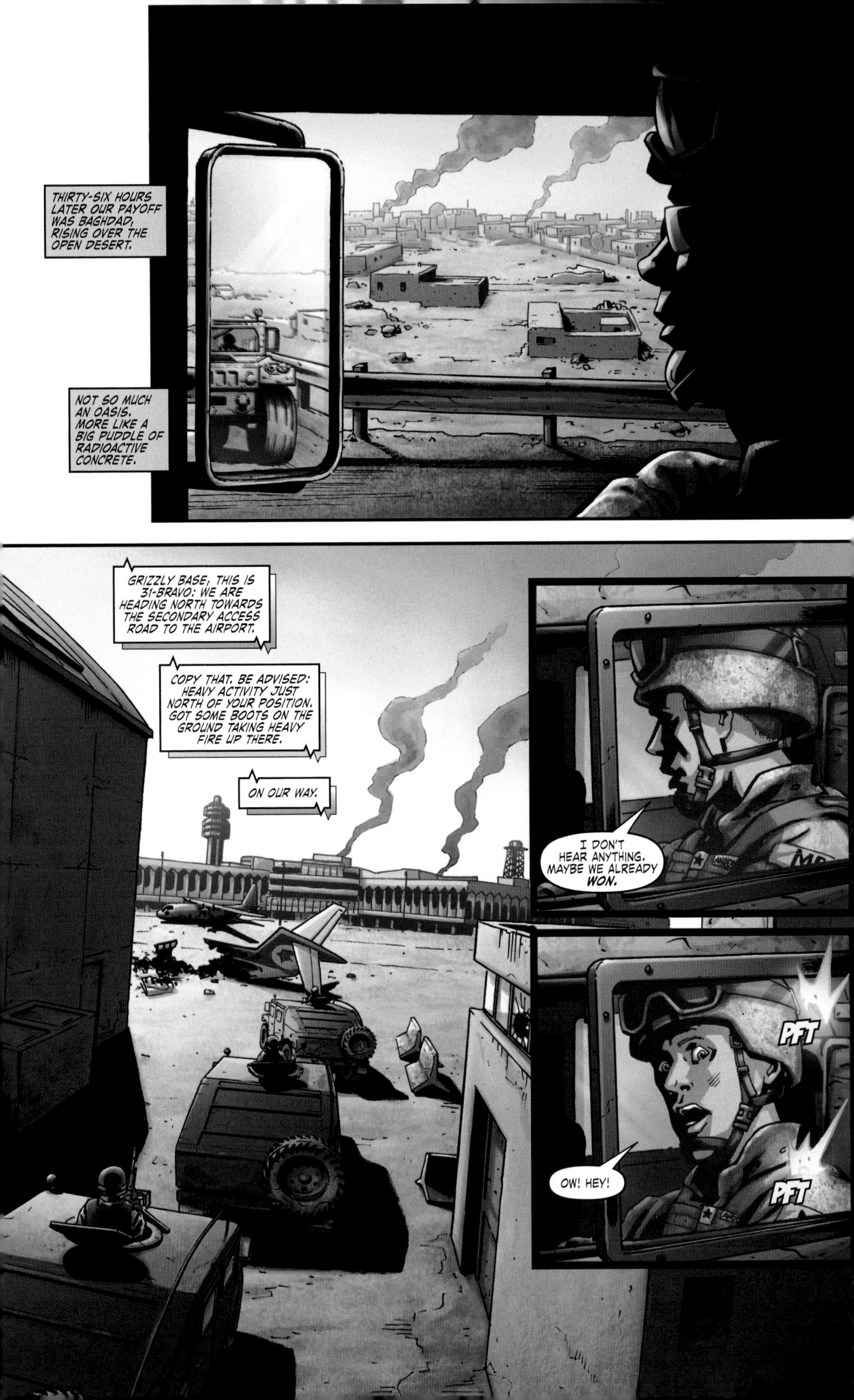
THIRTY-SIX HOURS LATER OUR PAYOFF WAS BAGHDAD, RISING OVER THE OPEN DESERT.
NOT SO MUCH AN OASIS. MORE LIKE A BIG PUDDLE OF RADIOACTIVE CONCRETE.
GRIZZLY BASE, THIS IS 31-BRAVO: WE ARE HEADING NORTH TOWARDS THE SECONDARY ACCESS ROAD TO THE AIRPORT.
COPY THAT. BE ADVISED: HEAVY ACTIVITY JUST NORTH OF YOUR POSITION. GOT SOME BOOTS ON THE GROUND TAKING HEAVY FIRE UP THERE.
ON OUR WAY.
I DON'T HEAR ANYTHING. MAYBE WE ALREADY WON.
PFT
OW! HEY!
PFT

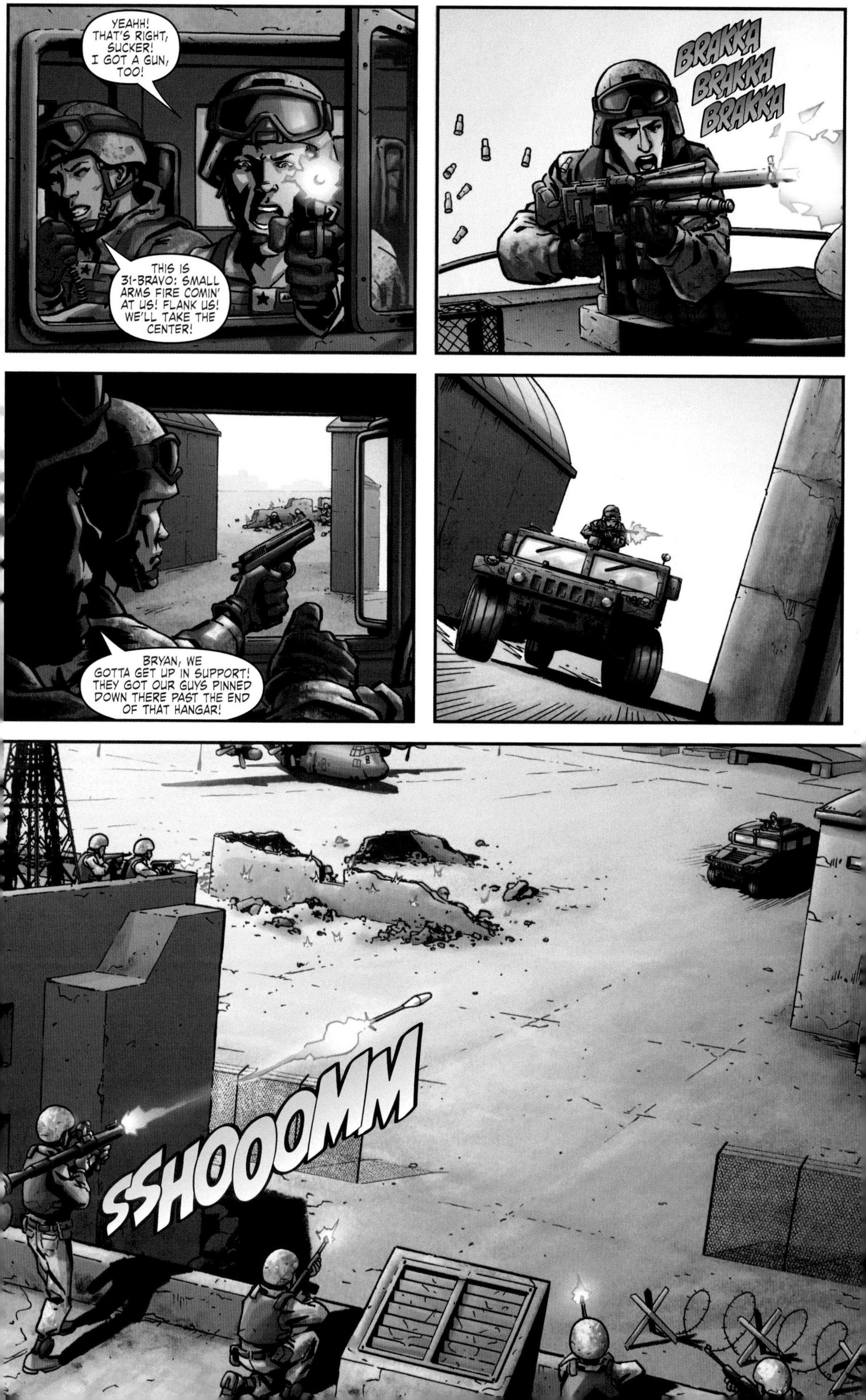
YEAHH! THAT'S RIGHT, SUCKER! I GOT A GUN, TOO!
THIS IS 31-BRAVO: SMALL ARMS FIRE COMIN' AT US! FLANK US! WE'LL TAKE THE CENTER!
BRAKKA BRAKKA BRAKKA
BRYAN, WE GOTTA GET UP IN SUPPORT! THEY GOT OUR GUYS PINNED DOWN THERE PAST THE END OF THAT HANGAR!
SSHOOOMM

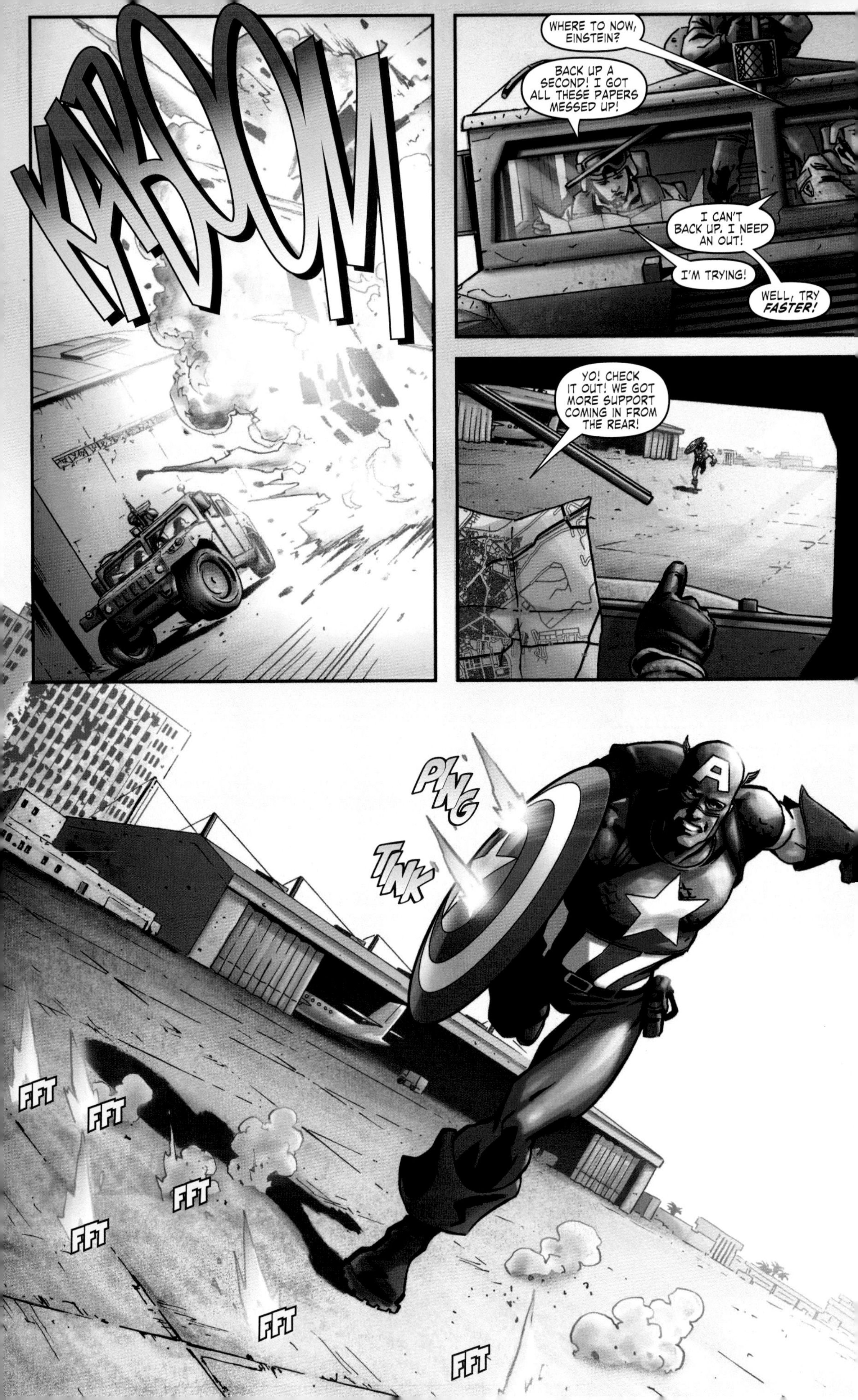
KABOOM
WHERE TO NOW, EINSTEIN?
BACK UP A SECOND! I GOT ALL THESE PAPERS MESSED UP!
I CAN'T BACK UP. I NEED AN OUT!
I'M TRYING!
WELL, TRY FASTER!
YO! CHECK IT OUT! WE GOT MORE SUPPORT COMING IN FROM THE REAR!
PING
TINK
FFT
FFT
FFT
FFT
FFT
FFT

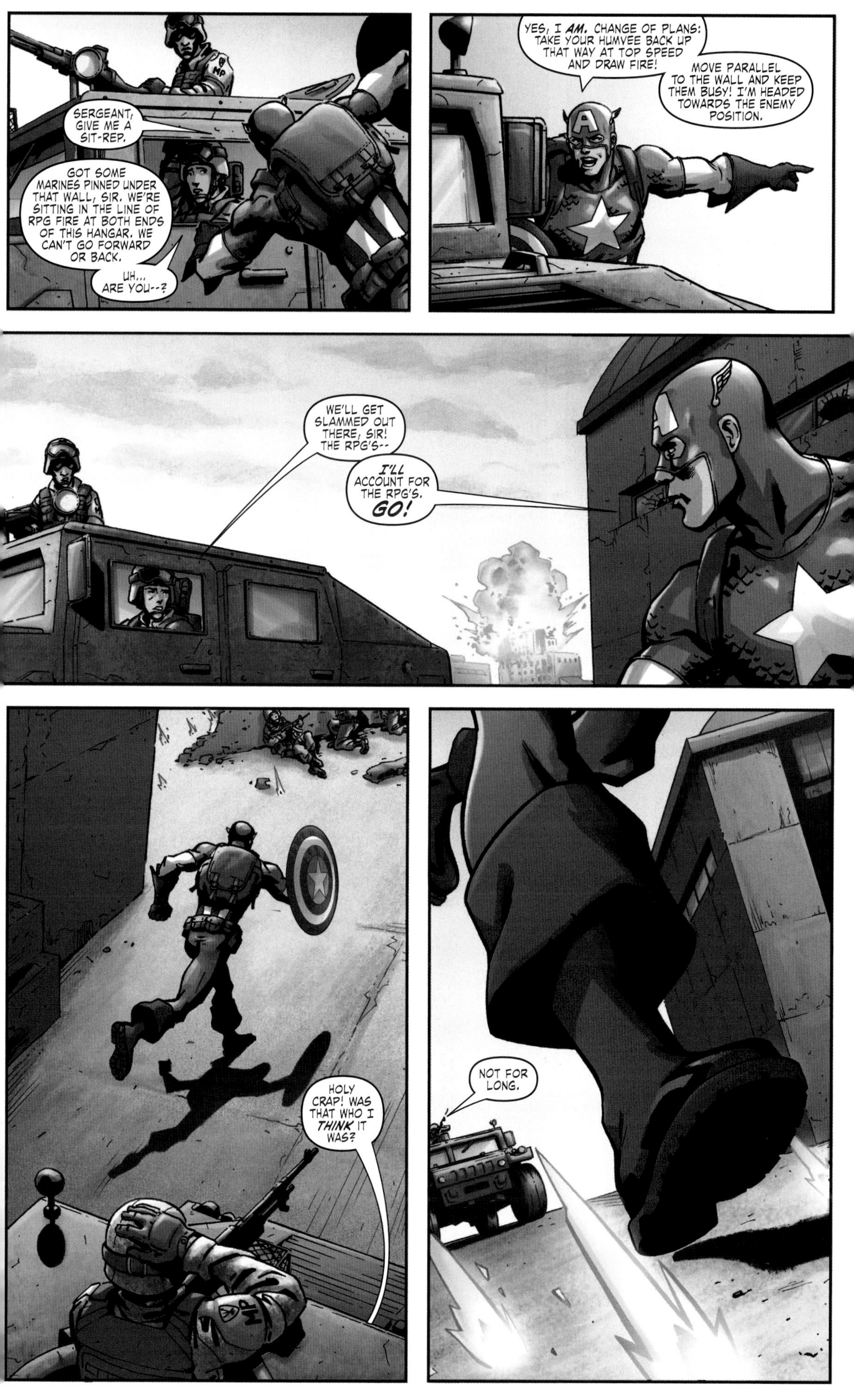
SERGEANT, GIVE ME A SIT-REP.
GOT SOME MARINES PINNED UNDER THAT WALL, SIR. WE'RE SITTING IN THE LINE OF RPG FIRE AT BOTH ENDS OF THIS HANGAR. WE CAN'T GO FORWARD OR BACK.
UH... ARE YOU--?
YES, I AM. CHANGE OF PLANS: TAKE YOUR HUMVEE BACK UP THAT WAY AT TOP SPEED AND DRAW FIRE!
MOVE PARALLEL TO THE WALL AND KEEP THEM BUSY! I'M HEADED TOWARDS THE ENEMY POSITION.
WE'LL GET SLAMMED OUT THERE, SIR! THE RPG'S--
I'LL ACCOUNT FOR THE RPG'S. GO!
HOLY CRAP! WAS THAT WHO I THINK IT WAS?
NOT FOR LONG.

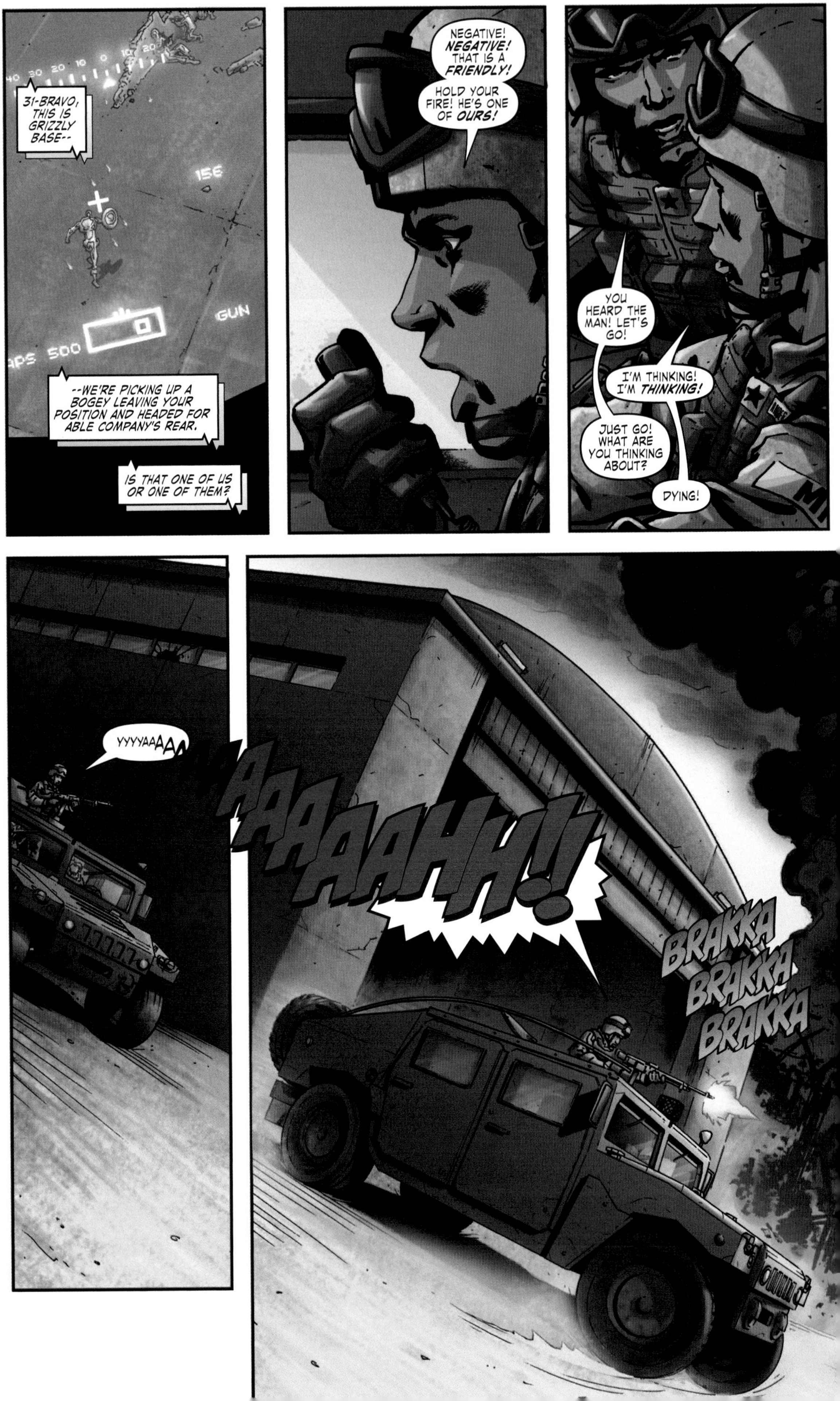
31-BRAVO, THIS IS GRIZZLY BASE--
--WE'RE PICKING UP A BOGEY LEAVING YOUR POSITION AND HEADED FOR ABLE COMPANY'S REAR.
IS THAT ONE OF US OR ONE OF THEM?
NEGATIVE! NEGATIVE! THAT IS A FRIENDLY!
HOLD YOUR FIRE! HE'S ONE OF OURS!
YOU HEARD THE MAN! LET'S GO!
I'M THINKING! I'M THINKING!
JUST GO! WHAT ARE YOU THINKING ABOUT?
DYING!
YYYYAAAAAAAAAAAHH!!
BRAKKA BRAKKA BRAKKA

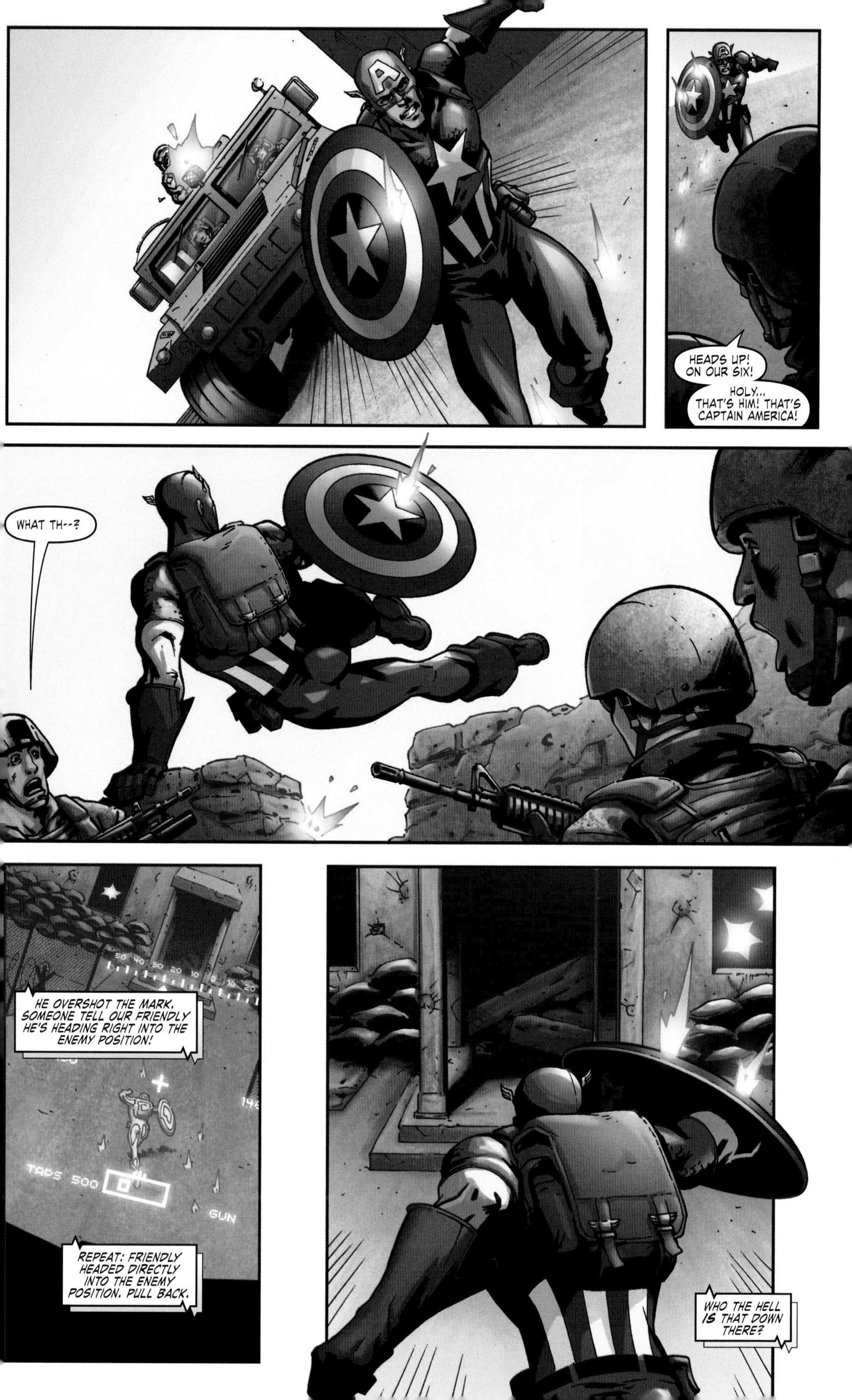
HEADS UP! ON OUR SIX!
HOLY... THAT'S HIM! THAT'S CAPTAIN AMERICA!
WHAT TH--?
HE OVERSHOT THE MARK. SOMEONE TELL OUR FRIENDLY HE'S HEADING RIGHT INTO THE ENEMY POSITION!
TADS 500
GUN
REPEAT: FRIENDLY HEADED DIRECTLY INTO THE ENEMY POSITION. PULL BACK.
WHO THE HELL IS THAT DOWN THERE?

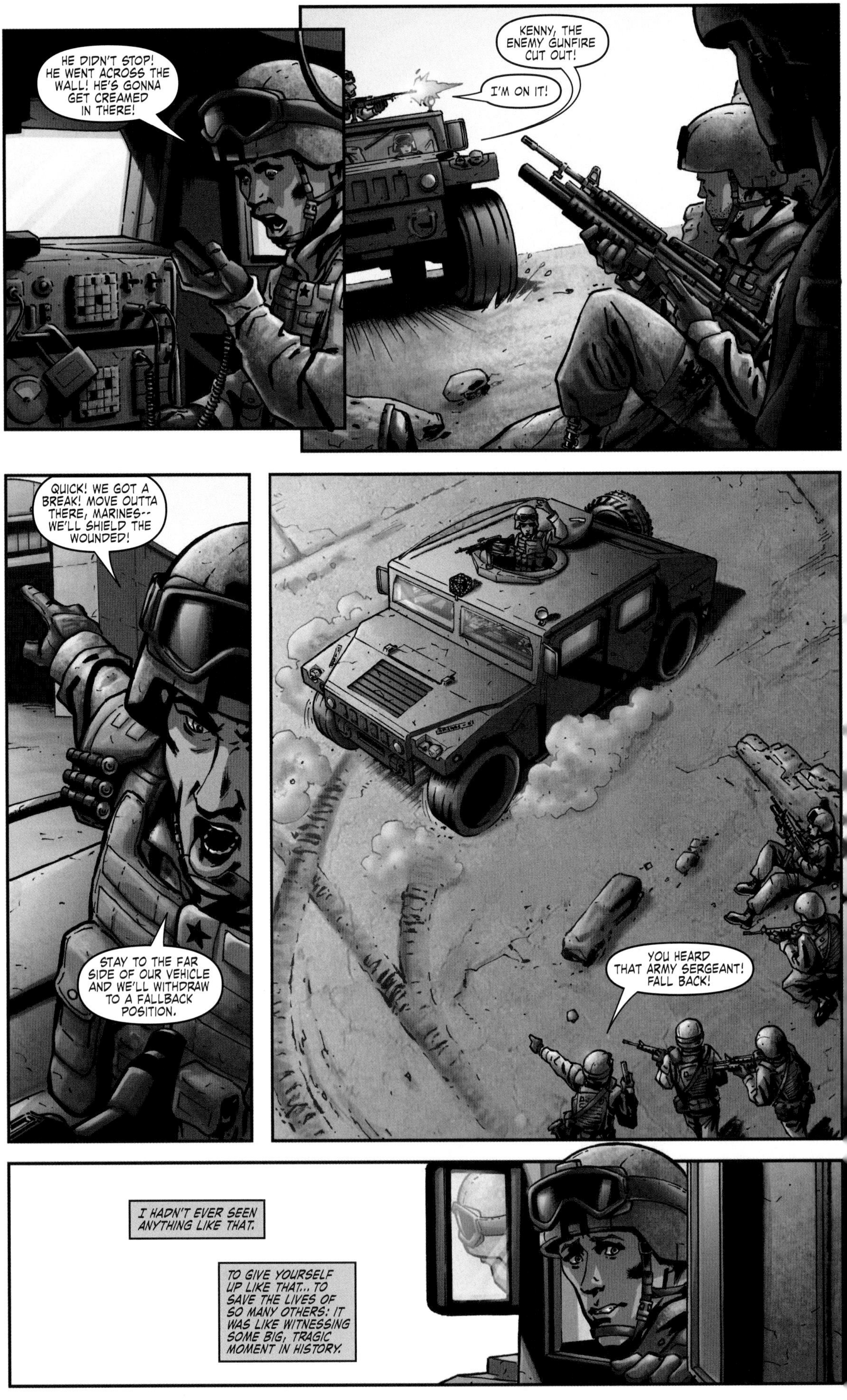
HE DIDN'T STOP! HE WENT ACROSS THE WALL! HE'S GONNA GET CREAMED IN THERE!
KENNY, THE ENEMY GUNFIRE CUT OUT!
I'M ON IT!
QUICK! WE GOT A BREAK! MOVE OUTTA THERE, MARINES-- WE'LL SHIELD THE WOUNDED!
STAY TO THE FAR SIDE OF OUR VEHICLE AND WE'LL WITHDRAW TO A FALLBACK POSITION.
YOU HEARD THAT ARMY SERGEANT! FALL BACK!
I HADN'T EVER SEEN ANYTHING LIKE THAT.
TO GIVE YOURSELF UP LIKE THAT... TO SAVE THE LIVES OF SO MANY OTHERS: IT WAS LIKE WITNESSING SOME BIG, TRAGIC MOMENT IN HISTORY.

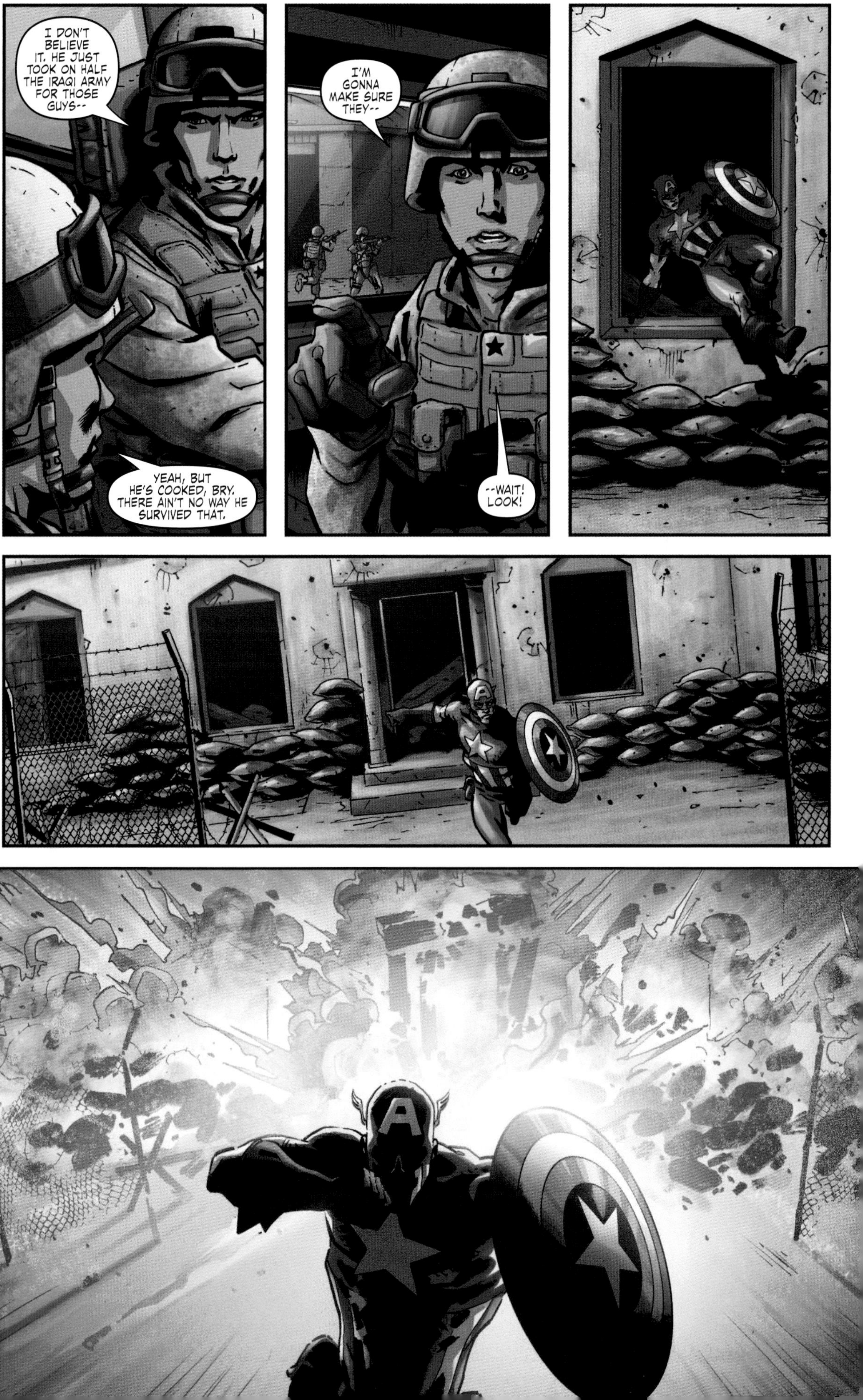
I DON'T BELIEVE IT. HE JUST TOOK ON HALF THE IRAQI ARMY FOR THOSE GUYS--
YEAH, BUT HE'S COOKED, BRY. THERE AIN'T NO WAY HE SURVIVED THAT.
I'M GONNA MAKE SURE THEY--
--WAIT! LOOK!

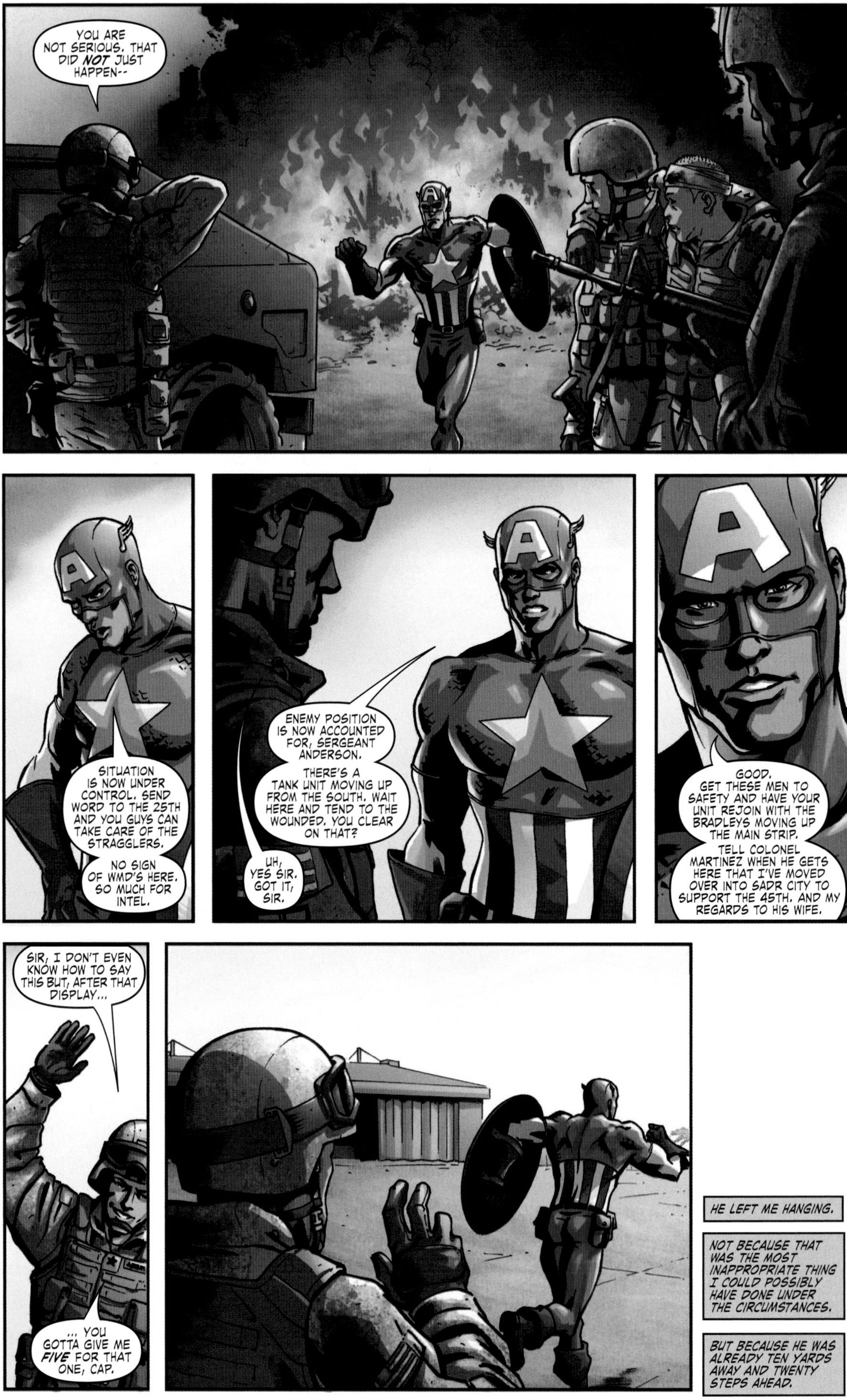
YOU ARE NOT SERIOUS. THAT DID *NOT* JUST HAPPEN--
SITUATION IS NOW UNDER CONTROL. SEND WORD TO THE 25TH AND YOU GUYS CAN TAKE CARE OF THE STRAGGLERS.
NO SIGN OF WMD'S HERE. SO MUCH FOR INTEL.
ENEMY POSITION IS NOW ACCOUNTED FOR, SERGEANT ANDERSON.
THERE'S A TANK UNIT MOVING UP FROM THE SOUTH. WAIT HERE AND TEND TO THE WOUNDED. YOU CLEAR ON THAT?
UH, YES SIR. GOT IT, SIR.
GOOD. GET THESE MEN TO SAFETY AND HAVE YOUR UNIT REJOIN WITH THE BRADLEYS MOVING UP THE MAIN STRIP.
TELL COLONEL MARTINEZ WHEN HE GETS HERE THAT I'VE MOVED OVER INTO SADR CITY TO SUPPORT THE 45TH. AND MY REGARDS TO HIS WIFE.
SIR, I DON'T EVEN KNOW HOW TO SAY THIS BUT, AFTER THAT DISPLAY...
... YOU GOTTA GIVE ME *FIVE* FOR THAT ONE, CAP.
HE LEFT ME HANGING.
NOT BECAUSE THAT WAS THE MOST INAPPROPRIATE THING I COULD POSSIBLY HAVE DONE UNDER THE CIRCUMSTANCES.
BUT BECAUSE HE WAS ALREADY TEN YARDS AWAY AND TWENTY STEPS AHEAD.

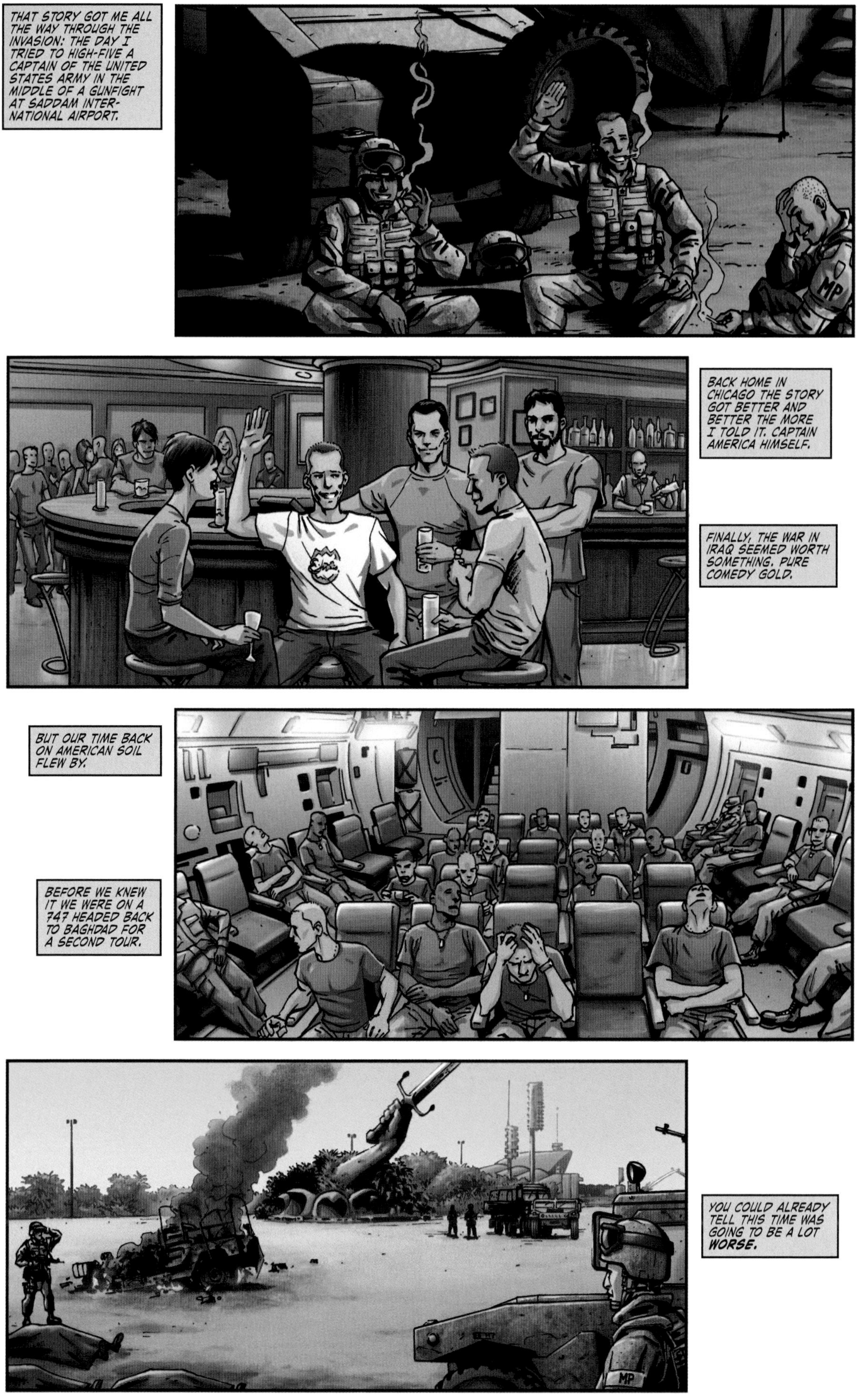
THAT STORY GOT ME ALL THE WAY THROUGH THE INVASION: THE DAY I TRIED TO HIGH-FIVE A CAPTAIN OF THE UNITED STATES ARMY IN THE MIDDLE OF A GUNFIGHT AT SADDAM INTER-NATIONAL AIRPORT.
MP
BACK HOME IN CHICAGO THE STORY GOT BETTER AND BETTER THE MORE I TOLD IT. CAPTAIN AMERICA HIMSELF.
FINALLY, THE WAR IN IRAQ SEEMED WORTH SOMETHING. PURE COMEDY GOLD.
BUT OUR TIME BACK ON AMERICAN SOIL FLEW BY.
BEFORE WE KNEW IT WE WERE ON A 747 HEADED BACK TO BAGHDAD FOR A SECOND TOUR.
YOU COULD ALREADY TELL THIS TIME WAS GOING TO BE A LOT **WORSE.**
MP

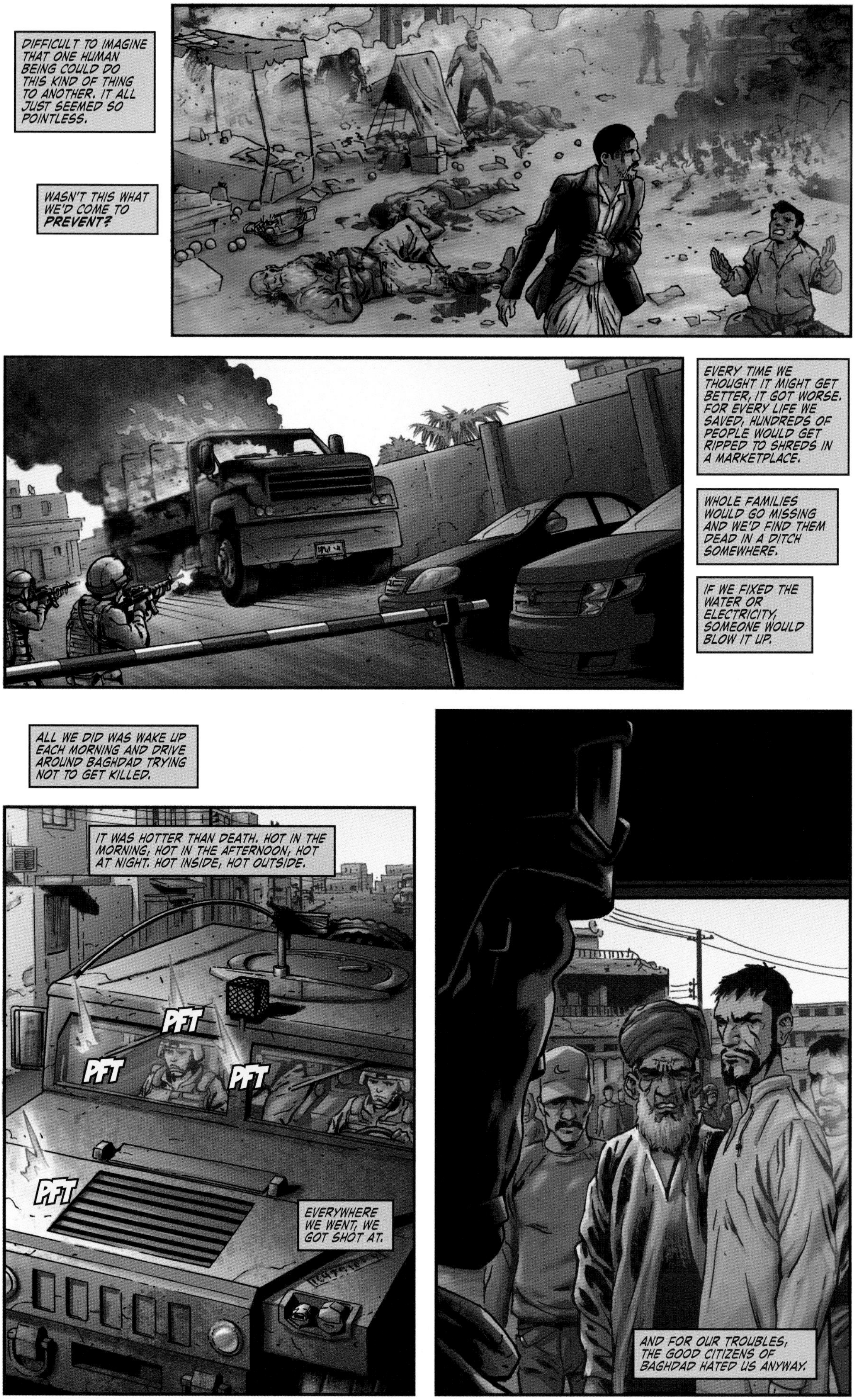
DIFFICULT TO IMAGINE THAT ONE HUMAN BEING COULD DO THIS KIND OF THING TO ANOTHER. IT ALL JUST SEEMED SO POINTLESS.
WASN'T THIS WHAT WE'D COME TO PREVENT?
EVERY TIME WE THOUGHT IT MIGHT GET BETTER, IT GOT WORSE. FOR EVERY LIFE WE SAVED, HUNDREDS OF PEOPLE WOULD GET RIPPED TO SHREDS IN A MARKETPLACE.
WHOLE FAMILIES WOULD GO MISSING AND WE'D FIND THEM DEAD IN A DITCH SOMEWHERE.
IF WE FIXED THE WATER OR ELECTRICITY, SOMEONE WOULD BLOW IT UP.
ALL WE DID WAS WAKE UP EACH MORNING AND DRIVE AROUND BAGHDAD TRYING NOT TO GET KILLED.
IT WAS HOTTER THAN DEATH. HOT IN THE MORNING, HOT IN THE AFTERNOON, HOT AT NIGHT. HOT INSIDE, HOT OUTSIDE.
PFT
PFT
PFT
PFT
EVERYWHERE WE WENT, WE GOT SHOT AT.
AND FOR OUR TROUBLES, THE GOOD CITIZENS OF BAGHDAD HATED US ANYWAY.

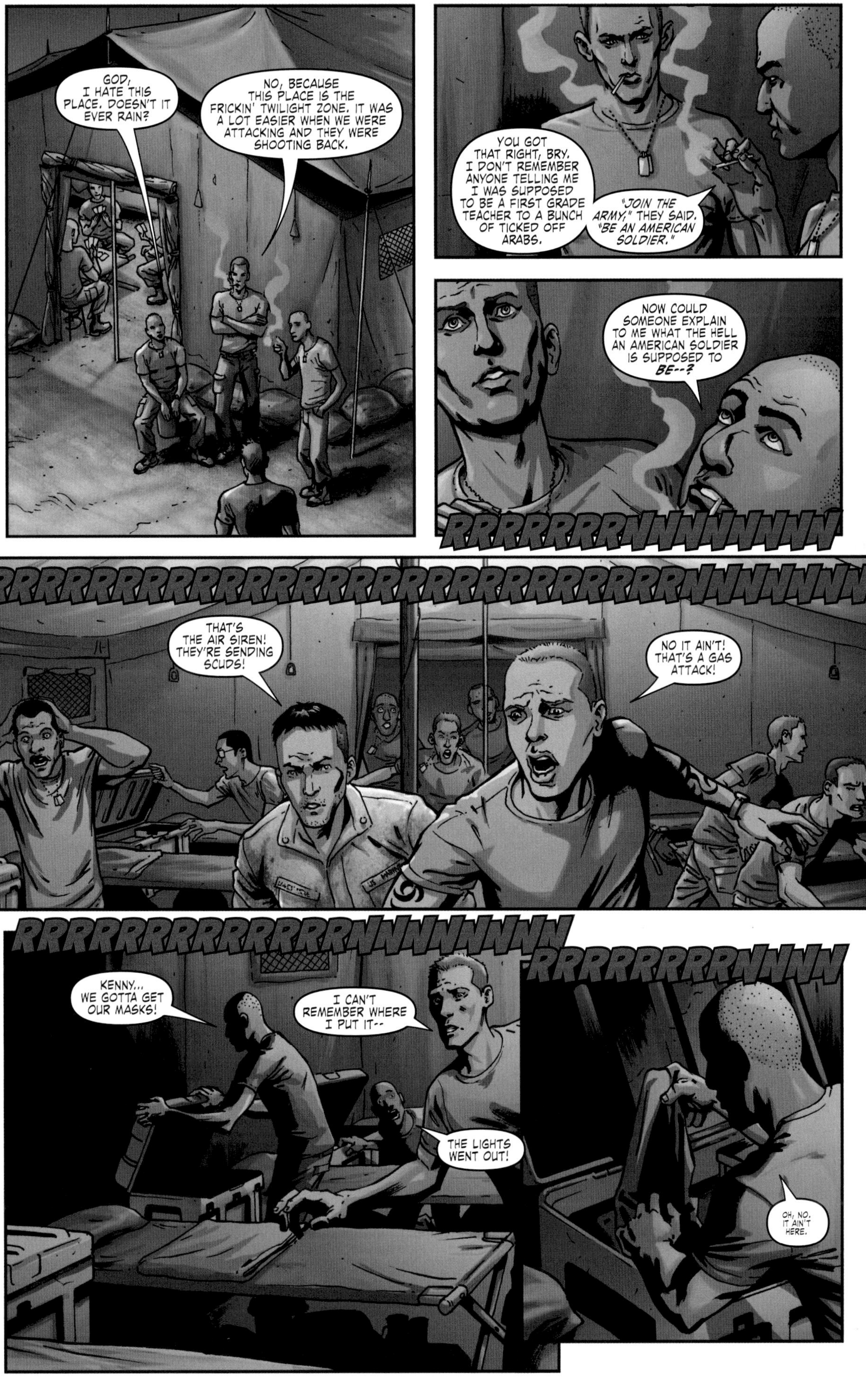
GOD, I HATE THIS PLACE. DOESN'T IT EVER RAIN?
NO, BECAUSE THIS PLACE IS THE FRICKIN' TWILIGHT ZONE. IT WAS A LOT EASIER WHEN WE WERE ATTACKING AND THEY WERE SHOOTING BACK.
YOU GOT THAT RIGHT, BRY. I DON'T REMEMBER ANYONE TELLING ME I WAS SUPPOSED TO BE A FIRST GRADE TEACHER TO A BUNCH OF TICKED OFF ARABS.
"JOIN THE ARMY," THEY SAID. "BE AN AMERICAN SOLDIER."
NOW COULD SOMEONE EXPLAIN TO ME WHAT THE HELL AN AMERICAN SOLDIER IS SUPPOSED TO BE--?
RRRRRRRRNNNNNNNN
RRRRRRRRRRRRRRRRRRRRRRRRRRRRRRNNNNNNN
THAT'S THE AIR SIREN! THEY'RE SENDING SCUDS!
NO IT AIN'T! THAT'S A GAS ATTACK!
RRRRRRRRRRRRRRRRNNNNNNNNN
RRRRRRRRRRNNNN
KENNY... WE GOTTA GET OUR MASKS!
I CAN'T REMEMBER WHERE I PUT IT--
THE LIGHTS WENT OUT!
OH, NO. IT AIN'T HERE.

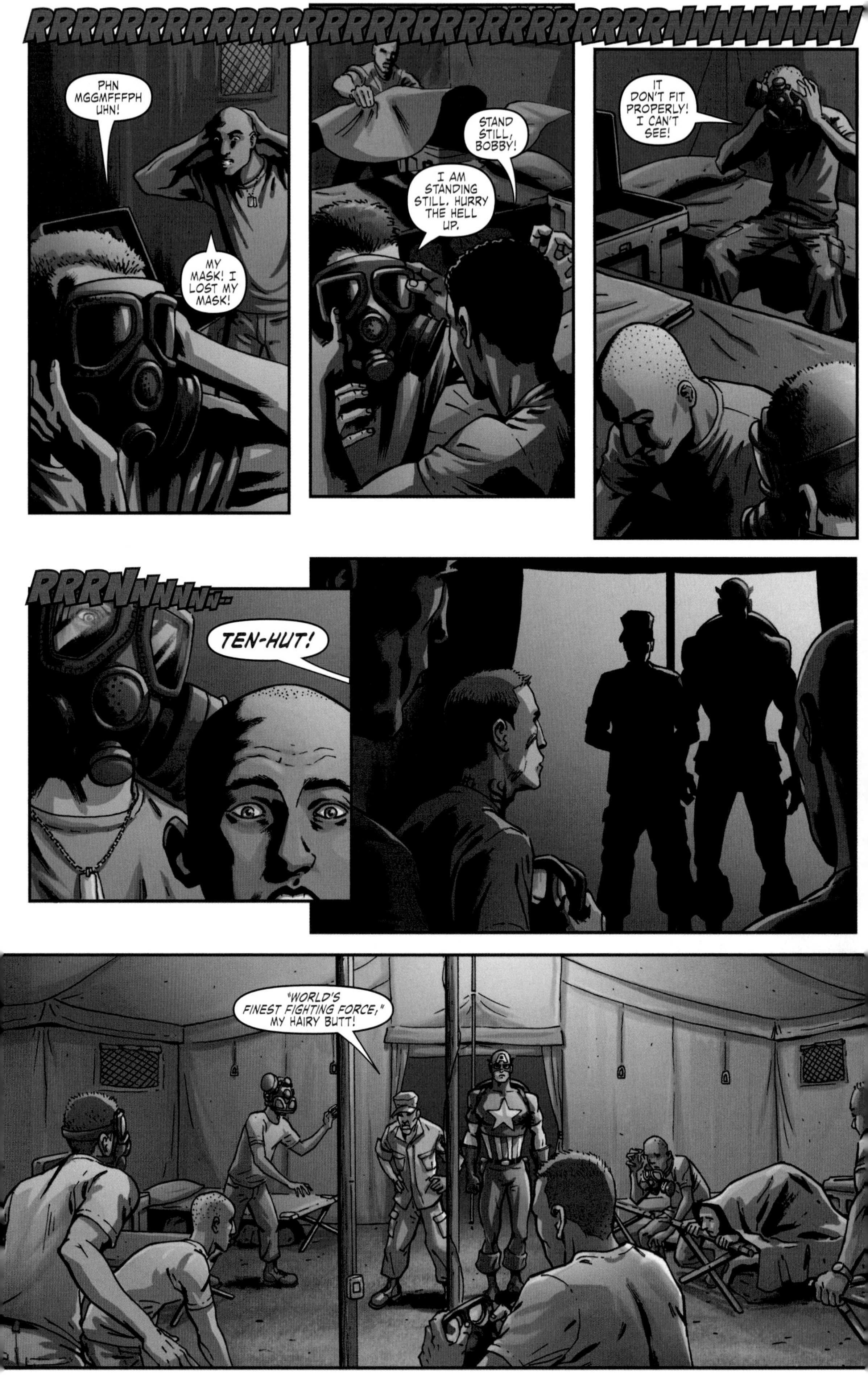
RRRRRRRRRRRRRRRRRRRRRRRRRRRRRRRRRNNNNNNNNN
PHN MGGMFFFPH UHN!
MY MASK! I LOST MY MASK!
STAND STILL, BOBBY!
I AM STANDING STILL. HURRY THE HELL UP.
IT DON'T FIT PROPERLY! I CAN'T SEE!
RRRNNNNNN--
TEN-HUT!
"WORLD'S FINEST FIGHTING FORCE," MY HAIRY BUTT!

YOU MEN DO REALIZE THAT IF THIS HAD BEEN AN *ACTUAL* ATTACK MOST OF YOU WOULD BE DEAD?

WANT *ME* TO KILL THEM FOR YOU, SIR? SAVE THE ENEMY THE TROUBLE.

NOT RIGHT NOW, SERGEANT.

ANDERSON, WAIT, OLSON... YOU THREE COME WITH ME.

THE REST OF YOU WAIT HERE. BUT DON'T GET COMFORTABLE, 'CAUSE I'LL BE BACK FOR YOU REAL *SOON*, YOU BUNCH OF SALLIES.

THE CAPTAIN HAS REQUESTED THREE VOLUNTEERS FOR A NEW MISSION. YOU THREE ARE JUST SLIGHTLY LESS STUPID THAN THE OTHERS SO I'VE DECIDED *YOU* WILL BE THOSE THREE VOLUNTEERS.

THANK YOU, SERGEANT.

YOU MEN CAN STAND AT EASE.

I WANT YOU TO KNOW THIS IS NOT GOING TO BE EASY. THINGS HAVE TAKEN A TURN FOR THE WORSE HERE IN THE CITY AND I'M BEING ASKED BY THE BRASS TO REVISE OUR TACTICS. ANY QUESTIONS?

WHAT'S THE NEW TACTICS, SIR?

LET'S JUST SAY WE'RE GOING TO BE DRINKING A LOT OF *TEA*.

AS IT TURNED OUT, ONLY HE GOT TO DRINK THE TEA.

SOMEONE'S IDEA OF A JOKE, I GUESS. OUR JOB WAS TO DRIVE THE CAPTAIN AROUND THE STREETS OF BAGHDAD AND GO VISIT LOCAL MULLAHS.

IT WAS SUDDENLY IMPORTANT TO WIN THE HEARTS AND MINDS OF THE SAME PEOPLE WE'D BEEN SHOOTING AT THE PREVIOUS YEAR.

THE SAME PEOPLE WHO WERE NOW LEAVING BOMBS BY THE SIDE OF THE ROAD FOR US, KILLING AND TORTURING CIVILIANS, AND LAUGHING IN OUR FACES AS THEY LIED THROUGH THEIR TEETH.

WE'D DRIVE THROUGH DOWNTOWN, EXPOSED TO EVERY INSURGENT WITH A GUN AND A GRUDGE.

NO WATER.
NO AIR CONDITIONING.
NO ELECTRICITY.

NO FRONT LINES.
NO MISSION.

EVERY DAY WAS HOTTER THAN THE DAY BEFORE.

AND NO END IN SIGHT.

WELL, *THIS* SUCKS.

WHAT, YOU JUST CAME TO THAT DECISION AFTER WEEKS OF CAREFUL STUDY?

HEY, DON'T GET PISSY WITH ME. IT AIN'T MY FAULT.

YES, IT IS.

YOU KNOW WHAT I HEARD? WHEN THE SECRETARY OF DEFENSE CAME HERE LAST WEEK THEY DROVE HIM AROUND IN A HALF-MILLION-DOLLAR RHINO RUNNER.

I'D LIKE TO BRING HIM OUT ON PATROL IN ONE OF *THESE* UNDERARMORED TIN CANS FOR HALF A DAY AND SEE HOW HE FEELS THEN.

I DON'T GET WHY WE'RE EVEN *OUT* HERE.

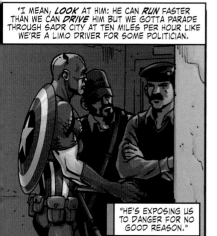

"I MEAN, *LOOK* AT HIM: HE CAN *RUN* FASTER THAN WE CAN *DRIVE* HIM BUT WE GOTTA PARADE THROUGH SADR CITY AT TEN MILES PER HOUR LIKE WE'RE A LIMO DRIVER FOR SOME POLITICIAN.

"HE'S EXPOSING US TO DANGER FOR NO GOOD REASON."

TRUE 'DAT. MAYBE WE CAN ASK HIM TO PUT IN A WORD AND FIX THE HUMVEE'S AIR CONDITIONING--

BRYAN... *LOOK!*

ALLAH *AKHBAR!*

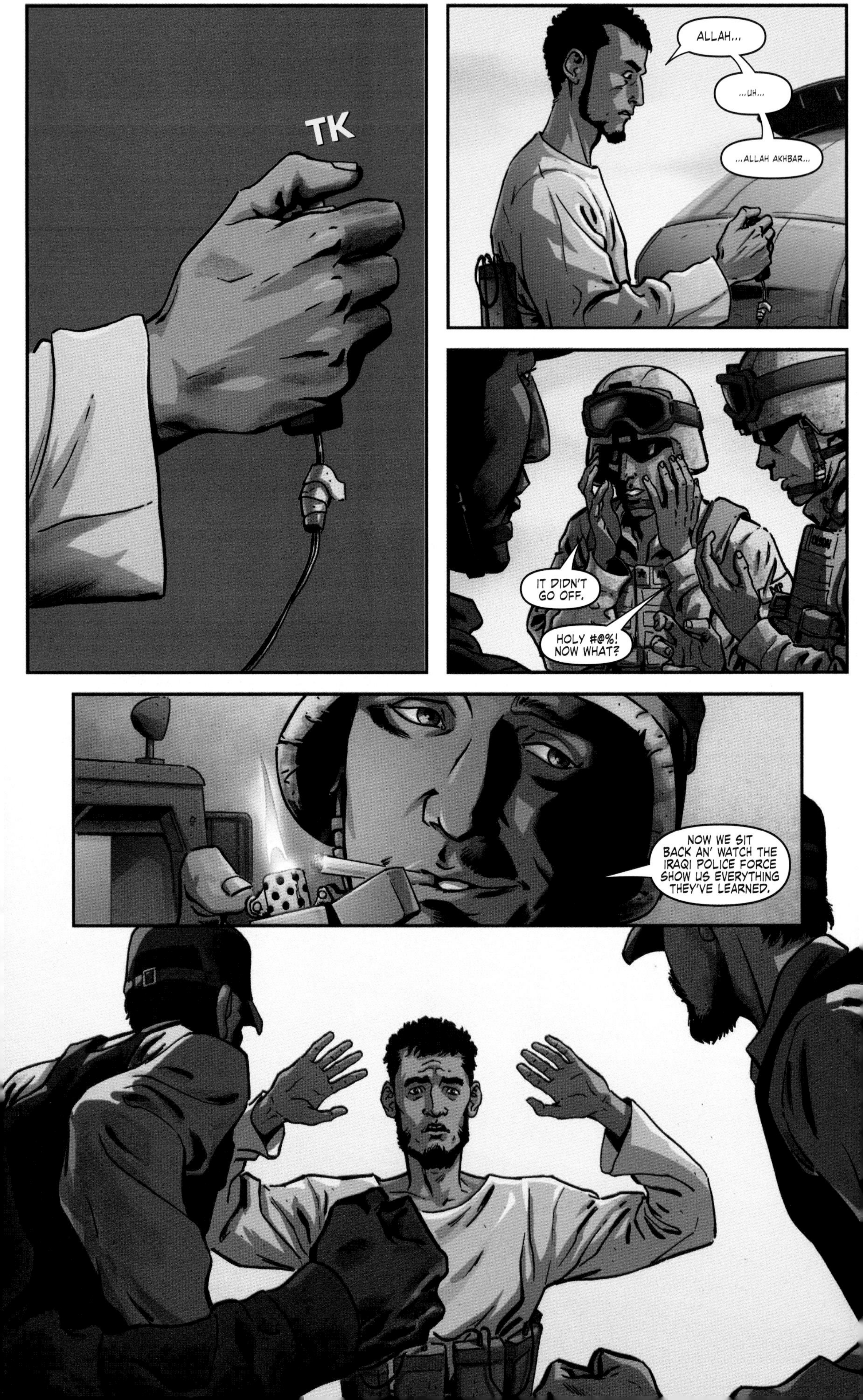
TK
ALLAH...
...UH...
...ALLAH AKHBAR...
IT DIDN'T GO OFF.
HOLY #@%! NOW WHAT?
NOW WE SIT BACK AN' WATCH THE IRAQI POLICE FORCE SHOW US EVERYTHING THEY'VE LEARNED.

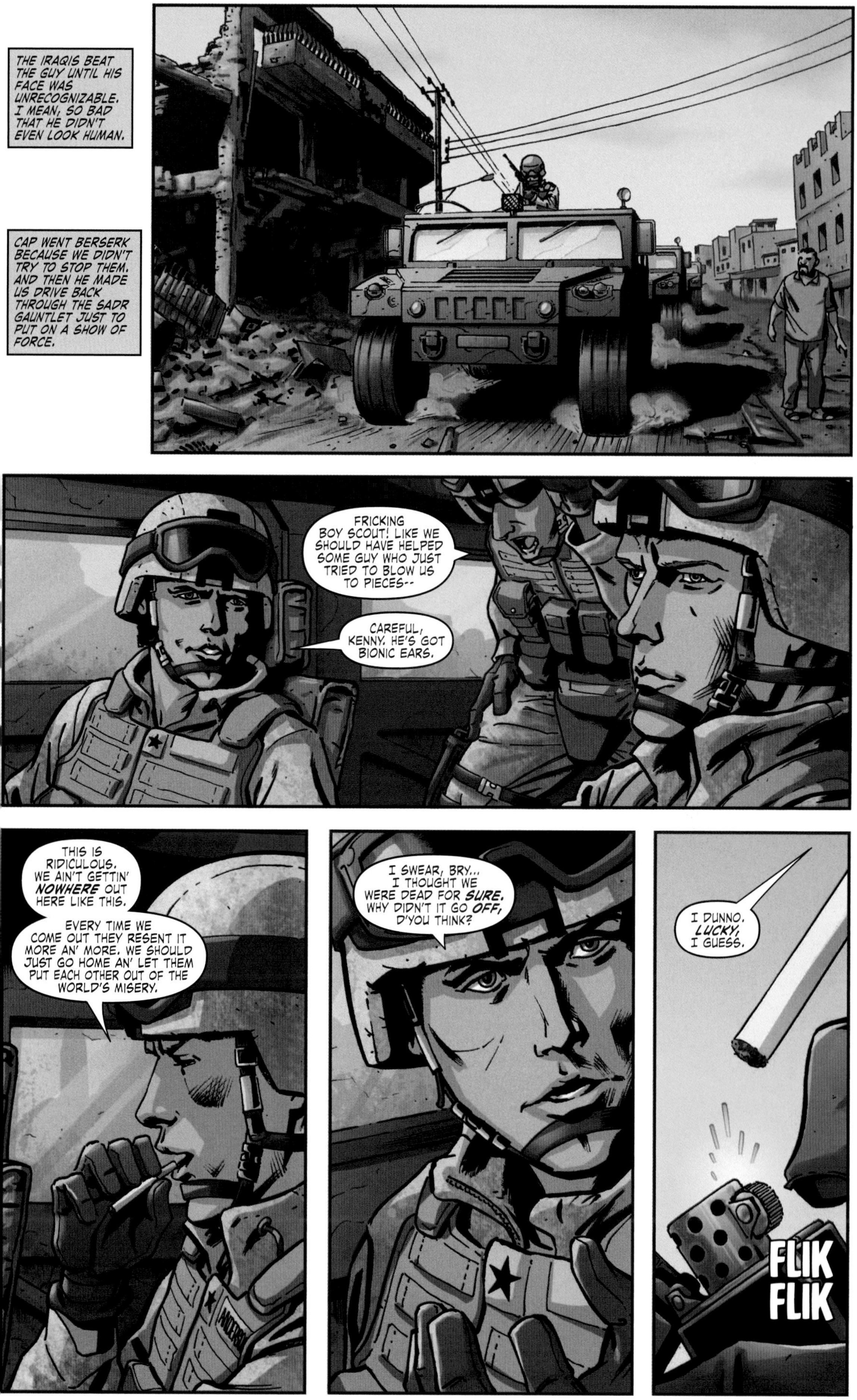
THE IRAQIS BEAT THE GUY UNTIL HIS FACE WAS UNRECOGNIZABLE. I MEAN, SO BAD THAT HE DIDN'T EVEN LOOK HUMAN.
CAP WENT BERSERK BECAUSE WE DIDN'T TRY TO STOP THEM. AND THEN HE MADE US DRIVE BACK THROUGH THE SADR GAUNTLET JUST TO PUT ON A SHOW OF FORCE.
FRICKING BOY SCOUT! LIKE WE SHOULD HAVE HELPED SOME GUY WHO JUST TRIED TO BLOW US TO PIECES--
CAREFUL, KENNY. HE'S GOT BIONIC EARS.
THIS IS RIDICULOUS. WE AIN'T GETTIN' NOWHERE OUT HERE LIKE THIS.
EVERY TIME WE COME OUT THEY RESENT IT MORE AN' MORE. WE SHOULD JUST GO HOME AN' LET THEM PUT EACH OTHER OUT OF THE WORLD'S MISERY.
I SWEAR, BRY... I THOUGHT WE WERE DEAD FOR SURE. WHY DIDN'T IT GO OFF, D'YOU THINK?
I DUNNO. LUCKY, I GUESS.
FLIK FLIK

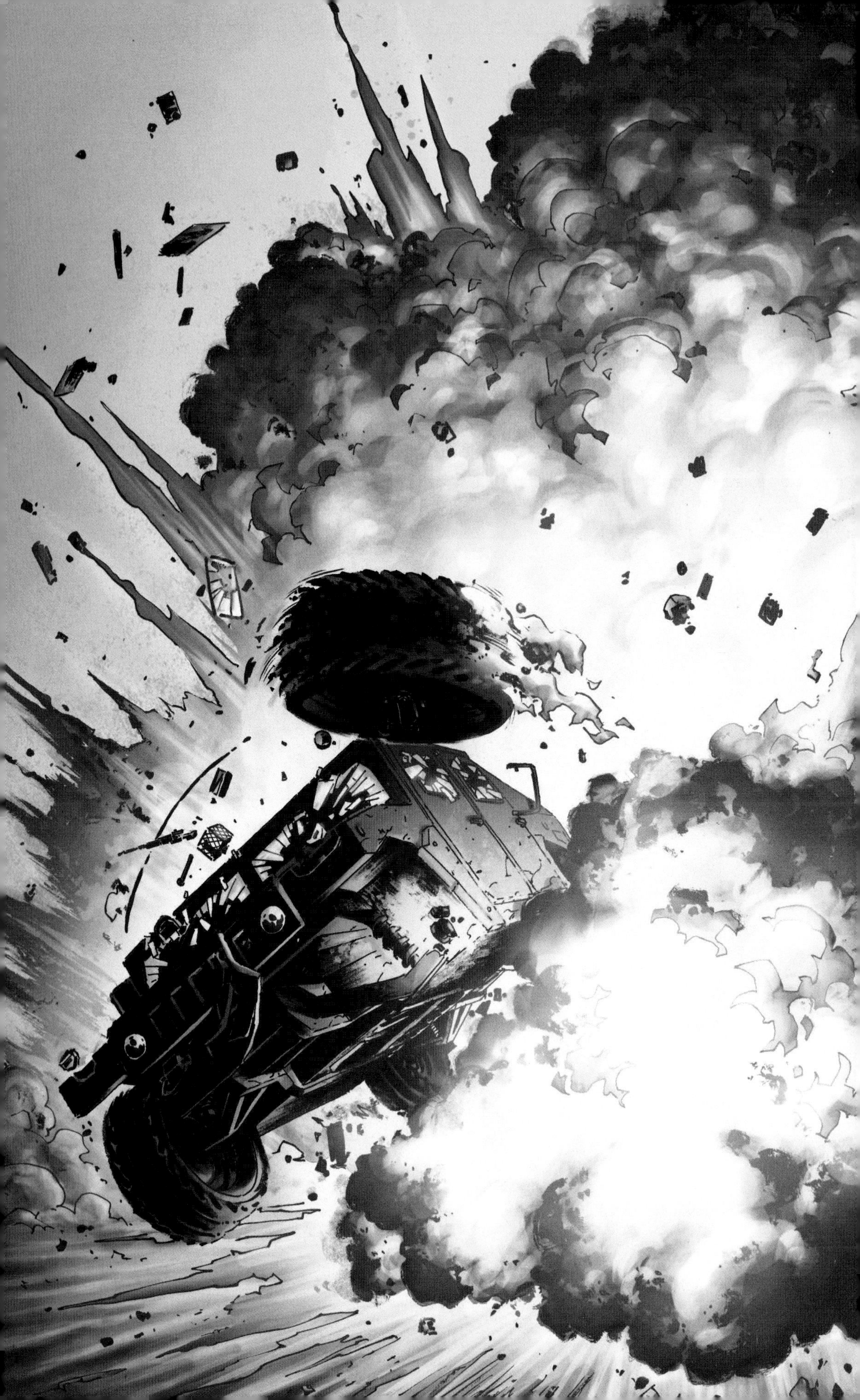

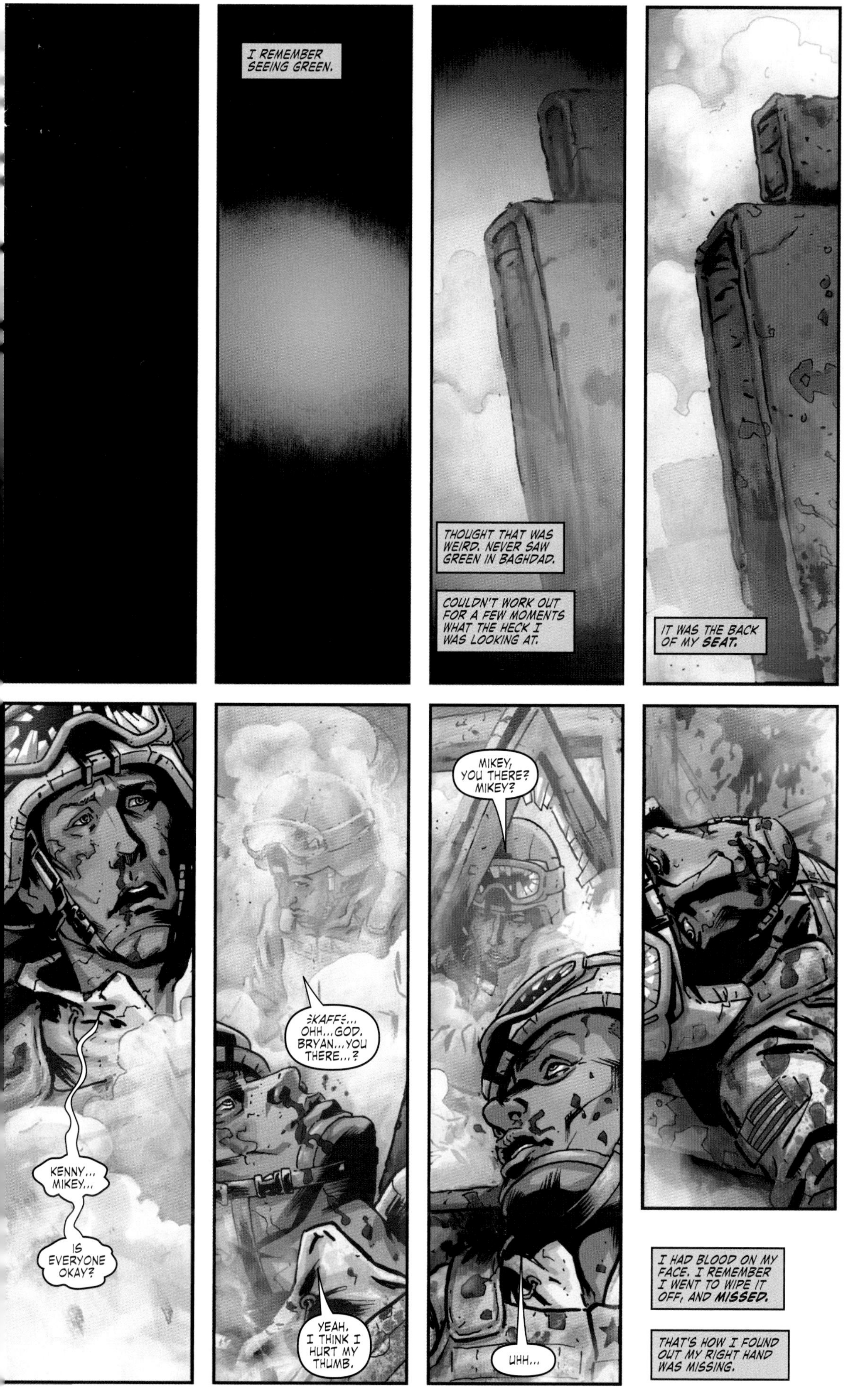
I REMEMBER SEEING GREEN.
THOUGHT THAT WAS WEIRD. NEVER SAW GREEN IN BAGHDAD.
COULDN'T WORK OUT FOR A FEW MOMENTS WHAT THE HECK I WAS LOOKING AT.
IT WAS THE BACK OF MY SEAT.
KENNY... MIKEY...
IS EVERYONE OKAY?
KAFF... OHH...GOD. BRYAN...YOU THERE...?
YEAH. I THINK I HURT MY THUMB.
MIKEY, YOU THERE? MIKEY?
UHH...
I HAD BLOOD ON MY FACE. I REMEMBER I WENT TO WIPE IT OFF, AND MISSED.
THAT'S HOW I FOUND OUT MY RIGHT HAND WAS MISSING.

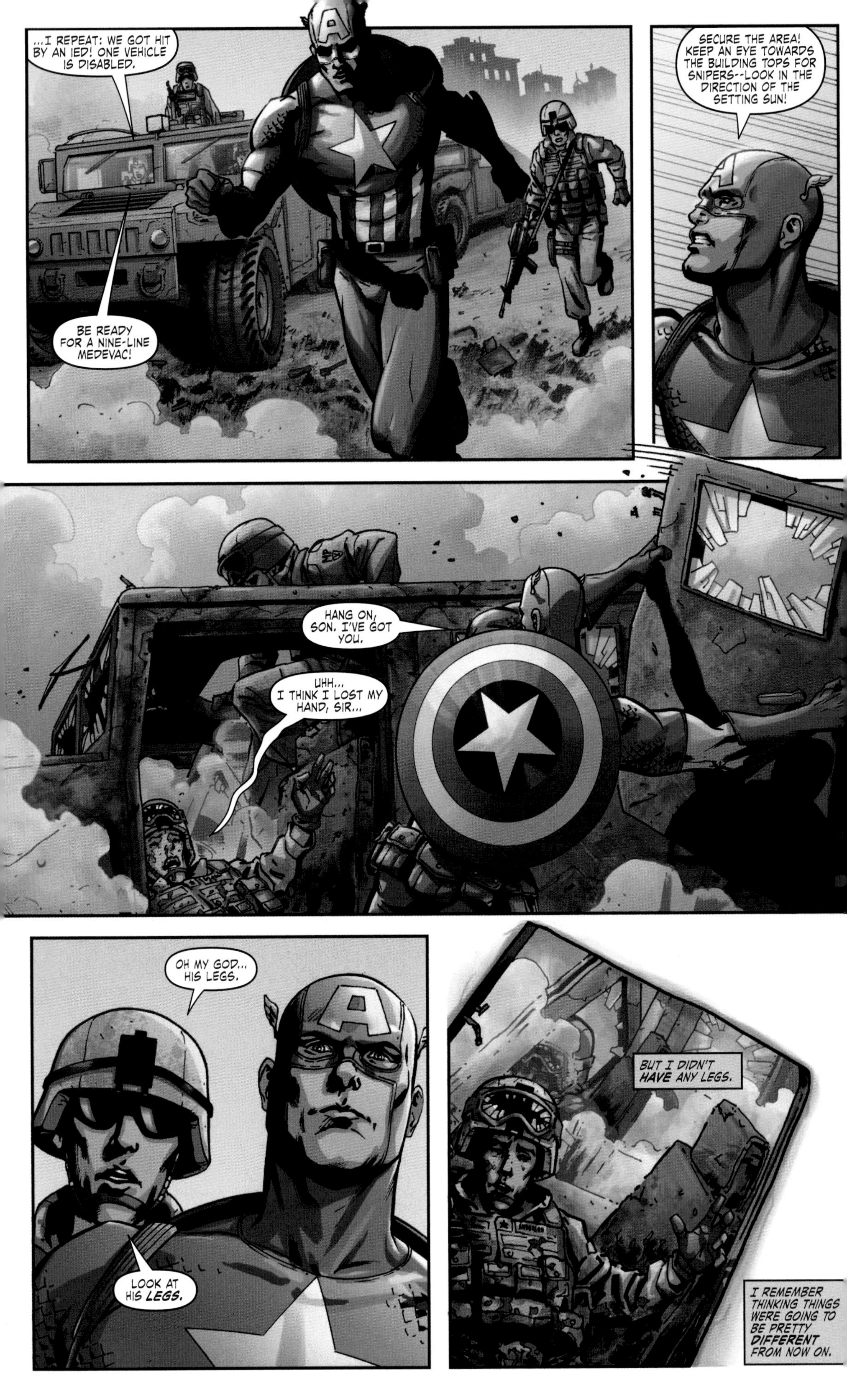

...I REPEAT: WE GOT HIT BY AN IED! ONE VEHICLE IS DISABLED.
BE READY FOR A NINE-LINE MEDEVAC!
SECURE THE AREA! KEEP AN EYE TOWARDS THE BUILDING TOPS FOR SNIPERS--LOOK IN THE DIRECTION OF THE SETTING SUN!
HANG ON, SON. I'VE GOT YOU.
UHH... I THINK I LOST MY HAND, SIR...
OH MY GOD... HIS LEGS.
LOOK AT HIS LEGS.
BUT I DIDN'T HAVE ANY LEGS.
I REMEMBER THINKING THINGS WERE GOING TO BE PRETTY DIFFERENT FROM NOW ON.

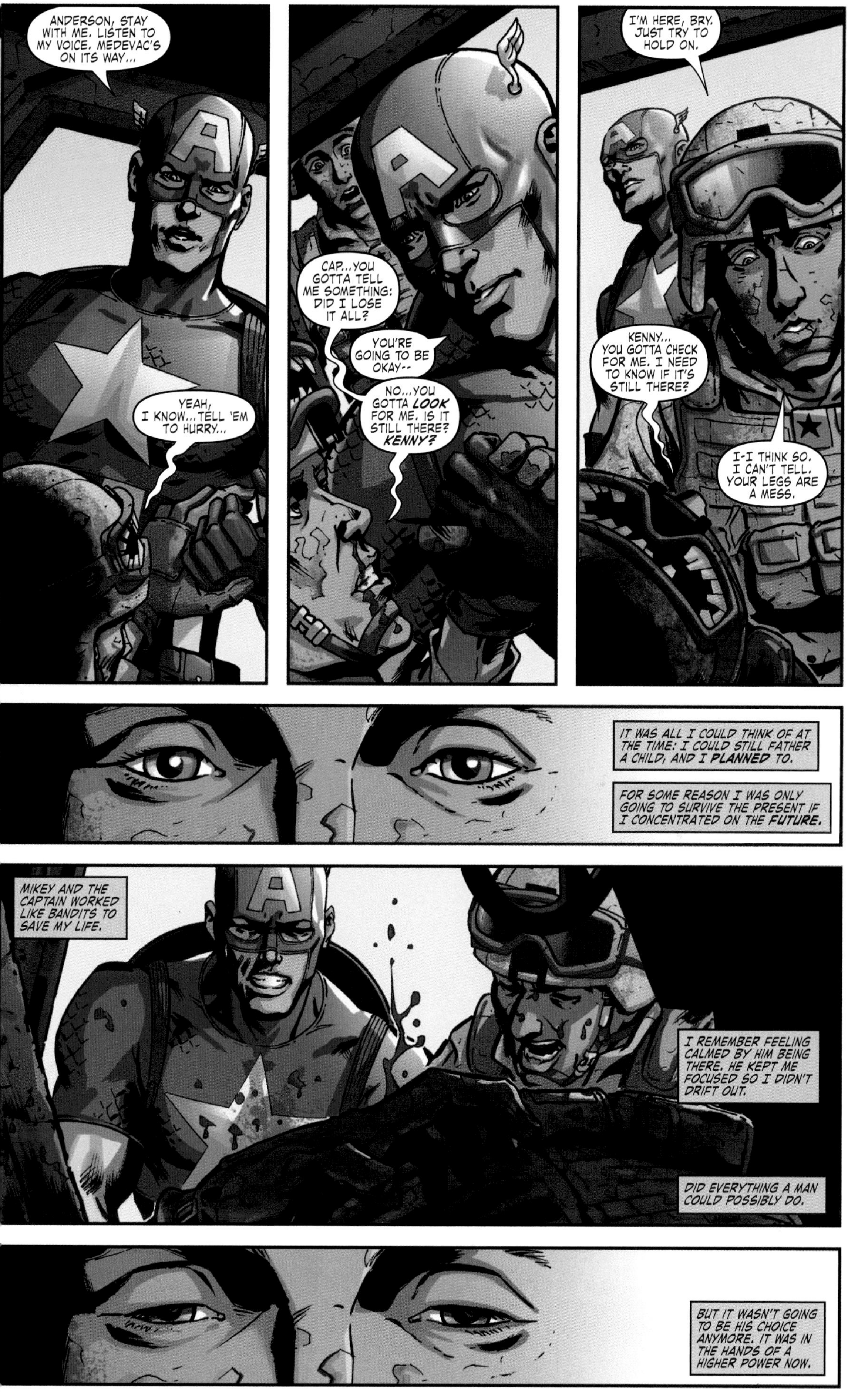
ANDERSON, STAY WITH ME. LISTEN TO MY VOICE. MEDEVAC'S ON ITS WAY...
YEAH, I KNOW...TELL 'EM TO HURRY...
CAP...YOU GOTTA TELL ME SOMETHING: DID I LOSE IT ALL?
YOU'RE GOING TO BE OKAY--
NO...YOU GOTTA LOOK FOR ME. IS IT STILL THERE? KENNY?
I'M HERE, BRY. JUST TRY TO HOLD ON.
KENNY... YOU GOTTA CHECK FOR ME. I NEED TO KNOW IF IT'S STILL THERE?
I-I THINK SO. I CAN'T TELL. YOUR LEGS ARE A MESS.
IT WAS ALL I COULD THINK OF AT THE TIME: I COULD STILL FATHER A CHILD, AND I PLANNED TO.
FOR SOME REASON I WAS ONLY GOING TO SURVIVE THE PRESENT IF I CONCENTRATED ON THE FUTURE.
MIKEY AND THE CAPTAIN WORKED LIKE BANDITS TO SAVE MY LIFE.
I REMEMBER FEELING CALMED BY HIM BEING THERE. HE KEPT ME FOCUSED SO I DIDN'T DRIFT OUT.
DID EVERYTHING A MAN COULD POSSIBLY DO.
BUT IT WASN'T GOING TO BE HIS CHOICE ANYMORE. IT WAS IN THE HANDS OF A HIGHER POWER NOW.

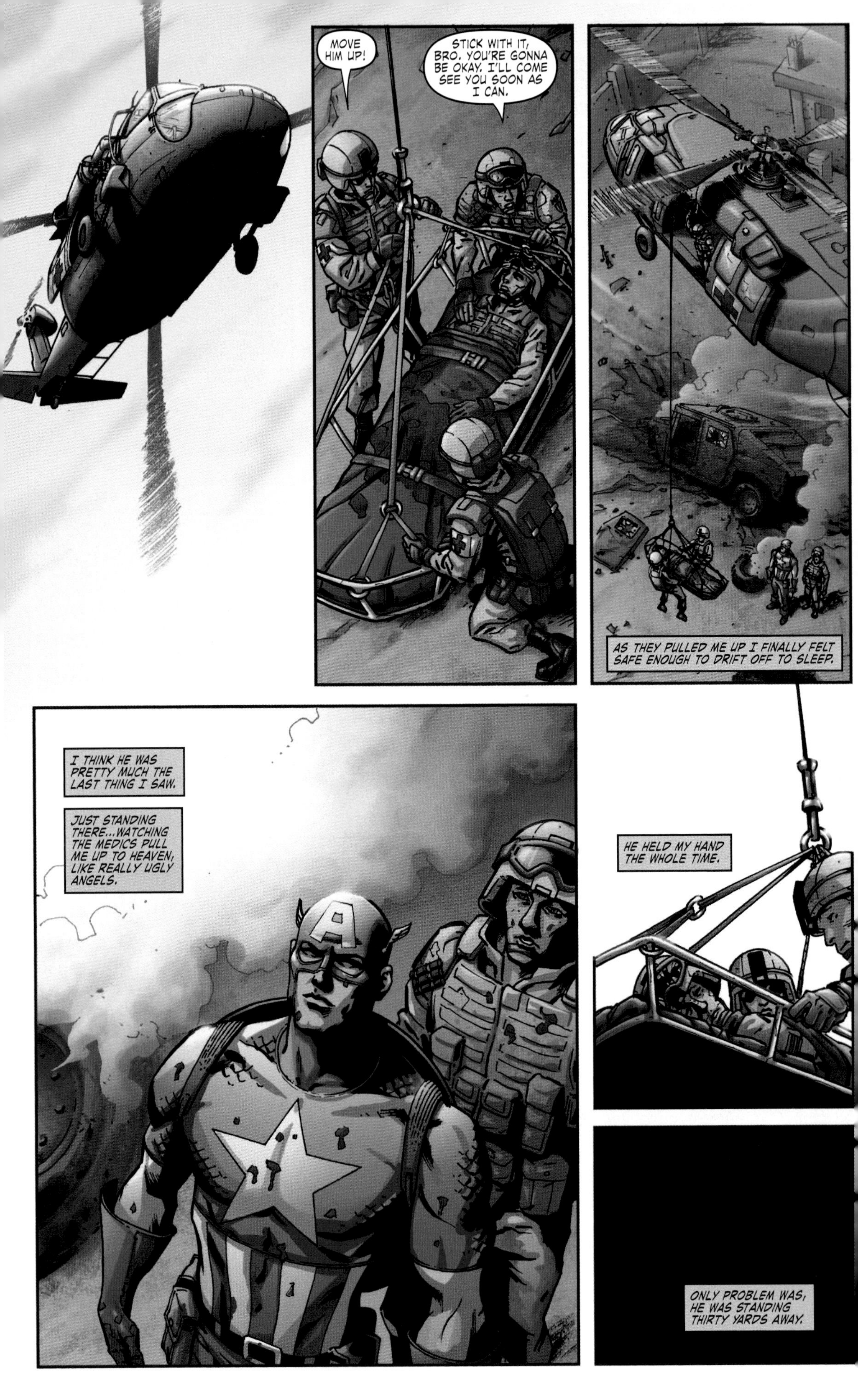
MOVE HIM UP!
STICK WITH IT, BRO. YOU'RE GONNA BE OKAY. I'LL COME SEE YOU SOON AS I CAN.
AS THEY PULLED ME UP I FINALLY FELT SAFE ENOUGH TO DRIFT OFF TO SLEEP.
I THINK HE WAS PRETTY MUCH THE LAST THING I SAW.
JUST STANDING THERE...WATCHING THE MEDICS PULL ME UP TO HEAVEN, LIKE REALLY UGLY ANGELS.
HE HELD MY HAND THE WHOLE TIME.
ONLY PROBLEM WAS, HE WAS STANDING THIRTY YARDS AWAY.

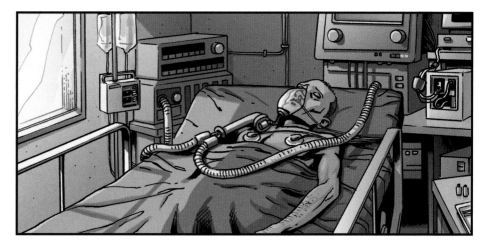

THEY KEPT ME IN AN INDUCED COMA FOR ALMOST TWO MONTHS.

THE ARMY BROUGHT MY MOM AND DAD OVER TO BE WITH ME. MY BROTHER CAME TOO.

DAD DIDN'T LEAVE MY SIDE FOR A MOMENT, EVEN IF THEY TOLD HIM TO. HE HELPED PACK AND DRESS MY WOUNDS.

FORTY-SEVEN SURGERIES IN THE FIRST THREE WEEKS. TWELVE MORE AFTER THAT.

THEY DID ALL THEY COULD TO SAVE ALL THE PIECES OF ME THAT WERE LEFT.

WAKING UP WAS A LOT HARDER THAN IT HAD ANY RIGHT TO *BE*.

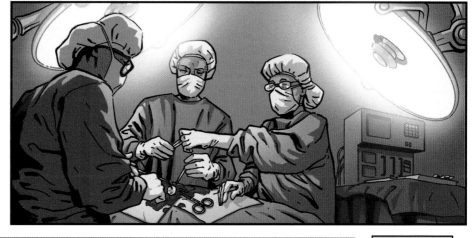

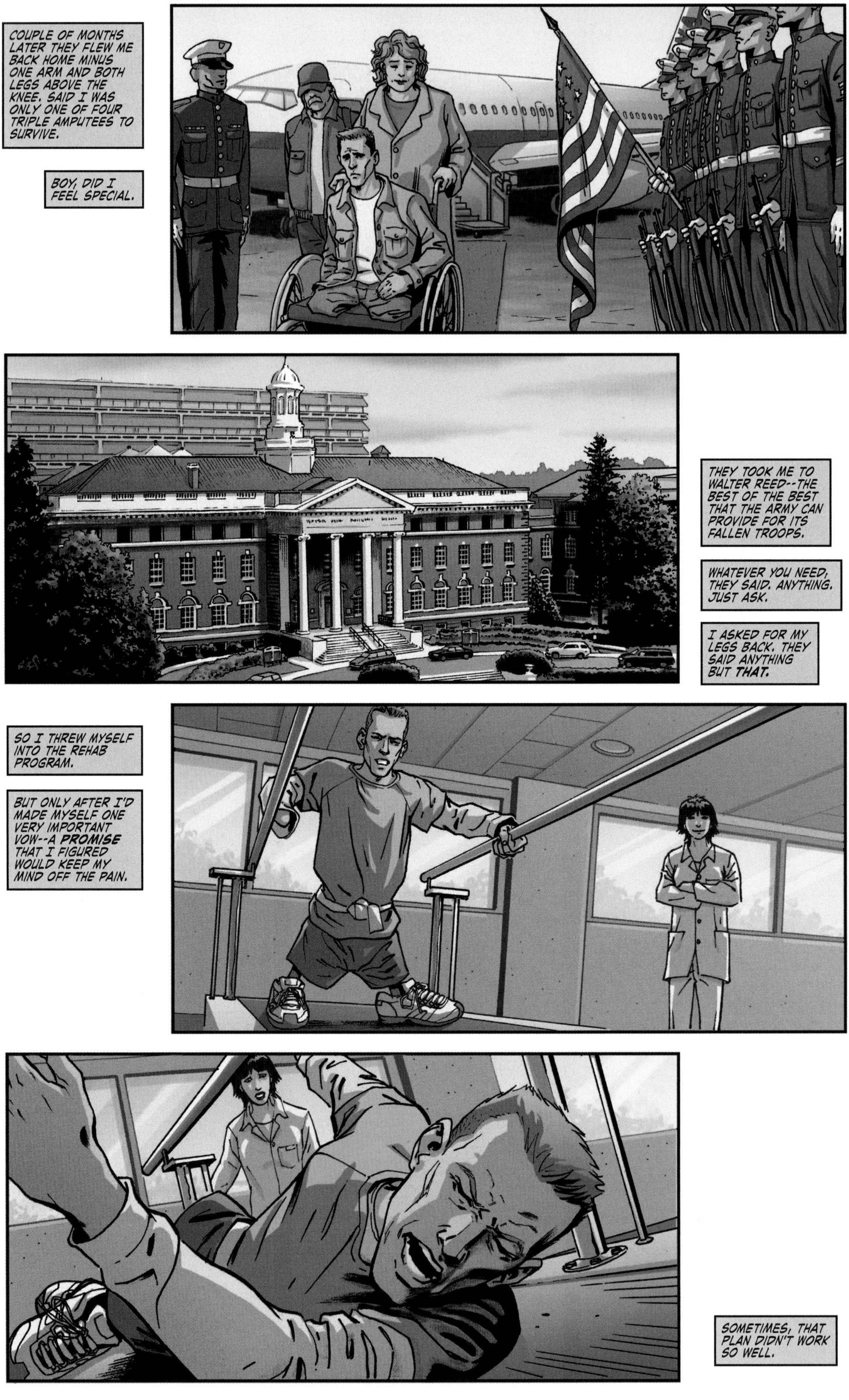
COUPLE OF MONTHS LATER THEY FLEW ME BACK HOME MINUS ONE ARM AND BOTH LEGS ABOVE THE KNEE. SAID I WAS ONLY ONE OF FOUR TRIPLE AMPUTEES TO SURVIVE.
BOY, DID I FEEL SPECIAL.
THEY TOOK ME TO WALTER REED--THE BEST OF THE BEST THAT THE ARMY CAN PROVIDE FOR ITS FALLEN TROOPS.
WHATEVER YOU NEED, THEY SAID. ANYTHING. JUST ASK.
I ASKED FOR MY LEGS BACK. THEY SAID ANYTHING BUT THAT.
SO I THREW MYSELF INTO THE REHAB PROGRAM.
BUT ONLY AFTER I'D MADE MYSELF ONE VERY IMPORTANT VOW--A PROMISE THAT I FIGURED WOULD KEEP MY MIND OFF THE PAIN.
SOMETIMES, THAT PLAN DIDN'T WORK SO WELL.

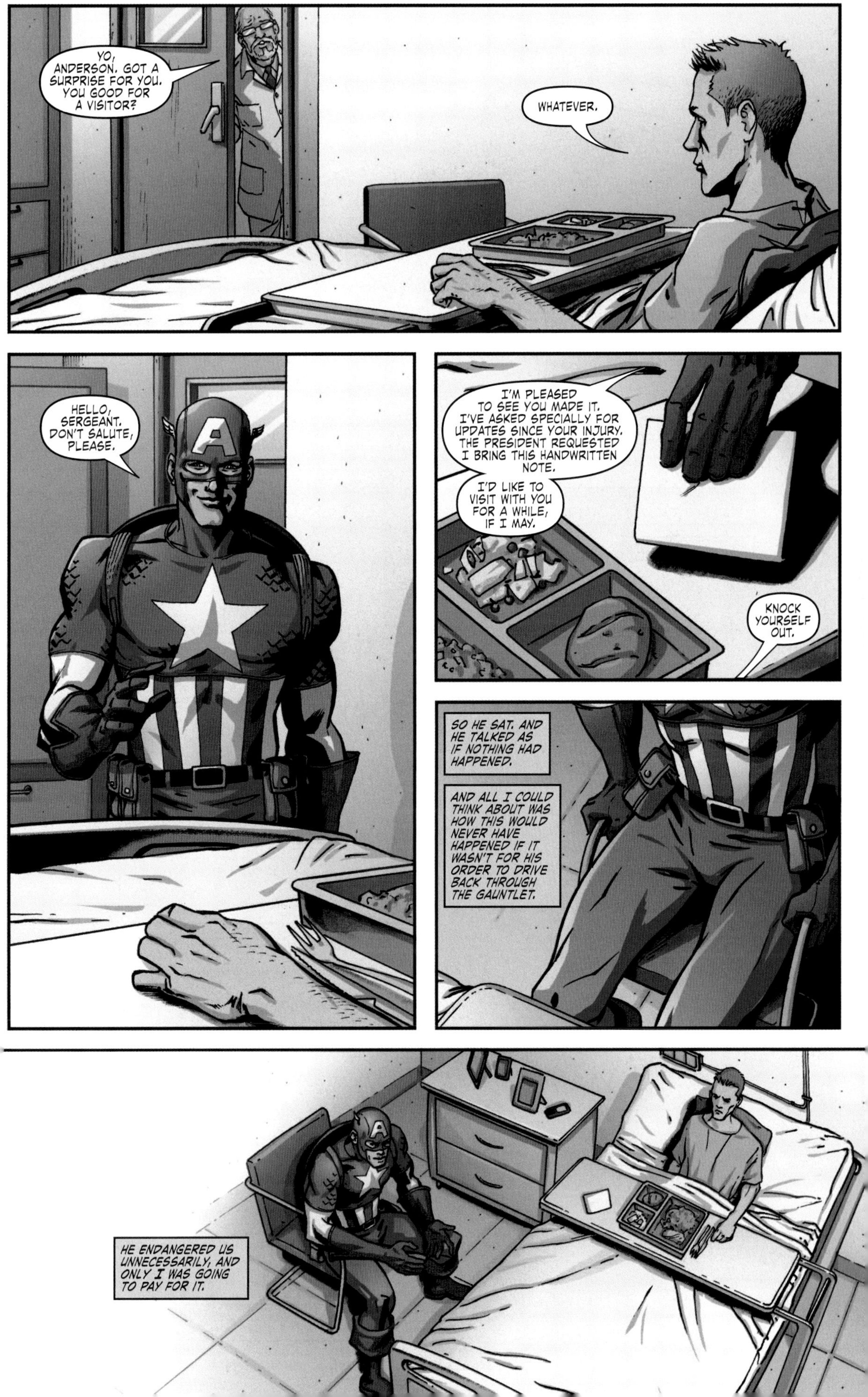
YO, ANDERSON. GOT A SURPRISE FOR YOU. YOU GOOD FOR A VISITOR?
WHATEVER.
HELLO, SERGEANT. DON'T SALUTE, PLEASE.
I'M PLEASED TO SEE YOU MADE IT. I'VE ASKED SPECIALLY FOR UPDATES SINCE YOUR INJURY. THE PRESIDENT REQUESTED I BRING THIS HANDWRITTEN NOTE.
I'D LIKE TO VISIT WITH YOU FOR A WHILE, IF I MAY.
KNOCK YOURSELF OUT.
SO HE SAT. AND HE TALKED AS IF NOTHING HAD HAPPENED.
AND ALL I COULD THINK ABOUT WAS HOW THIS WOULD NEVER HAVE HAPPENED IF IT WASN'T FOR HIS ORDER TO DRIVE BACK THROUGH THE GAUNTLET.
HE ENDANGERED US UNNECESSARILY, AND ONLY I WAS GOING TO PAY FOR IT.

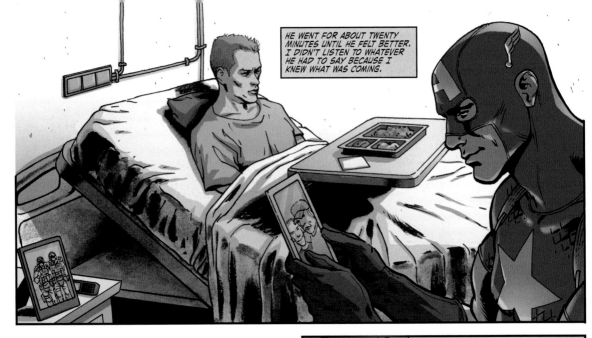

HE WENT FOR ABOUT TWENTY MINUTES UNTIL HE FELT BETTER. I DIDN'T LISTEN TO WHATEVER HE HAD TO SAY BECAUSE I KNEW WHAT WAS COMING.

WHEN HE WAS DONE, HE STOOD UP TO WALK OUT OF THE ROOM.

BECAUSE HE *COULD*.

I KEPT THINKING, "TELL HIM. TELL HIM." BUT WHAT WAS I GOING TO SAY?

THERE'S NO PLACE TO TELL A CAPTAIN THAT HE PUT YOUR LIFE IN JEOPARDY AND COST YOU THREE OF YOUR LIMBS.

DESPITE HIS GENEROUS REQUEST I SALUTED AS HE LEFT.

WITH MY HAND MISSING YOU COULDN'T EVEN SEE WHICH FINGER I WAS HOLDING UP.

I STAYED AT WALTER REED FOR AN ENTIRE YEAR. WENT TO A PRETTY DARK PLACE THAT I ALMOST DIDN'T CLIMB *OUT* OF.

GOT FIT WITH AN ELECTRIC HAND THAT COULD SWIVEL ALL THE WAY AROUND, LIKE A FRICKIN' *OWL.*

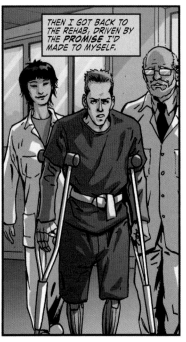

THEN I GOT BACK TO THE REHAB, DRIVEN BY THE *PROMISE* I'D MADE TO MYSELF.

AAHW!

THAT WHOLE TIME DOING REHAB MADE ME THINK OF THIS SHERYL CROW SONG: "NO ONE SAID IT WOULD BE EASY.

"NO ONE SAID IT WOULD BE THIS *HARD.*"

WHEN THE YEAR WAS UP I WENT BACK HOME. IT WAS KIND OF EMOTIONAL LEAVING ALL THOSE DOCTORS AND NURSES.

I HAD NO IDEA WHAT I WAS GOING *HOME* TO.

WELLCOME HOME

THANKS BRYAN

TRULY...

I HAD NO IDEA.

...TODAY, A HEARTWARMING HOMECOMING FOR ARMY SERGEANT BRYAN ANDERSON. WE'RE HERE AT CHICAGO'S O'HARE AIRPORT WHERE HUNDREDS HAVE GATHERED AT THE GATE TO WELCOME BACK AN AMERICAN HERO...

BRYAN OUR HERO

LIFE HAS A FUNNY WAY OF EVENING OUT SOMETIMES. FOR EVERYTHING YOU LOSE, THERE'S SOMETHING YOU GAIN.

I HAD LOST TWO LEGS AND MY RIGHT ARM. YET I HAD THE LOVE AND ADMIRATION OF ALL THESE PEOPLE.

THANK YOU

COUPLE OF WEEKS AFTER I GOT HOME I THREW OUT THE FIRST PITCH AT THE CUBBIES. IT WAS FUNNY 'CAUSE MY DAD WAS SO IMPRESSED.

I ASKED HIM IF HE WASN'T IMPRESSED WHEN I GOT BLOWN UP AND HE SAID, "NO, I WAS *ANNOYED.*"

The Meaning of... Esquire

MAN AT HIS BEST

WISDOM & DAMN GOOD ADVICE

SOMEONE AT A MAGAZINE SAW IT ON TV, AND THEY CALLED ME IN TO DO AN ARTICLE.

I THOUGHT IT WOULD BE IN THE MIDDLE SOMEWHERE. AND INSTEAD, THEY PUT ME ON THE COVER.

NEXT THING YOU KNOW, I'D BECOME A CERTIFIED *CELEBRITY.*

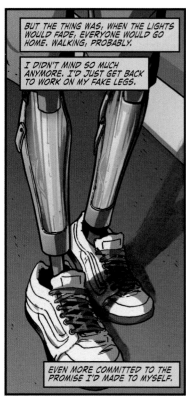

BUT THE THING WAS, WHEN THE LIGHTS WOULD FADE, EVERYONE WOULD GO HOME. WALKING, PROBABLY.

I DIDN'T MIND SO MUCH ANYMORE. I'D JUST GET BACK TO WORK ON MY FAKE LEGS.

EVEN MORE COMMITTED TO THE PROMISE I'D MADE TO MYSELF.

I GOT FITTED WITH SOME ELECTRIC LEGS TO GO WITH MY ELECTRIC HAND.

GERMAN ENGINEERING AT ITS FINEST, THEY SAID.

AAHWW!

I KEPT THINKING I WAS NEVER GOING TO MAKE IT.

TIME WAS RUNNING OUT.

BUT I MADE IT JUST IN TIME. AND A FEW MONTHS LATER, I KEPT THE PROMISE I'D MADE TO MYSELF BACK AT WALTER REED.

WHEN KENNY, MIKEY, AND THE REST OF THE GUYS RETURNED FROM THEIR SECOND TOUR, I WAS THE FIRST PERSON TO MEET THEM.

STANDING.

WELCOME HEROES

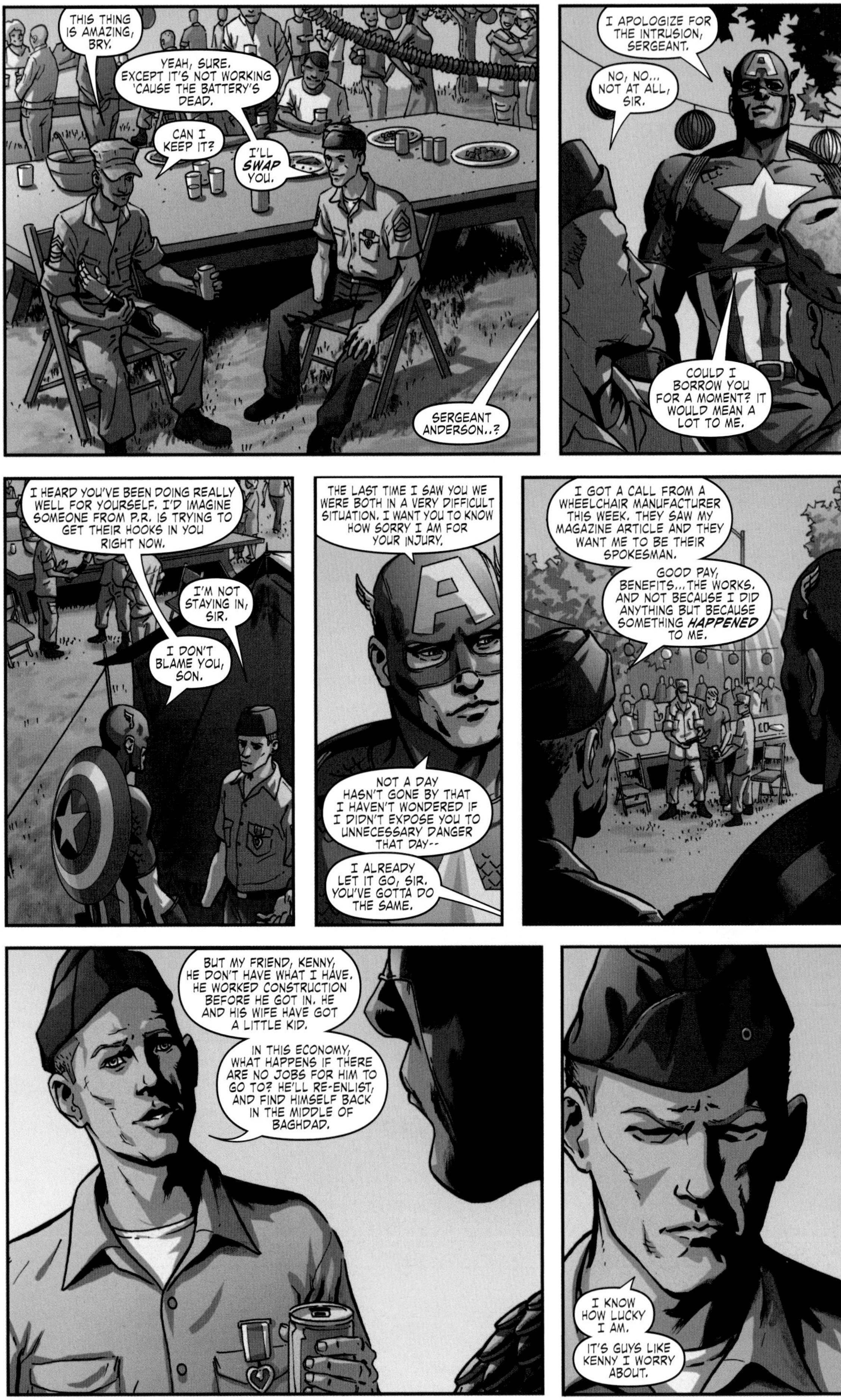
THIS THING IS AMAZING, BRY.
YEAH, SURE. EXCEPT IT'S NOT WORKING 'CAUSE THE BATTERY'S DEAD.
CAN I KEEP IT?
I'LL SWAP YOU.
SERGEANT ANDERSON..?
I APOLOGIZE FOR THE INTRUSION, SERGEANT.
NO, NO... NOT AT ALL, SIR.
COULD I BORROW YOU FOR A MOMENT? IT WOULD MEAN A LOT TO ME.
I HEARD YOU'VE BEEN DOING REALLY WELL FOR YOURSELF. I'D IMAGINE SOMEONE FROM P.R. IS TRYING TO GET THEIR HOOKS IN YOU RIGHT NOW.
I'M NOT STAYING IN, SIR.
I DON'T BLAME YOU, SON.
THE LAST TIME I SAW YOU WE WERE BOTH IN A VERY DIFFICULT SITUATION. I WANT YOU TO KNOW HOW SORRY I AM FOR YOUR INJURY.
NOT A DAY HASN'T GONE BY THAT I HAVEN'T WONDERED IF I DIDN'T EXPOSE YOU TO UNNECESSARY DANGER THAT DAY--
I ALREADY LET IT GO, SIR. YOU'VE GOTTA DO THE SAME.
I GOT A CALL FROM A WHEELCHAIR MANUFACTURER THIS WEEK. THEY SAW MY MAGAZINE ARTICLE AND THEY WANT ME TO BE THEIR SPOKESMAN.
GOOD PAY, BENEFITS... THE WORKS. AND NOT BECAUSE I DID ANYTHING BUT BECAUSE SOMETHING HAPPENED TO ME.
BUT MY FRIEND, KENNY, HE DON'T HAVE WHAT I HAVE. HE WORKED CONSTRUCTION BEFORE HE GOT IN. HE AND HIS WIFE HAVE GOT A LITTLE KID.
IN THIS ECONOMY, WHAT HAPPENS IF THERE ARE NO JOBS FOR HIM TO GO TO? HE'LL RE-ENLIST, AND FIND HIMSELF BACK IN THE MIDDLE OF BAGHDAD.
I KNOW HOW LUCKY I AM.
IT'S GUYS LIKE KENNY I WORRY ABOUT.

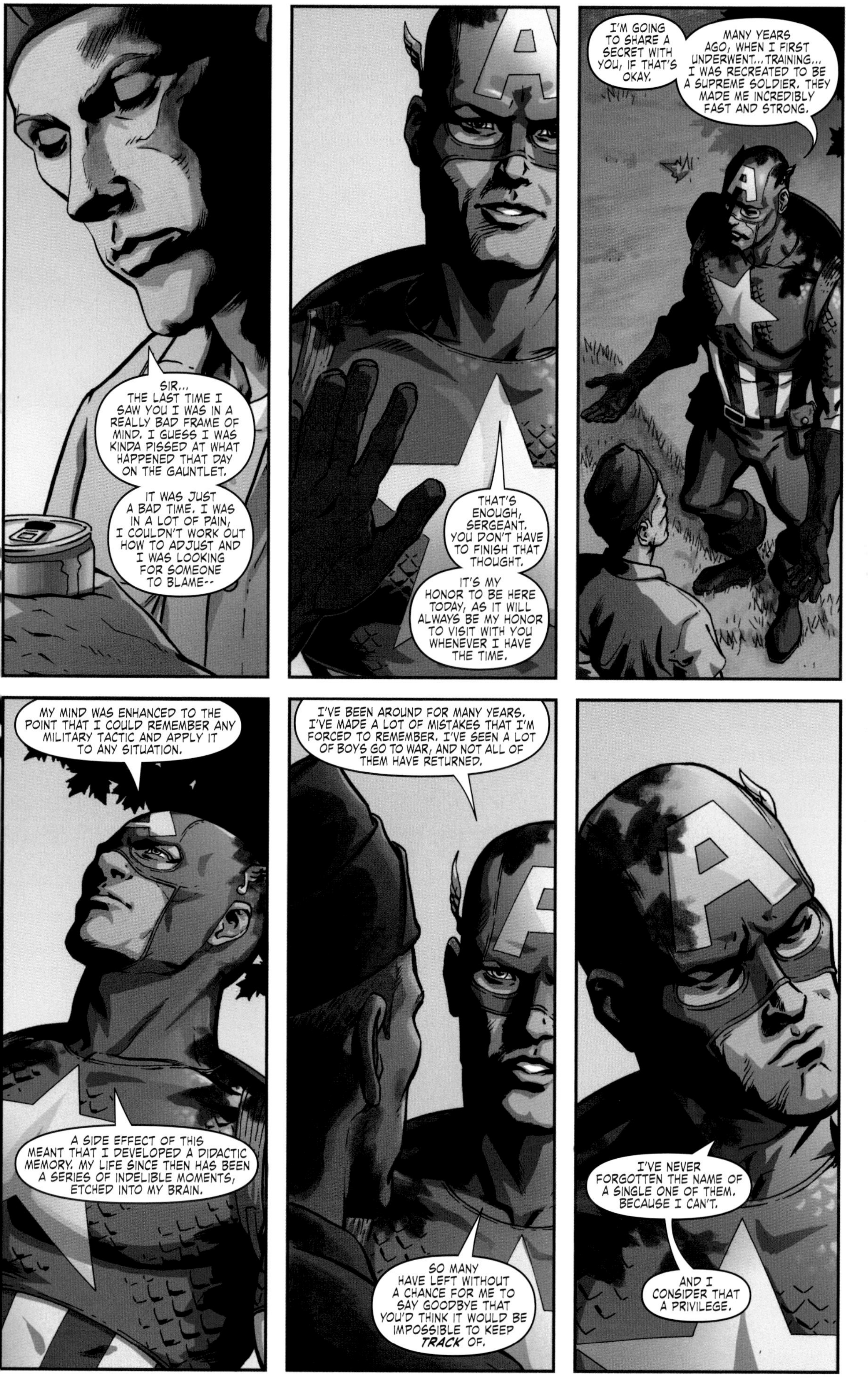
SIR... THE LAST TIME I SAW YOU I WAS IN A REALLY BAD FRAME OF MIND. I GUESS I WAS KINDA PISSED AT WHAT HAPPENED THAT DAY ON THE GAUNTLET.
IT WAS JUST A BAD TIME. I WAS IN A LOT OF PAIN, I COULDN'T WORK OUT HOW TO ADJUST AND I WAS LOOKING FOR SOMEONE TO BLAME--
THAT'S ENOUGH, SERGEANT. YOU DON'T HAVE TO FINISH THAT THOUGHT.
IT'S MY HONOR TO BE HERE TODAY, AS IT WILL ALWAYS BE MY HONOR TO VISIT WITH YOU WHENEVER I HAVE THE TIME.
I'M GOING TO SHARE A SECRET WITH YOU, IF THAT'S OKAY.
MANY YEARS AGO, WHEN I FIRST UNDERWENT... TRAINING... I WAS RECREATED TO BE A SUPREME SOLDIER. THEY MADE ME INCREDIBLY FAST AND STRONG.
MY MIND WAS ENHANCED TO THE POINT THAT I COULD REMEMBER ANY MILITARY TACTIC AND APPLY IT TO ANY SITUATION.
A SIDE EFFECT OF THIS MEANT THAT I DEVELOPED A DIDACTIC MEMORY. MY LIFE SINCE THEN HAS BEEN A SERIES OF INDELIBLE MOMENTS, ETCHED INTO MY BRAIN.
I'VE BEEN AROUND FOR MANY YEARS. I'VE MADE A LOT OF MISTAKES THAT I'M FORCED TO REMEMBER. I'VE SEEN A LOT OF BOYS GO TO WAR, AND NOT ALL OF THEM HAVE RETURNED.
SO MANY HAVE LEFT WITHOUT A CHANCE FOR ME TO SAY GOODBYE THAT YOU'D THINK IT WOULD BE IMPOSSIBLE TO KEEP TRACK OF.
I'VE NEVER FORGOTTEN THE NAME OF A SINGLE ONE OF THEM. BECAUSE I CAN'T.
AND I CONSIDER THAT A PRIVILEGE.

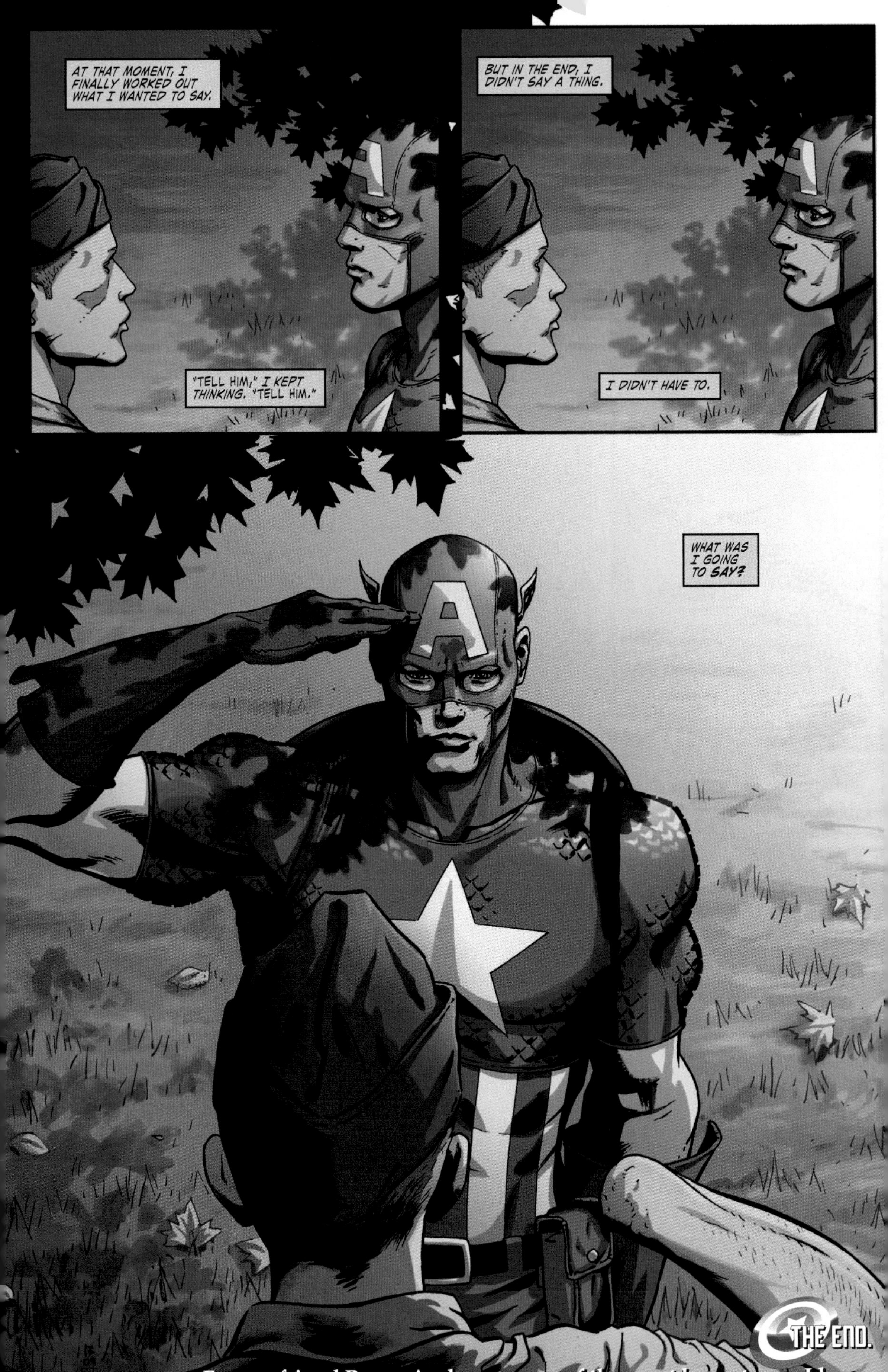
AT THAT MOMENT, I FINALLY WORKED OUT WHAT I WANTED TO SAY.
"TELL HIM," I KEPT THINKING. "TELL HIM."
BUT IN THE END, I DIDN'T SAY A THING.
I DIDN'T HAVE TO.
WHAT WAS I GOING TO SAY?
THE END.

For my friend Bryan Anderson: one of the most honest men I know.
For Kenny, who was there. And for Mike, who still is.

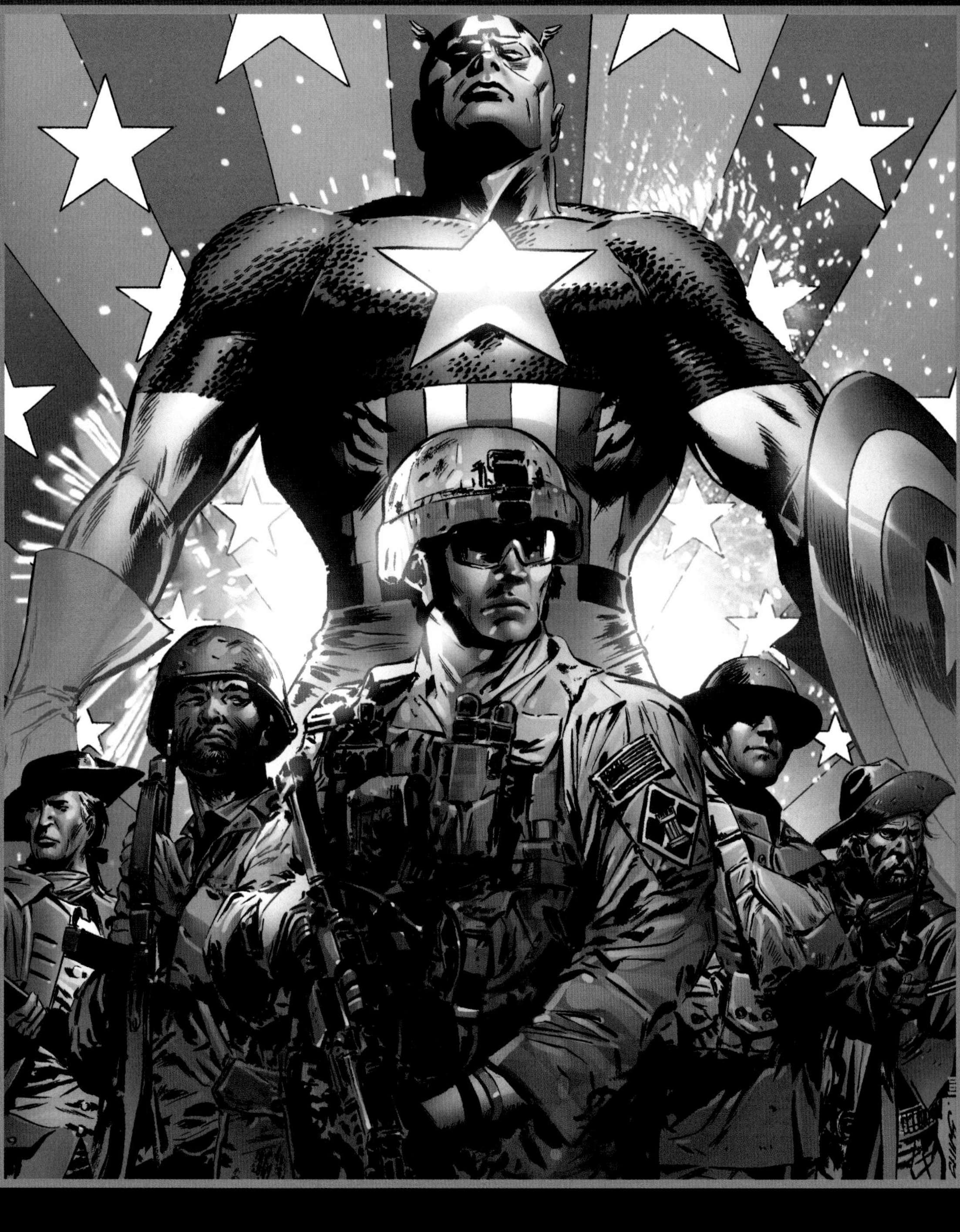

GHOSTS OF MY COUNTRY

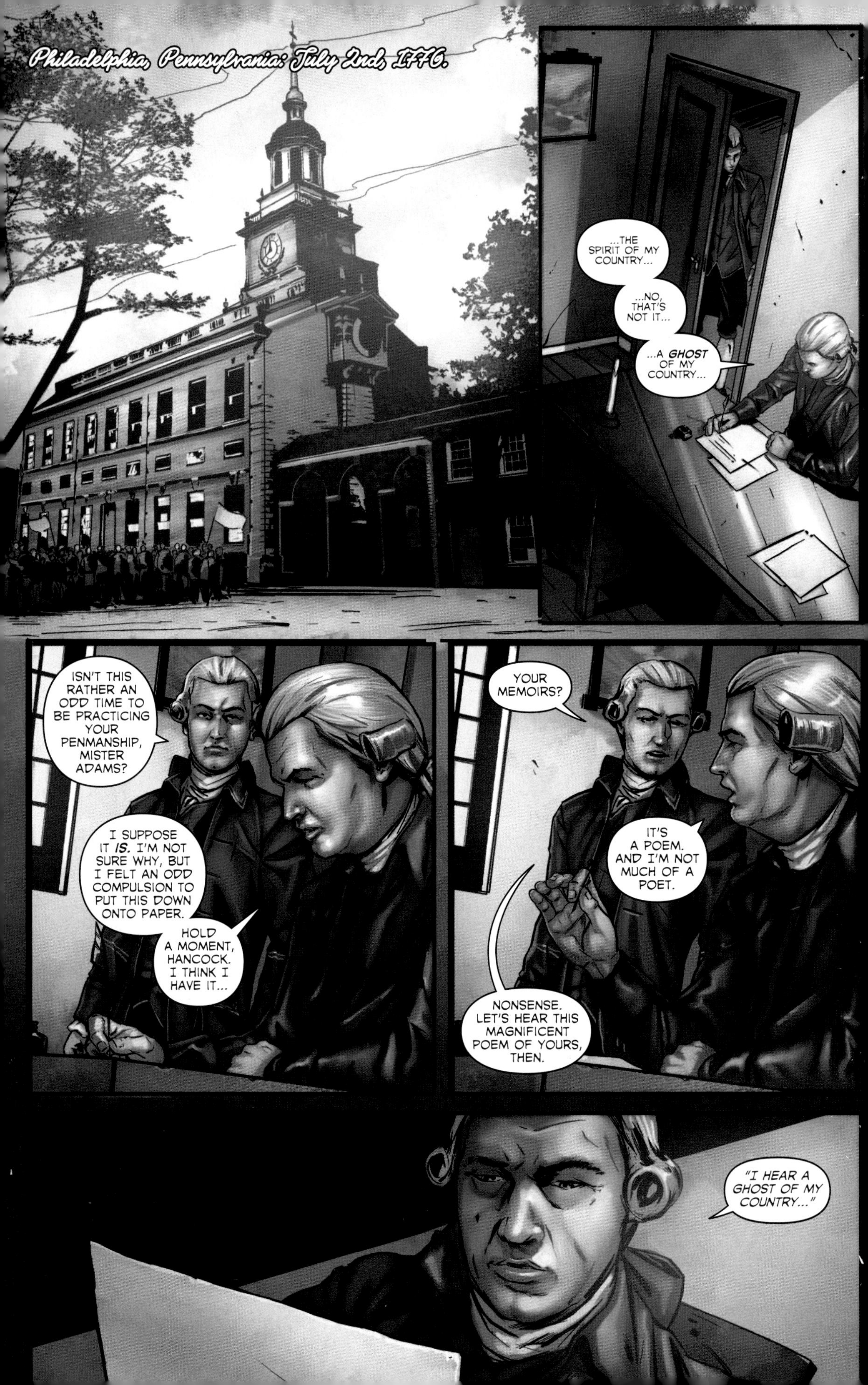
Philadelphia, Pennsylvania: July 2nd, 1776.
...THE SPIRIT OF MY COUNTRY...
...NO, THAT'S NOT IT...
...A GHOST OF MY COUNTRY...
ISN'T THIS RATHER AN ODD TIME TO BE PRACTICING YOUR PENMANSHIP, MISTER ADAMS?
I SUPPOSE IT IS. I'M NOT SURE WHY, BUT I FELT AN ODD COMPULSION TO PUT THIS DOWN ONTO PAPER.
HOLD A MOMENT, HANCOCK. I THINK I HAVE IT...
YOUR MEMOIRS?
IT'S A POEM. AND I'M NOT MUCH OF A POET.
NONSENSE. LET'S HEAR THIS MAGNIFICENT POEM OF YOURS, THEN.
"I HEAR A GHOST OF MY COUNTRY..."

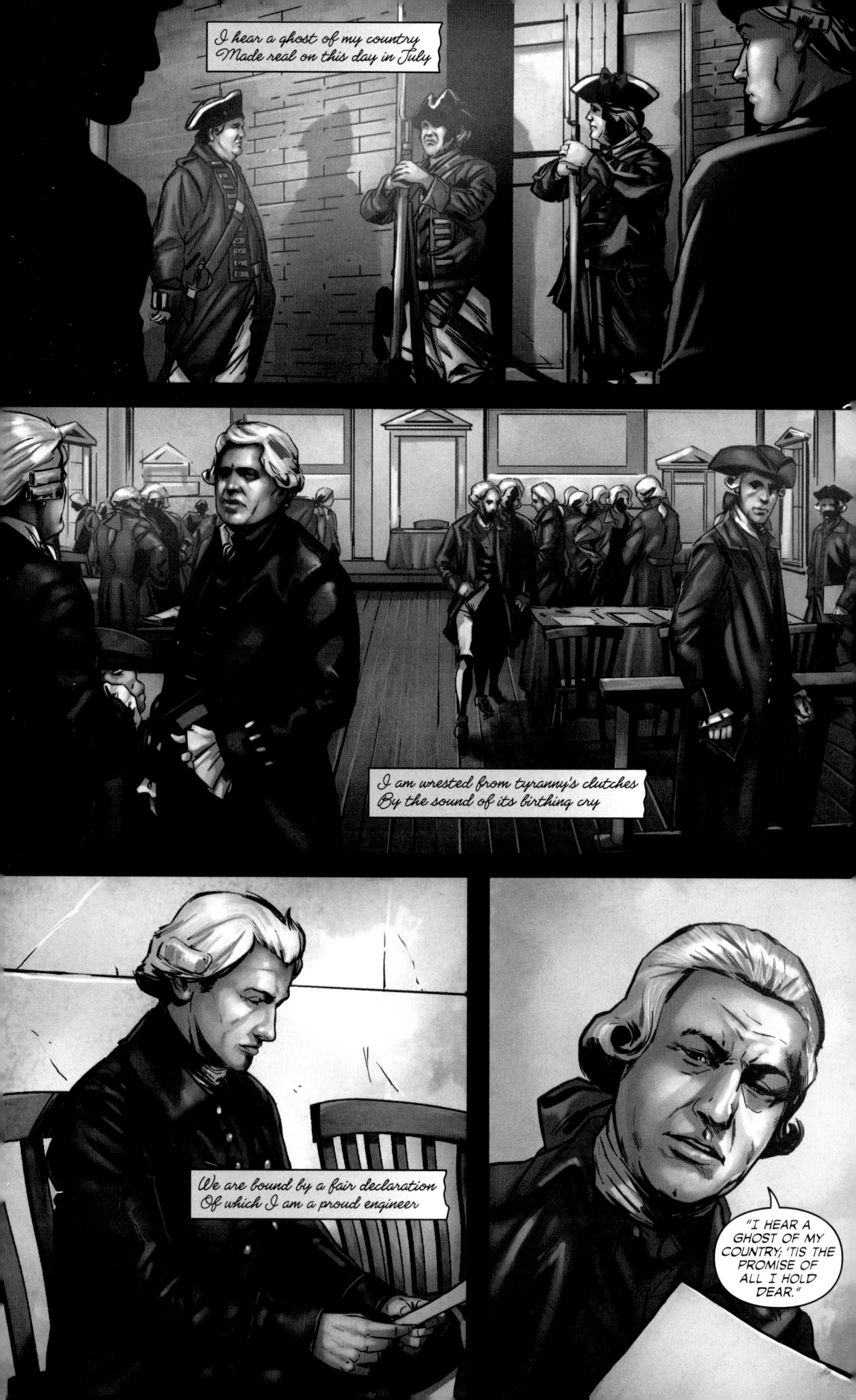
I hear a ghost of my country
Made real on this day in July
I am wrested from tyranny's clutches
By the sound of its birthing cry
We are bound by a fair declaration
Of which I am a proud engineer
"I HEAR A GHOST OF MY COUNTRY; 'TIS THE PROMISE OF ALL I HOLD DEAR."

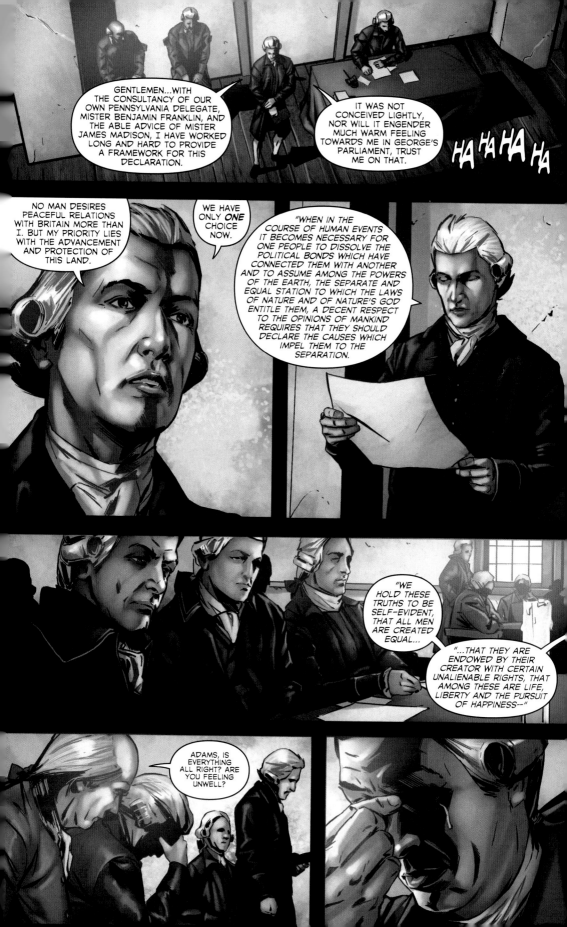

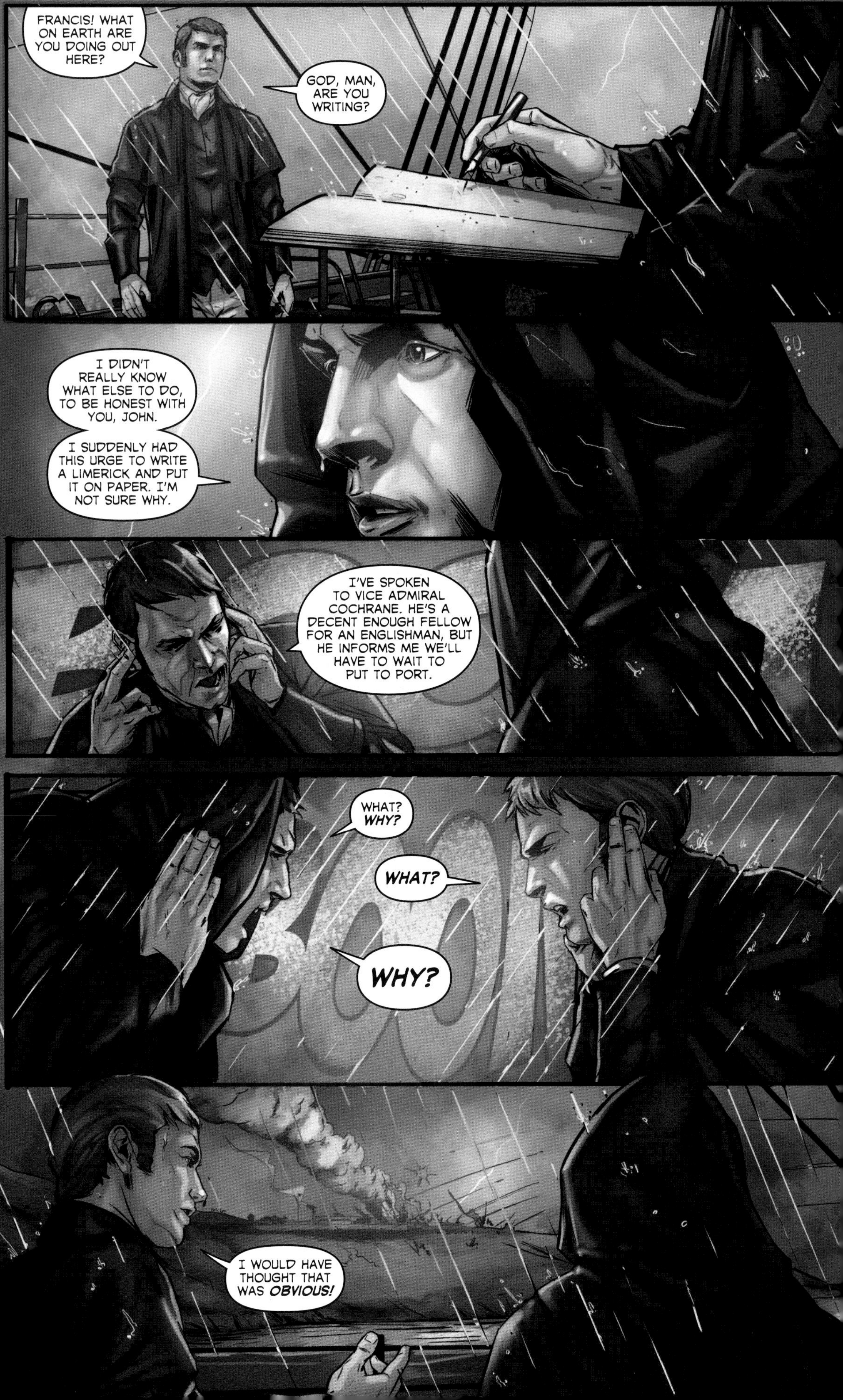
FRANCIS! WHAT ON EARTH ARE YOU DOING OUT HERE?
GOD, MAN, ARE YOU WRITING?
I DIDN'T REALLY KNOW WHAT ELSE TO DO, TO BE HONEST WITH YOU, JOHN.
I SUDDENLY HAD THIS URGE TO WRITE A LIMERICK AND PUT IT ON PAPER. I'M NOT SURE WHY.
I'VE SPOKEN TO VICE ADMIRAL COCHRANE. HE'S A DECENT ENOUGH FELLOW FOR AN ENGLISHMAN, BUT HE INFORMS ME WE'LL HAVE TO WAIT TO PUT TO PORT.
WHAT? *WHY?*
WHAT?
WHY?
I WOULD HAVE THOUGHT THAT WAS *OBVIOUS!*

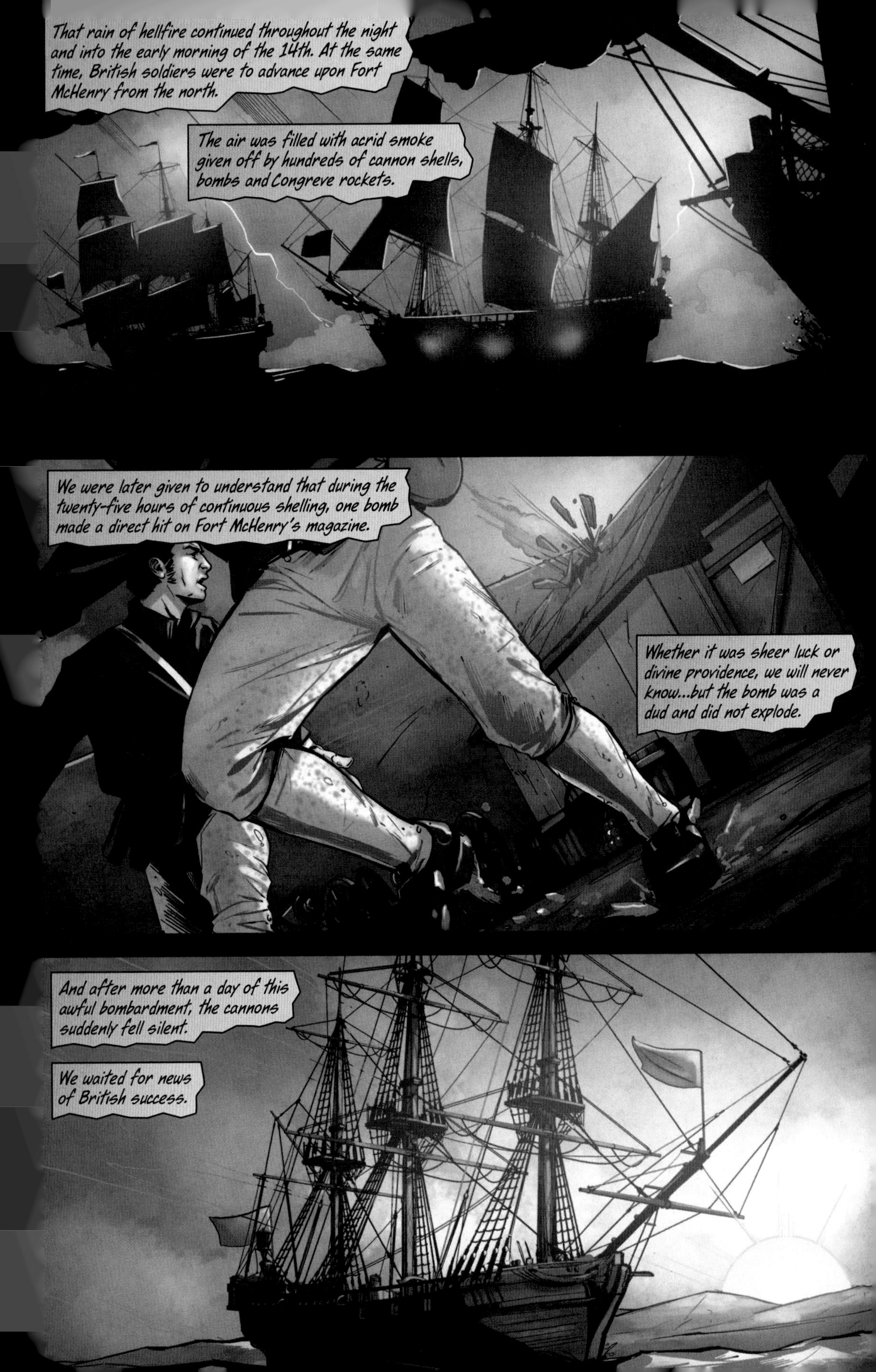
That rain of hellfire continued throughout the night and into the early morning of the 14th. At the same time, British soldiers were to advance upon Fort McHenry from the north.
The air was filled with acrid smoke given off by hundreds of cannon shells, bombs and Congreve rockets.
We were later given to understand that during the twenty-five hours of continuous shelling, one bomb made a direct hit on Fort McHenry's magazine.
Whether it was sheer luck or divine providence, we will never know...but the bomb was a dud and did not explode.
And after more than a day of this awful bombardment, the cannons suddenly fell silent.
We waited for news of British success.

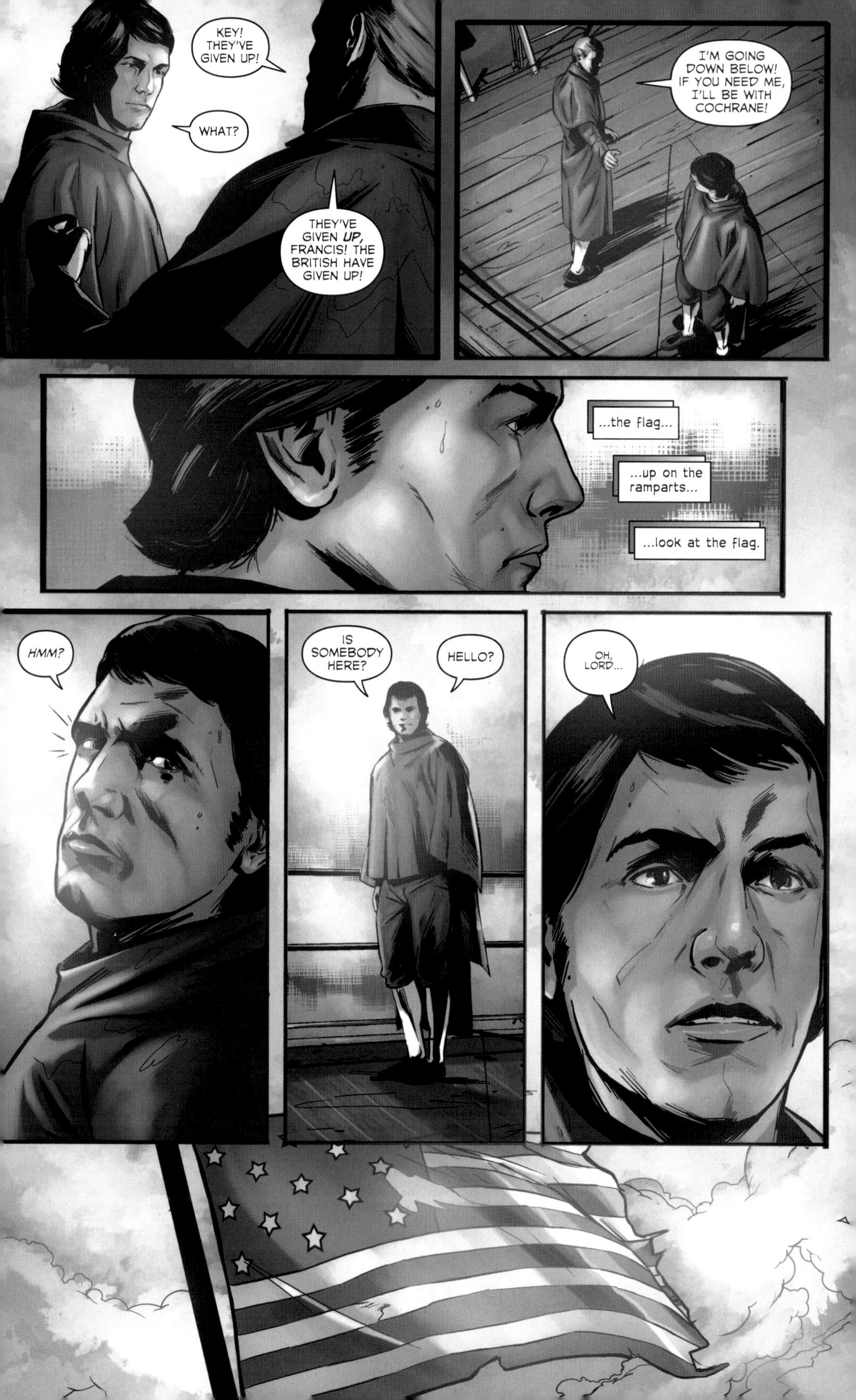
KEY! THEY'VE GIVEN UP!
WHAT?
THEY'VE GIVEN *UP,* FRANCIS! THE BRITISH HAVE GIVEN UP!
I'M GOING DOWN BELOW! IF YOU NEED ME, I'LL BE WITH COCHRANE!
...the flag...
...up on the ramparts...
...look at the flag.
HMM?
IS SOMEBODY HERE?
HELLO?
OH, LORD...

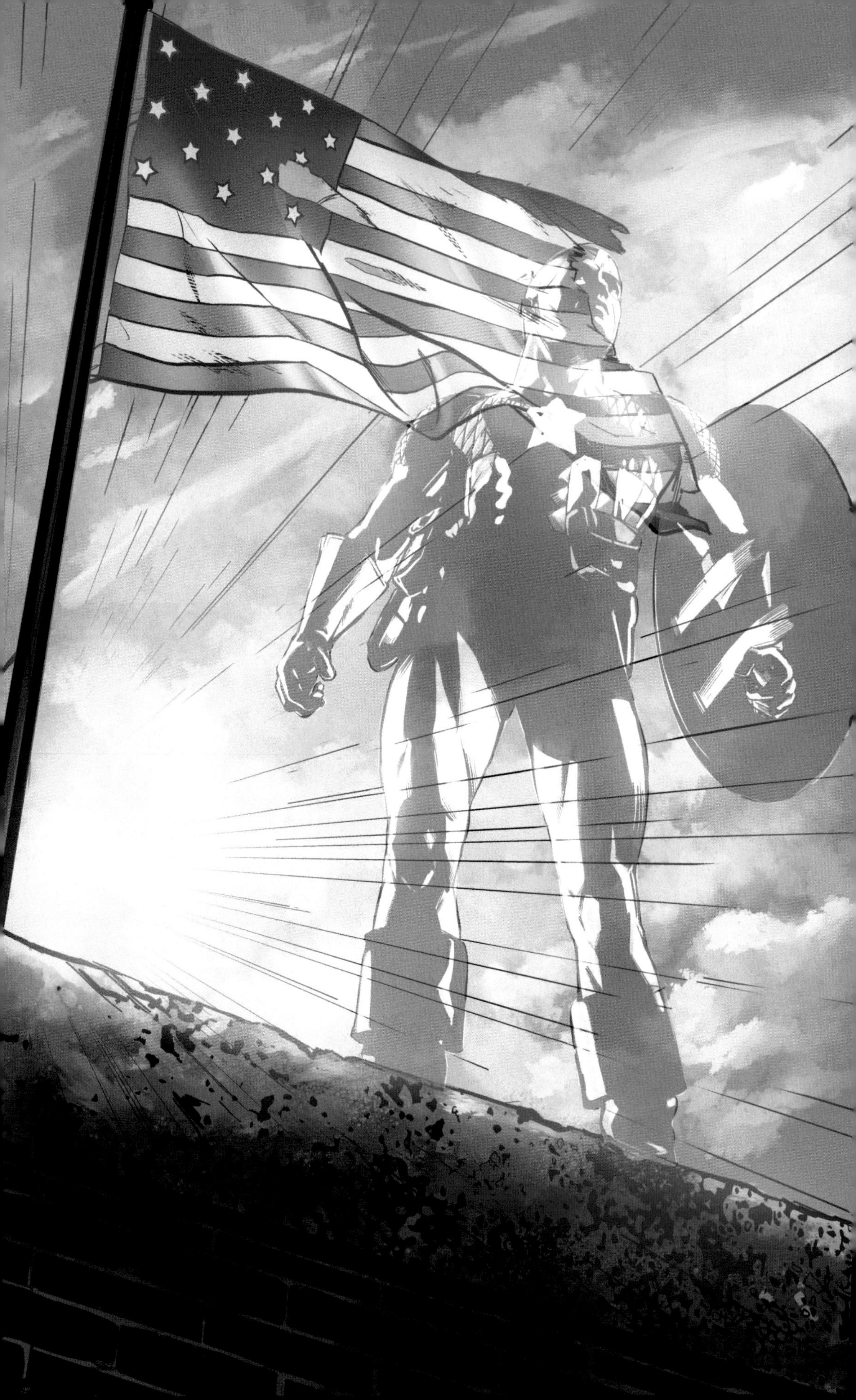

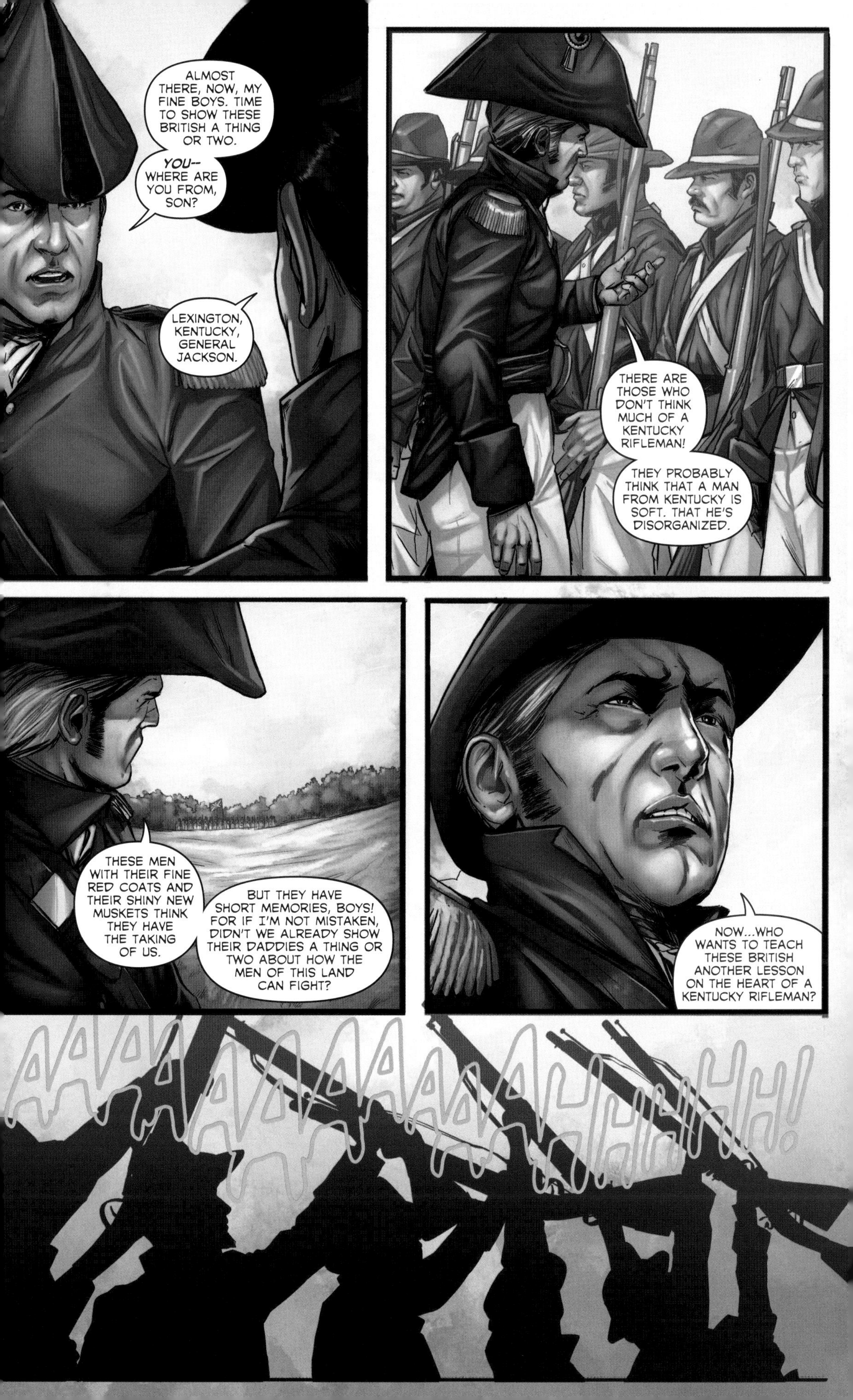
ALMOST THERE, NOW, MY FINE BOYS. TIME TO SHOW THESE BRITISH A THING OR TWO.
YOU-- WHERE ARE YOU FROM, SON?
LEXINGTON, KENTUCKY, GENERAL JACKSON.
THERE ARE THOSE WHO DON'T THINK MUCH OF A KENTUCKY RIFLEMAN!
THEY PROBABLY THINK THAT A MAN FROM KENTUCKY IS SOFT. THAT HE'S DISORGANIZED.
THESE MEN WITH THEIR FINE RED COATS AND THEIR SHINY NEW MUSKETS THINK THEY HAVE THE TAKING OF US.
BUT THEY HAVE SHORT MEMORIES, BOYS! FOR IF I'M NOT MISTAKEN, DIDN'T WE ALREADY SHOW THEIR DADDIES A THING OR TWO ABOUT HOW THE MEN OF THIS LAND CAN FIGHT?
NOW...WHO WANTS TO TEACH THESE BRITISH ANOTHER LESSON ON THE HEART OF A KENTUCKY RIFLEMAN?
AAAAAAAAAAAAHHHHHH!

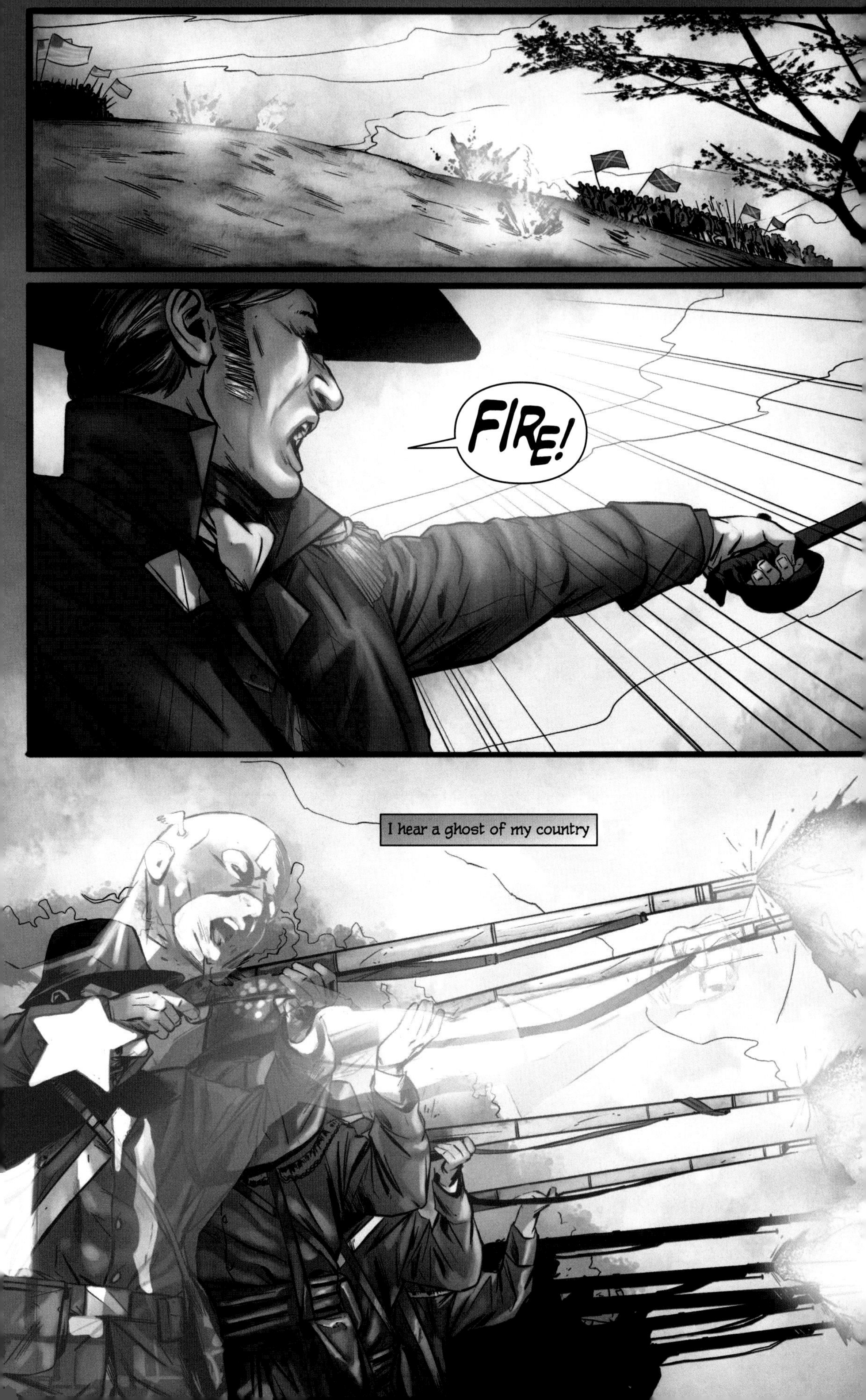
FIRE!
I hear a ghost of my country

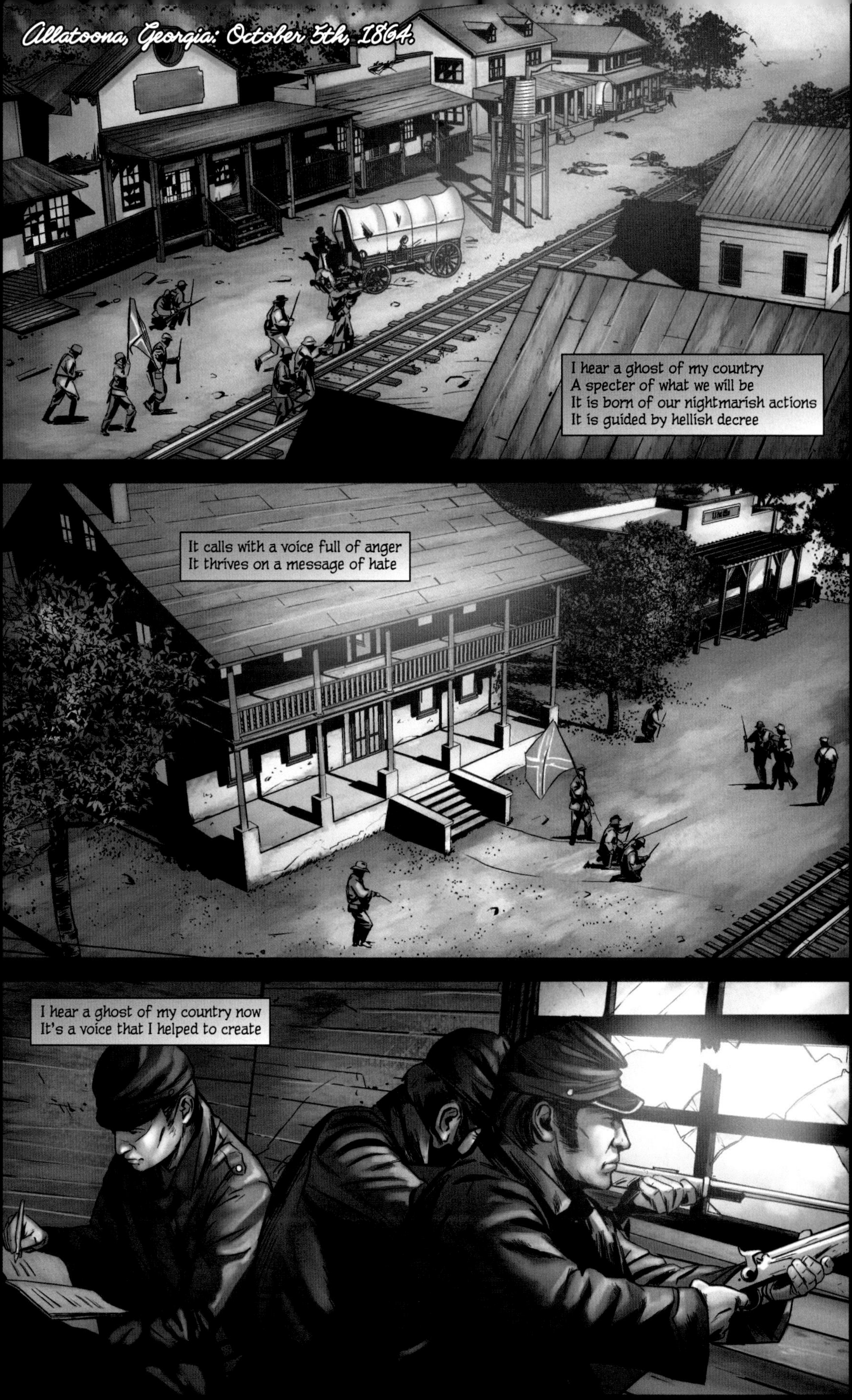
Allatoona, Georgia: October 5th, 1864.
I hear a ghost of my country
A specter of what we will be
It is born of our nightmarish actions
It is guided by hellish decree
It calls with a voice full of anger
It thrives on a message of hate
I hear a ghost of my country now
It's a voice that I helped to create

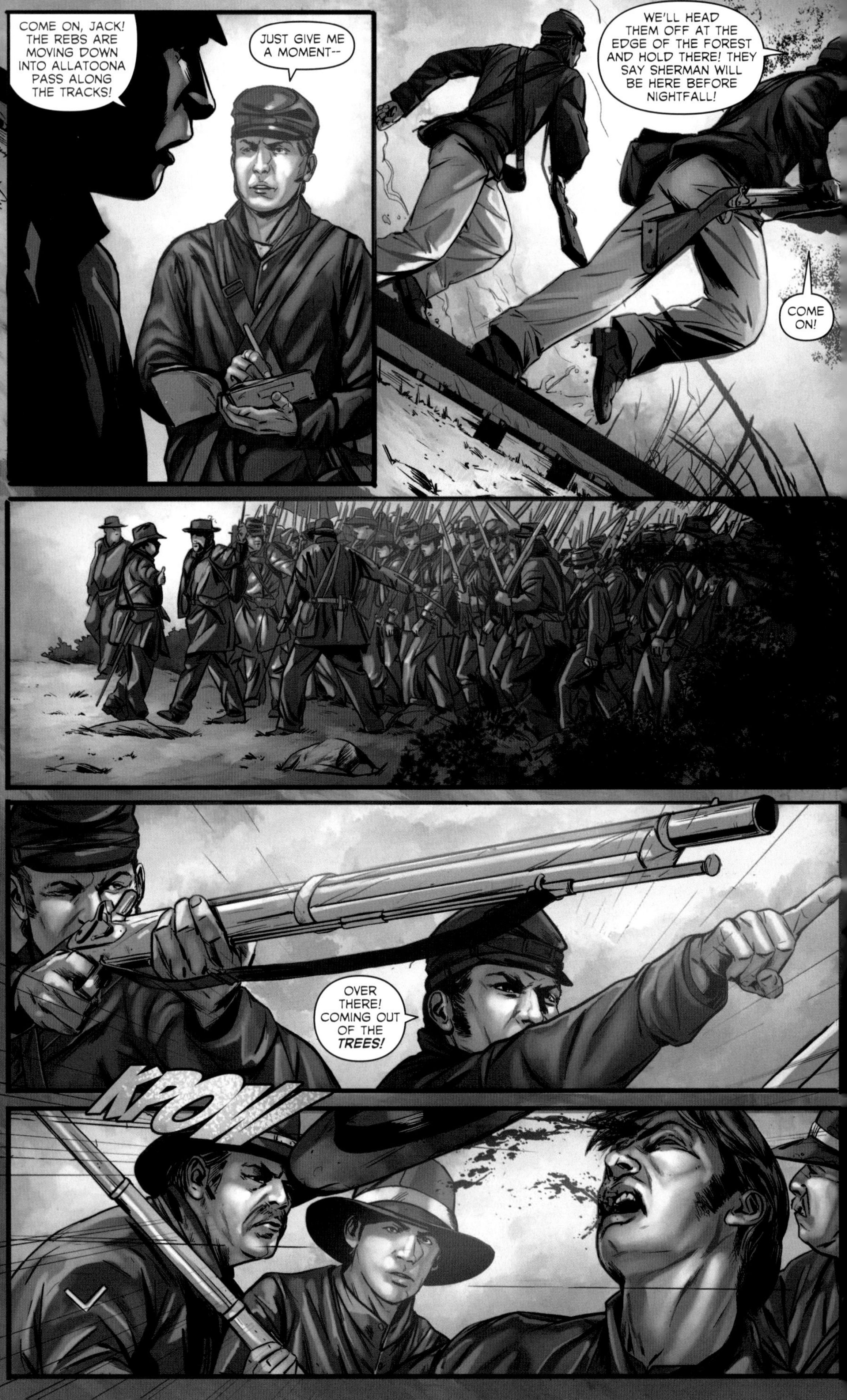
COME ON, JACK! THE REBS ARE MOVING DOWN INTO ALLATOONA PASS ALONG THE TRACKS!
JUST GIVE ME A MOMENT--
WE'LL HEAD THEM OFF AT THE EDGE OF THE FOREST AND HOLD THERE! THEY SAY SHERMAN WILL BE HERE BEFORE NIGHTFALL!
COME ON!
OVER THERE! COMING OUT OF THE *TREES!*
KPOW!!

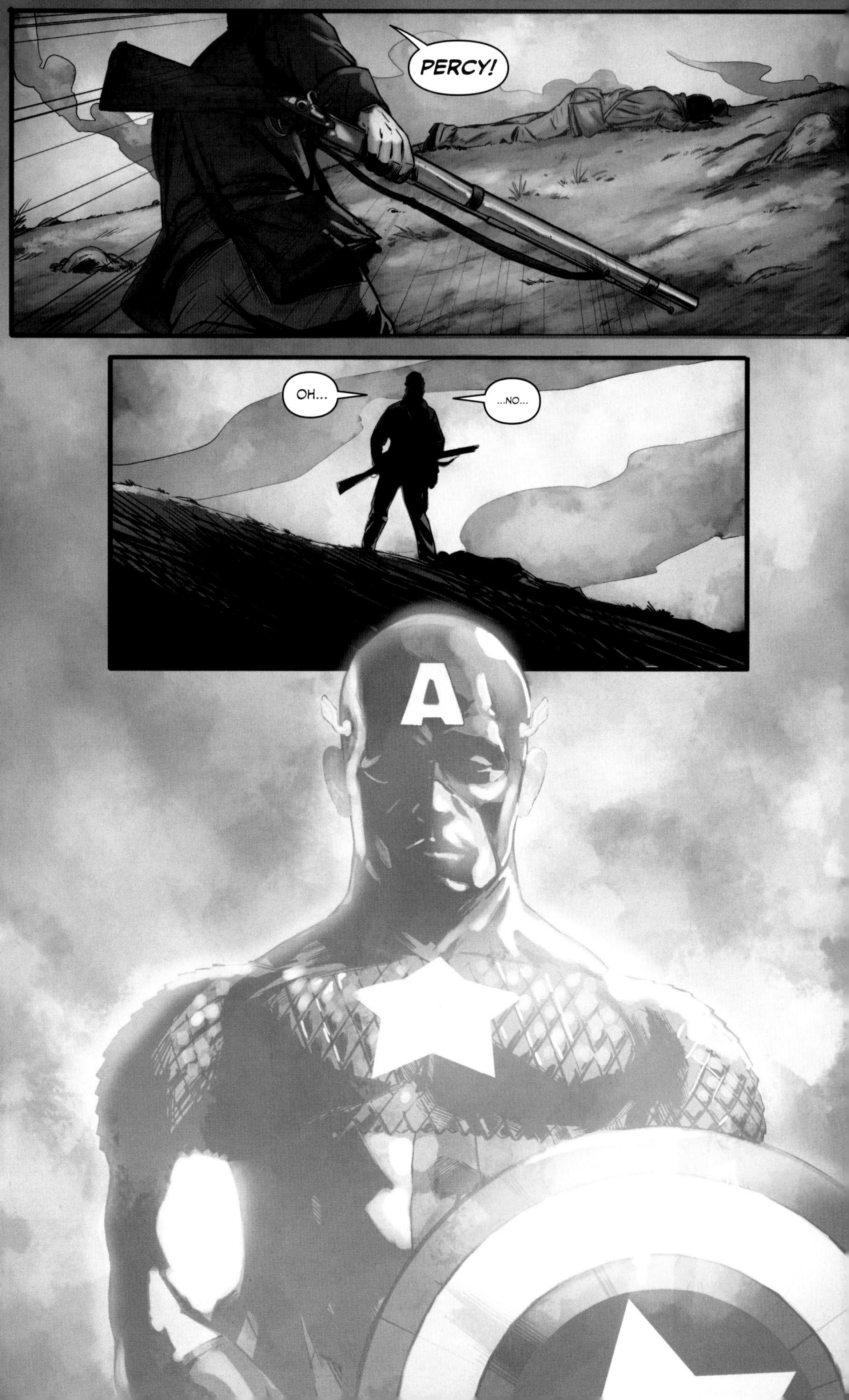
PERCY!
OH...
...NO...

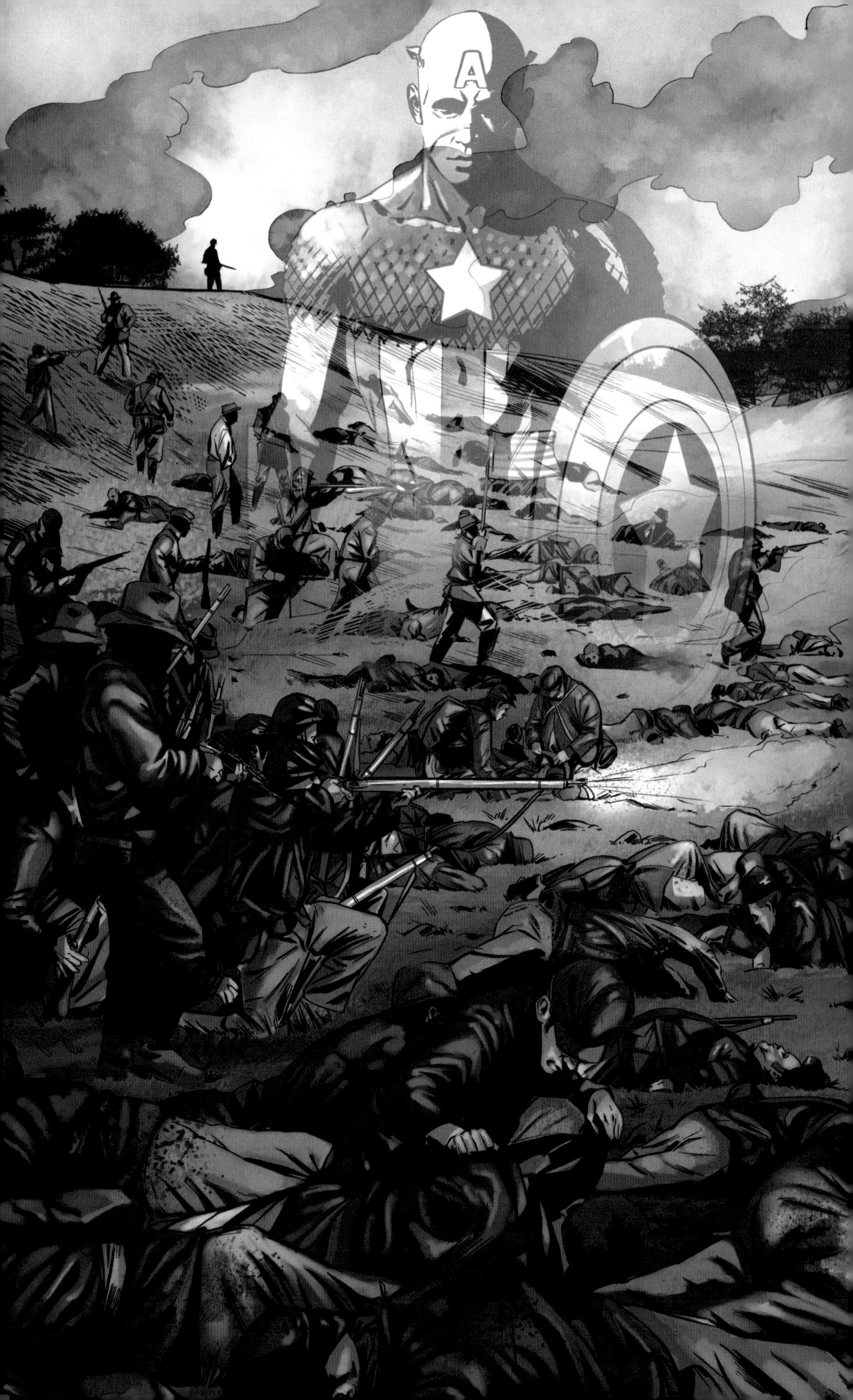

I dream of a ghost of my country

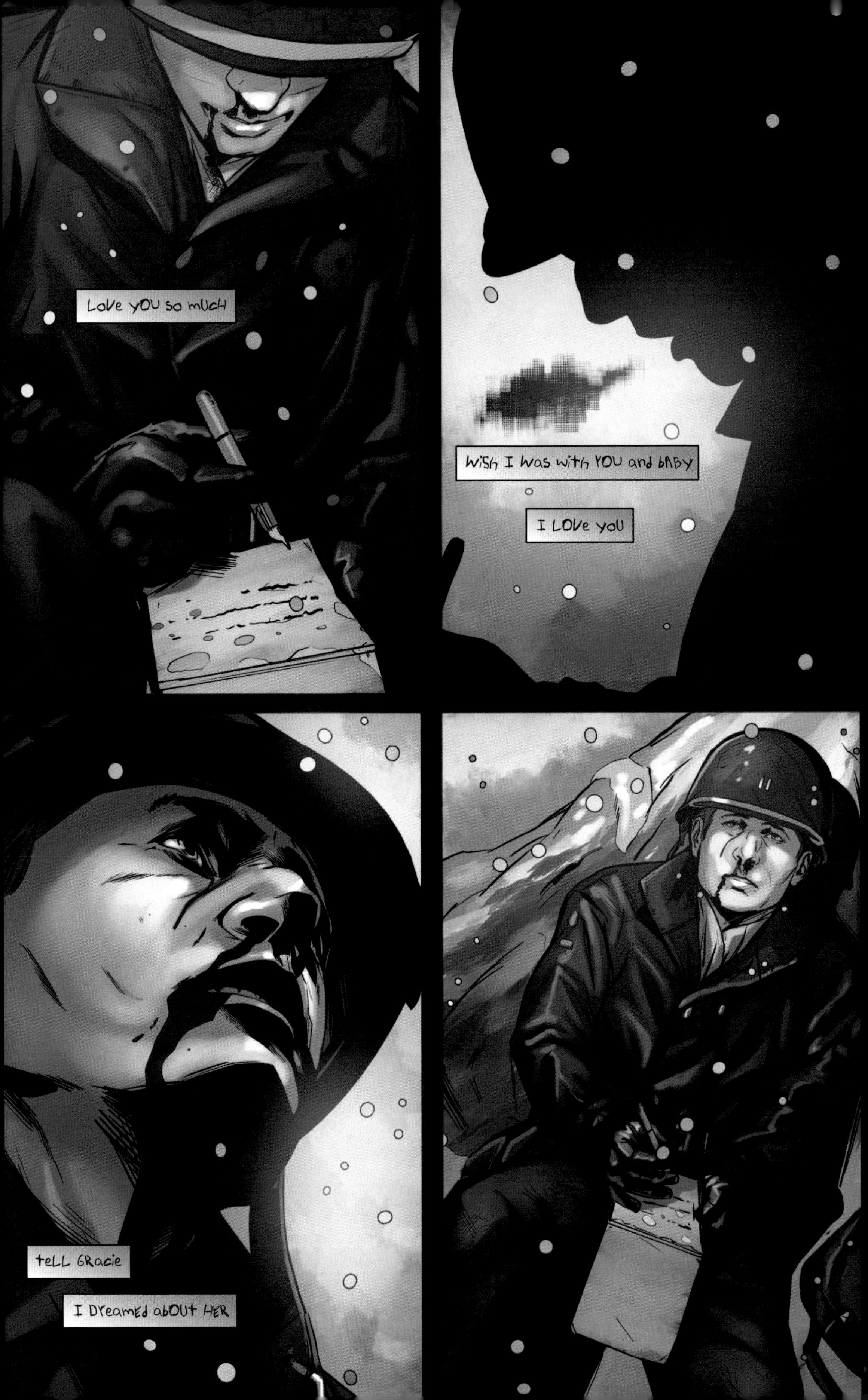
Love YOU so much
Wish I was with YOU and baby
I LOVe you
teLL Gracie
I Dreamed about HER

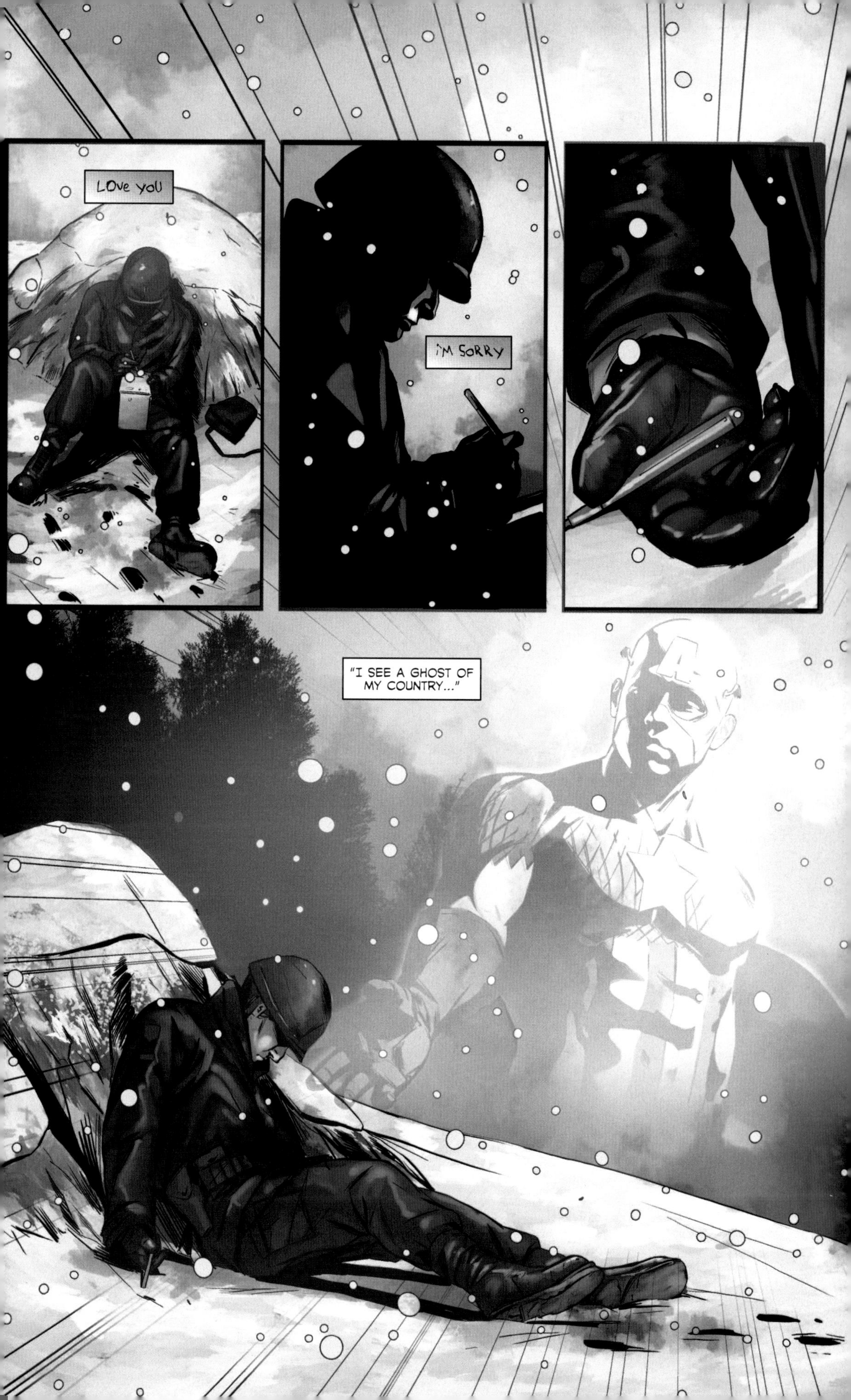
LOve yoU
I'M SORRY
"I SEE A GHOST OF MY COUNTRY..."

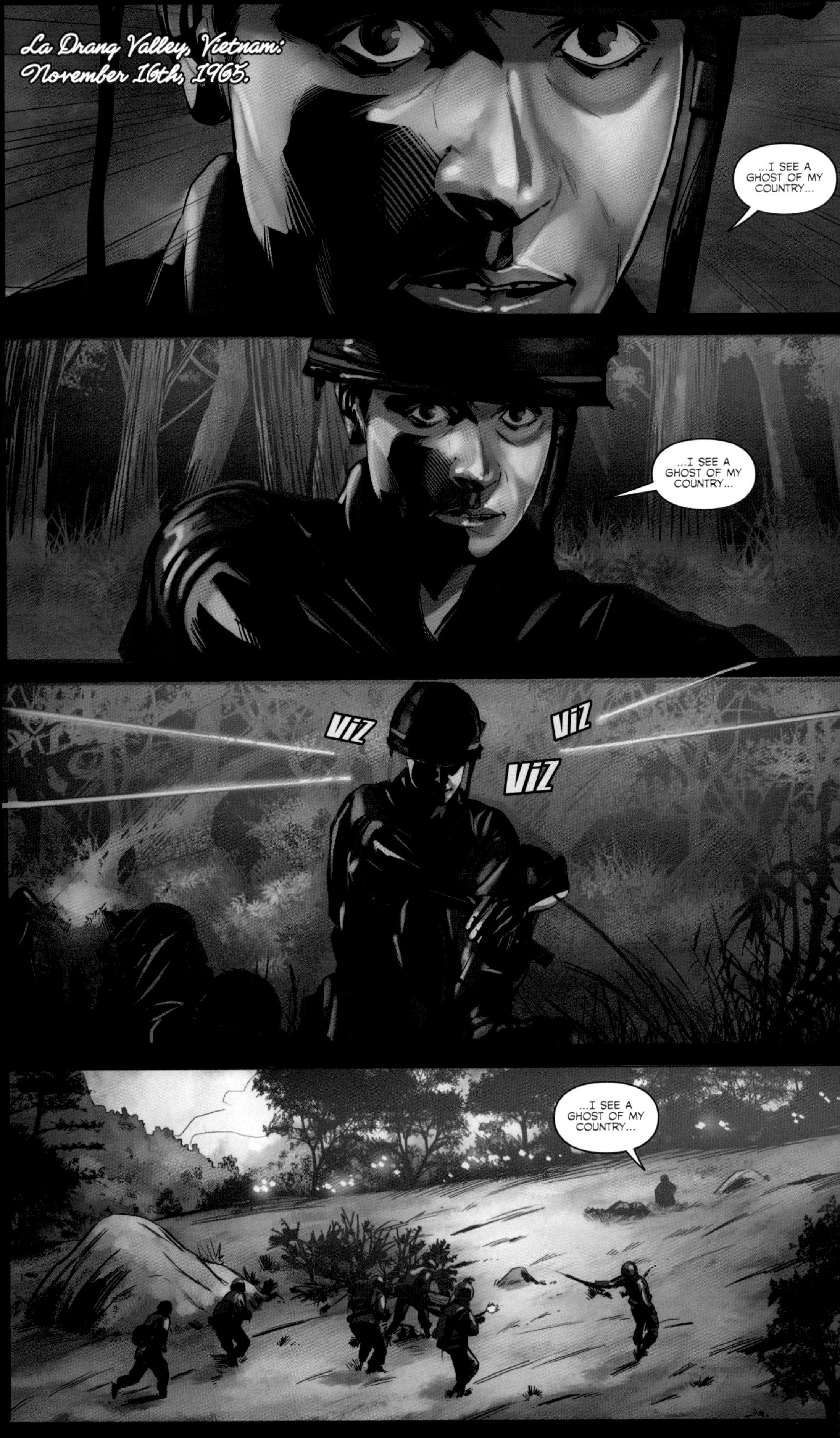
La Drang Valley, Vietnam:
November 16th, 1965.
...I SEE A GHOST OF MY COUNTRY...
...I SEE A GHOST OF MY COUNTRY...
VIZ
VIZ
VIZ
...I SEE A GHOST OF MY COUNTRY...

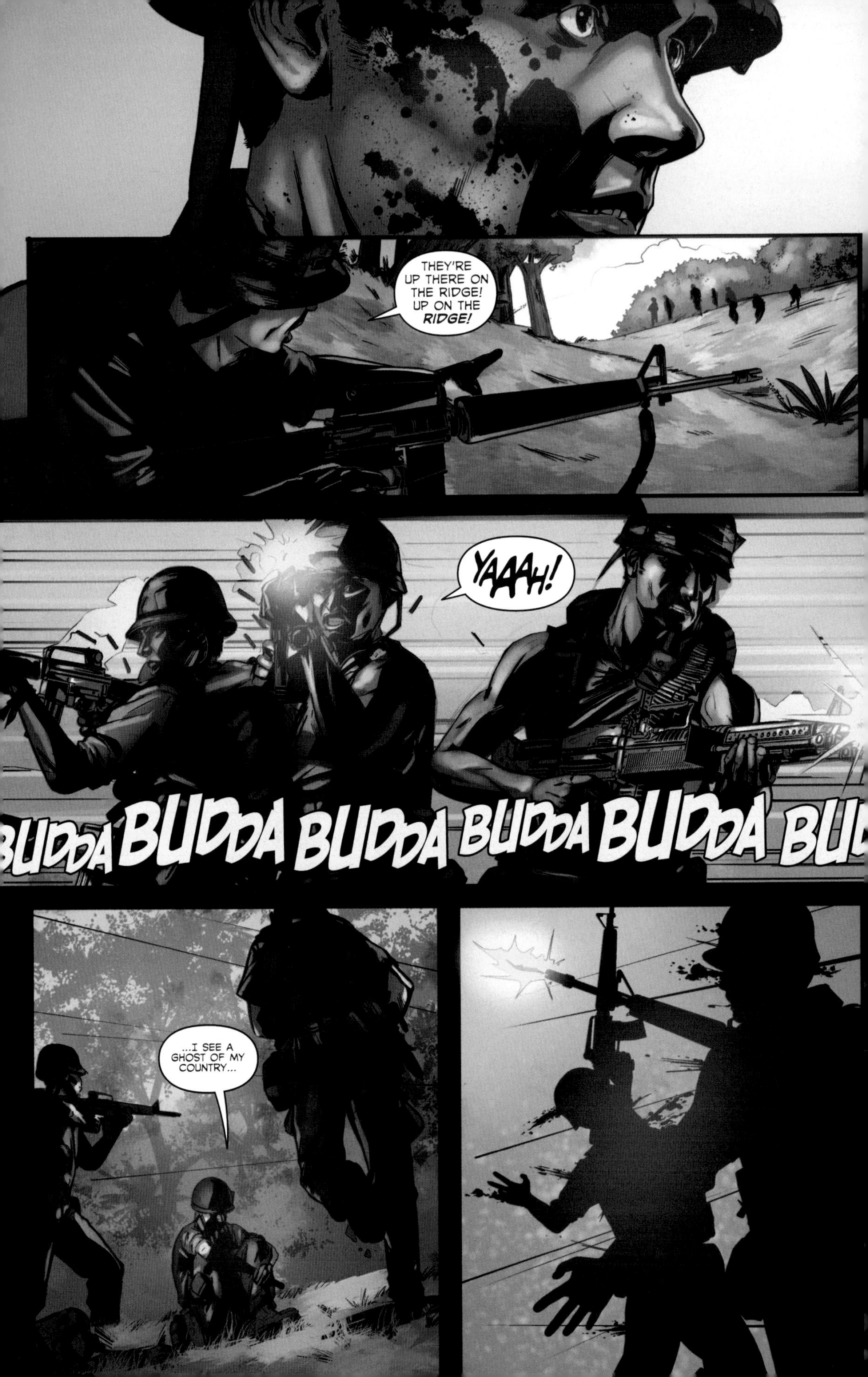
THEY'RE UP THERE ON THE RIDGE! UP ON THE RIDGE!
YAAAH!
BUDDA BUDDA BUDDA BUDDA BUDDA
...I SEE A GHOST OF MY COUNTRY...

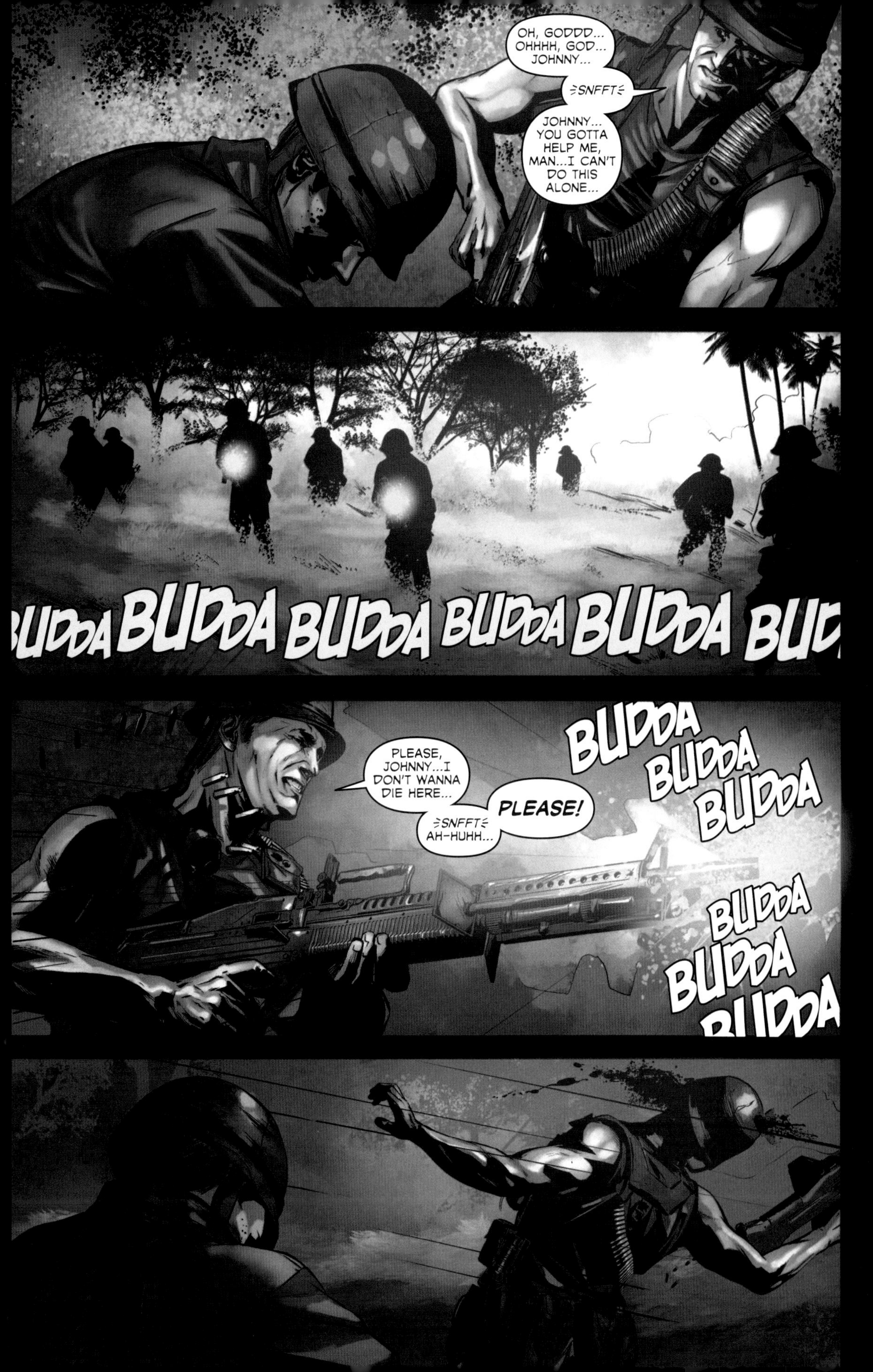
OH, GODDD... OHHHH, GOD... JOHNNY...
SNFFT
JOHNNY... YOU GOTTA HELP ME, MAN...I CAN'T DO THIS ALONE...
BUDDA BUDDA BUDDA BUDDA BUDDA
PLEASE, JOHNNY...I DON'T WANNA DIE HERE...
SNFFT AH-HUHH...
PLEASE!
BUDDA BUDDA BUDDA
BUDDA BUDDA BUDDA

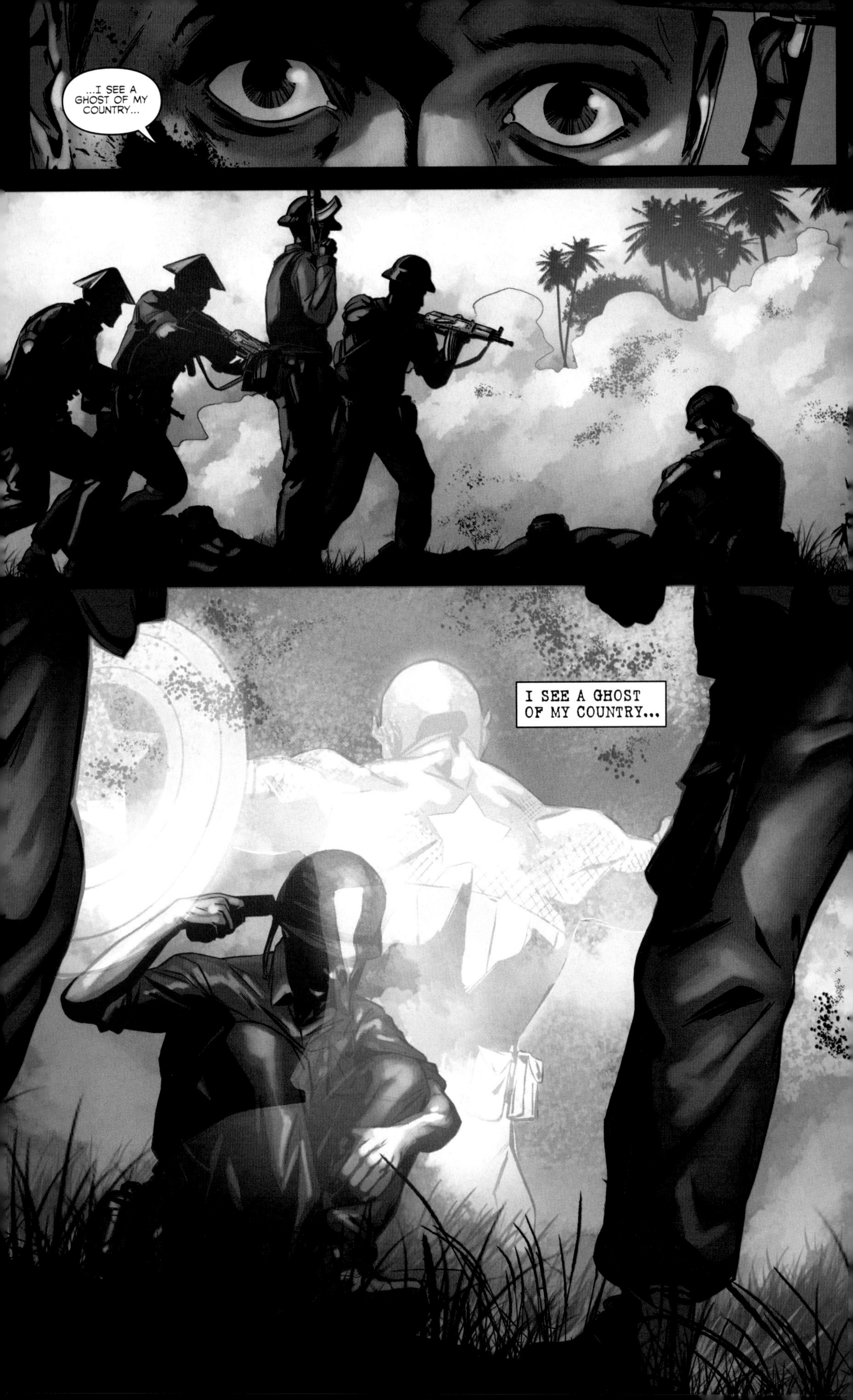
...I SEE A GHOST OF MY COUNTRY...
I SEE A GHOST OF MY COUNTRY...

21. **Governing Law**: This contract will be governed by and construed in accordance with of New York. Venue for any proceedings brought under this Agreement shall be a State or York City, NY.

22. **Consent to Breach Not Waiver**: No term or provision hereof shall be deemed waive excused, unless such waiver or consent is in writing and signed by the party claimed to have w No consent by either party to, or waiver of, a breach by the other party shall constitute a conse excuse of any other different or subsequent breach.

23. **Severability**: Should any portion of this Agreement be found unenforceable jurisdiction, but only in such jurisdiction, said portion of this Agreement shall be deleted or ig of this Agreement shall remain in full force and effect.

24. **Non-Waiver**: Failure or delay by either party on any occasion to exercise any right, this Agreement shall not be construed as a waiver or relinquishment for the future of such righ

25. **Force Majeure**: Neither party ~~All parties~~ will be liable to the other for delays in the Agreement if the delay is caused by stri

I SEE A GHOST OF MY COUNTRY

I SEE A GHOST OF MY COUNTRY

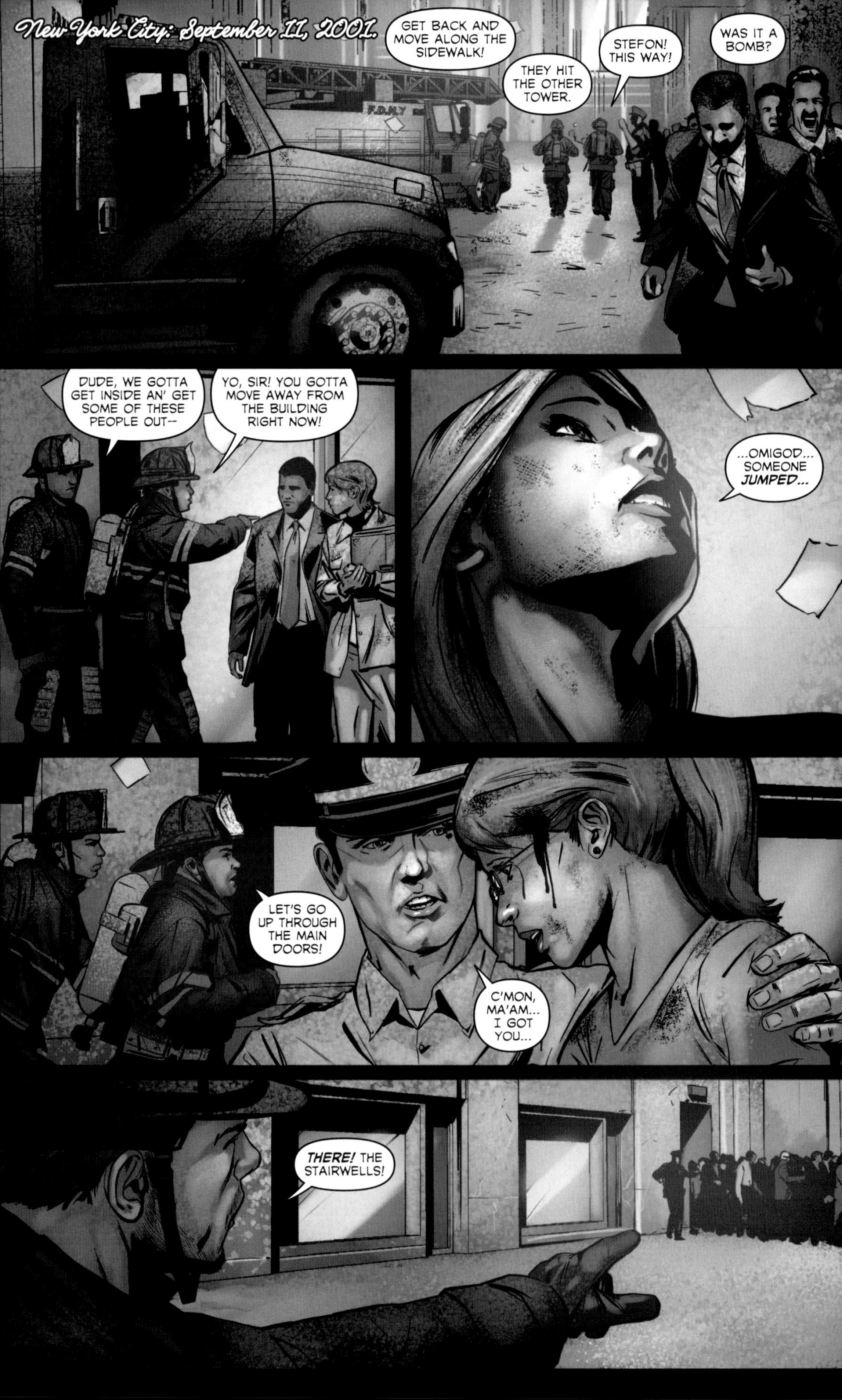
New York City: September 11, 2001.
GET BACK AND MOVE ALONG THE SIDEWALK!
THEY HIT THE OTHER TOWER.
STEFON! THIS WAY!
WAS IT A BOMB?
DUDE, WE GOTTA GET INSIDE AN' GET SOME OF THESE PEOPLE OUT--
YO, SIR! YOU GOTTA MOVE AWAY FROM THE BUILDING RIGHT NOW!
...OMIGOD... SOMEONE JUMPED...
LET'S GO UP THROUGH THE MAIN DOORS!
C'MON, MA'AM... I GOT YOU...
THERE! THE STAIRWELLS!
F.D.N.Y

Reprinted from *Marvel Spotlight: Captain America* (2009)

CAPTAIN AMERICA THEATER OF WAR

A SERIES OF ONE-SHOTS, LED BY WRITER PAUL JENKINS, EXPLORES CAP AND THE SACRIFICE OF THE WARRIOR CLASS

BY DUGAN TRODGLEN

Captain America: Theater of War is a series of one-shots designed to give us a different look at Captain America. As the name suggests, these are war stories, having thus far taken place back in World War II. They have been honest, touching, and at times brutal takes on the kinds of conflicts for which Captain America was created and the men and women of our armed forces continue to offer their lives for. The one-shots have included such creators as Howard Chaykin and Daniel and Charles Knauf, but a British writer has seized the reins, with no less than four entries either published or on their way to store shelves soon. ★ That writer, Paul Jenkins (now residing near Atlanta, Georgia), has had his name on all manner of projects for Marvel. Best known for bringing us Wolverine's *Origin*, he also won an Eisner for writing *Inhumans*, created the Sentry, and launched the *Frontline* series. Paul has now found himself neck deep in the war genre and wants to stick with it for a while. Despite not being born in America, Paul has a deep appreciation of the American military. As we'll find out in this moving *Spotlight* interview, he has many dear friends who are veterans and his family roots in the military go deep, resulting in some powerful tales.

SPOTLIGHT: Thanks for talking to us, Paul. You've done two *Theater of War* one-shots, with a third coming out...

PAUL: Actually there are going to be four total. It's the kind of material I really like to do so we kept going.

SPOTLIGHT: Originally these series of one-shots were conceived to feature rotating creative teams, but you've sort of taken them over as the writer. Was it your affinity for these war stories that led you to keep doing them?

PAUL: Yeah, it was. I like the material and I certainly have a lot to say on the subject. In the aftermath of me turning in the fourth script, my editor Tom Brevoort and I discussed future work and he said he wanted me to propose more war material. Not necessarily Cap, but war stories in general – we agree upon the fact that this material is clearly working for me right now.

SPOTLIGHT: I understand you have a lot of military history in your family.

PAUL: I lost two great-grandfathers in the Great War – the First World War. My dad in fact just sent me a locket that my great-grandfather took with him all through the war. In it is a photo of my great-grandmother and my grandfather at age 3. I have a son age 3 so this was so powerful to me – to try and see what he must have felt. I just went away to Los Angeles for a week and I was thinking about how I missed my family, but there he was all the way across the world – he died in Palestine a few days before the end of the war – it's just tremendously poignant to me. I also have a watch and chain he carried with him that I keep on a shelf.

I've done a little research and learned that another great-grandfather, Bill Eldridge, was killed in 1916 in Flanders. He's buried in a British cemetery in France and I've actually seen his grave and seen his military records. You realize he's just one of those guys – one of millions of guys who have died in war efforts.

Early on in writing about war I realized what heroism is really about. I've always tried – and I think I'm known for this – to make my stories about the characters foremost. Not so much the story elements like time warps and the things that are exploding, but "Why are these characters involved with this stuff?" I've learned that heroism isn't about people that go into battle unafraid; it's about people who go into battle terrified, but do it anyway. If I had to go to war, my fear would not be of dying; it would be of never seeing my wife and kid again. These people lived with it every day. To think about the guys who went up on Omaha Beach on D-Day. So many of them were killed, and you think about the Americans – they were not so much there to protect America directly. They were 3000 miles away trying to help people in another continent. That's incredibly noble to me.

When I wrote *Civil War: Frontline*, I included these four-page backup stories of each issue looking back, giving a historical perspective on war and why people fight, and the last issue was actually about my family – my dad, my grandfather, my great-grandfather. I have these bronze medallions in honor of my great-grandfather and my uncle. I keep them just outside my boy's room as a reminder that we have what we have because members of my family, along with many, many other families, went to war and laid their lives down for that.

As you can see, I have a lot to say on the subject!

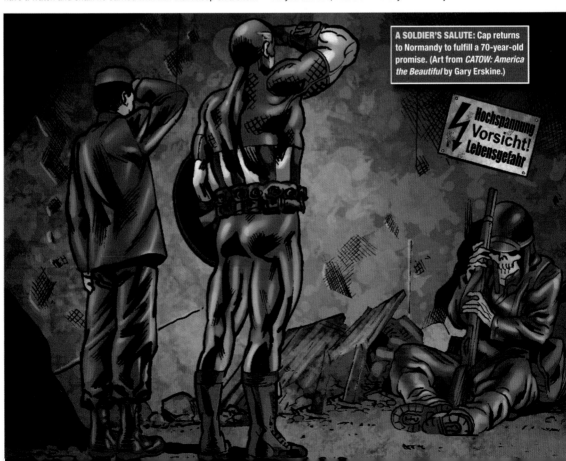

A SOLDIER'S SALUTE: Cap returns to Normandy to fulfill a 70-year-old promise. (Art from *CATOW: America the Beautiful* by Gary Erskine.)

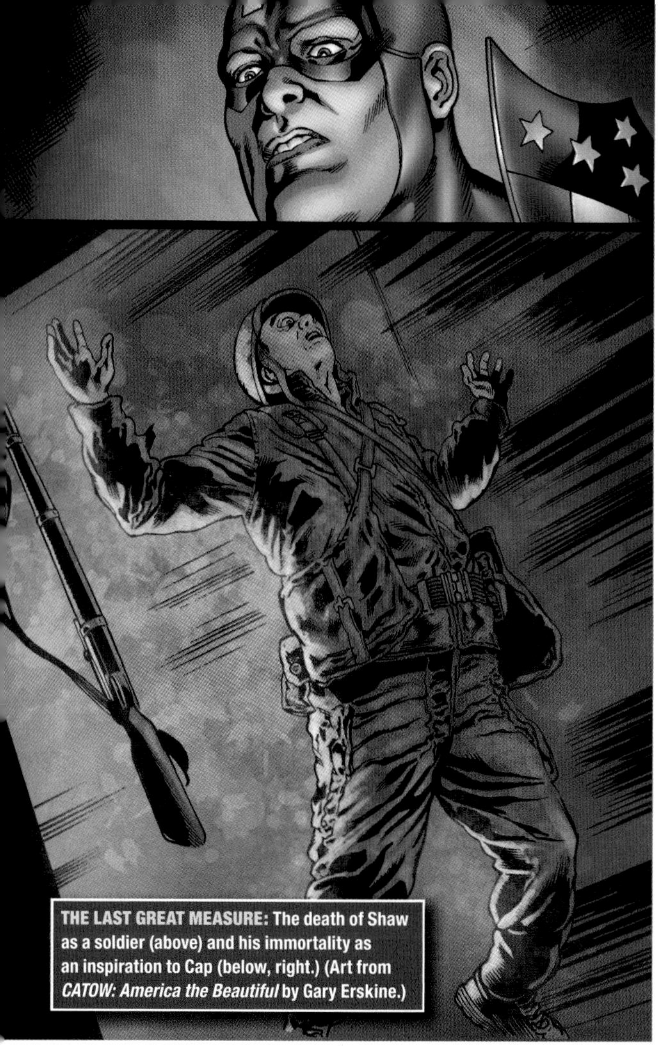

THE LAST GREAT MEASURE: The death of Shaw as a soldier (above) and his immortality as an inspiration to Cap (below, right.) (Art from *CATOW: America the Beautiful* by Gary Erskine.)

So at the end of that issue, after bringing the body home at last, as he had promised to do 70 years ago, Cap is speaking at a memorial service and says that this man, Bobby Shaw, was the bravest guy he's known because he was the most scared he'd ever known. That's how Cap sees things. And it's the epitome of these soldiers who go shed their blood in a foreign land. Like Rupert Brooke said, "If I should die, think only this of me: That there's some corner of a foreign field/ That is for ever England." That's such a beautiful line to me.

SPOTLIGHT: You dedicated that issue to your friend J. Douglas Huggins and his childhood friend who you named Bobby Shaw after, both veterans. How do you know Mr. Huggins?

PAUL: He's my neighbor. He is one of the most amazingly nice people I've ever met. Doug was at Pearl Harbor, where Bobby Shaw was killed. The picture in the back is Doug and Bobby. Doug was an electrician's mate on the USS St. Louis and Bobby was on the USS Arizona. That picture was taken two days before the attack. There they were smiling in Hawaii with no idea that two days later was the day that shall live in infamy. In comes this attack, and Doug loses his best friend. I went over to Doug's to interview him one time and he brings out this photo. He says, that's my best friend Bobby Shaw, and I thought he was going to tell me an anecdote about him. He said, "Two days after his picture was taken he was killed on the Arizona." My eyes just swelled up.

SPOTLIGHT: I've noticed that the two stories that have come out so far both feature the death of prominent, symbolic characters.

"CAP SAYS THAT THIS MAN, BOBBY SHAW, WAS THE BRAVEST GUY HE'S KNOWN BECAUSE HE WAS THE MOST SCARED HE'D EVER KNOWN." – WRITER PAUL JENKINS, DISCUSSING THE FEATURE CHARACTER OF *THEATER OF WAR: AMERICA THE BEAUTIFUL.*

SPOTLIGHT: Oh, yeah. That's the idea. We have plenty of folks talking about Captain America in this issue of *Spotlight*, and we want to get a different perspective here, just like your *Theater of War* books do.

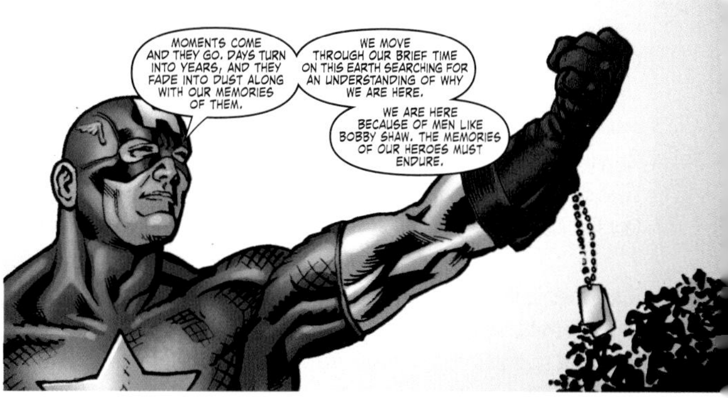
MOMENTS COME AND THEY GO. DAYS TURN INTO YEARS, AND THEY FADE INTO DUST ALONG WITH OUR MEMORIES OF THEM.
WE MOVE THROUGH OUR BRIEF TIME ON THIS EARTH SEARCHING FOR AN UNDERSTANDING OF WHY WE ARE HERE.
WE ARE HERE BECAUSE OF MEN LIKE BOBBY SHAW. THE MEMORIES OF OUR HEROES MUST ENDURE.

PAUL: Here's the thing about Captain America. I was given the job by Tom and he asked me if I had anything to say about war and of course I did. The first book ("America the Beautiful") came out and it was about someone who had gone off to a foreign field and had died. The idea was that he was small, afraid and ineffectual. He had a bad leg he claimed was from being shot but in reality he ran over his foot with a lawn mower. His story was bigger than he was, but in the end he did this incredibly heroic thing. At that crunch moment when you think he's going to fail – and he's failed twice in the story already – he kicks a grenade into a side shed and it kills him. His body is left there for 70 years. So many people found things they didn't think they could do like that. You wonder, "How would you react in that situation? What would you really do?"

PAUL: That's not necessarily true of the others. (*Laughter.*) Being a European who lives in America, I can really see how massive America really is. America can have a difficult time really seeing and grasping other cultures. It's not selfish or anything. It's just America is so large that it can be hard seeing beyond her borders because there is so much here to be concerned about. In the days before America's involvement in WWII there was a lot of isolationist sentiment: "Why should we? If they can't keep it together why should we go over there?" From the British perspective, we were right in the firing line; we were next. My mother and grandparents lived through the blitz of London. I grew up hearing about this. My mum ate her first banana because an American GI gave it to her.

So in the second issue I did – "A Brother In Arms" – one of the things I really wanted to say was that if you were a German patriot, you were fighting because you were fighting for your country, you're not necessarily a Nazi. So many of them were fighting because they were patriots and that was their job. The soldier in "Brother in Arms" in fact had no love for Hitler.

It talked about the Rules of Engagement. I have a good friend named Chris Dare, a Lt. Colonel in the army and he helped write the army's manual on the protocol of war and rules of engagement so I had an amazing conversation with him where he taught me how to handle this issue. In a way it was not quite accurate because the German soldier would have been ordered not to aid the enemy. But having said that, once his own guys shot at him he was free to choose his own course.

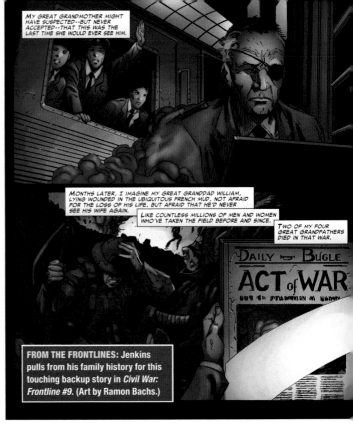

FROM THE FRONTLINES: Jenkins pulls from his family history for this touching backup story in *Civil War: Frontline #9*. (Art by Ramon Bachs.)

"IF I HAD TO GO TO WAR MY FEAR WOULD NOT BE OF DYING IT WOULD BE OF NEVER SEEING MY WIFE AND KID AGAIN" – JENKINS

SPOTLIGHT: Rules of Engagement and interrogation techniques aren't quite the same thing, but they certainly are both aspects of military ethics. Was the hot button interrogation issue on your mind as you wrote this issue?

PAUL: Very much so. One thing that was strange with *Civil War: Frontline* was that there was a lot of talk of my taking a political side, but no one could agree what side it was. I disassociate from the characters. Some people thought Sally Floyd was my leftwing mouthpiece but others said I was showing her in a bad light, as a fool, because I'm rightwing.

It's the same thing here. It doesn't take a rocket scientist, much less a Democrat or a Republican to see that torturing people – doing to them what they did to us – is the wrong way to go. As John McCain said, he just told them what they wanted to hear to get them to stop torturing him.

I felt that America's greatest strength is its high moral ground, and that strength is rendered ineffectual through things like torture. Looking back at soldiers in WWII, it may be hard to accept at times, but all soldiers are honorable and they must be treated in an honorable fashion.

PICTURES FROM PEARL HARBOR: Inspirations for Jenkins' *America the Beautiful.*

SPOTLIGHT: It was portrayed well in the story. It made them all human and sympathetic. You could see why the character of Molodec had such a hard time letting the German prisoner of war live after he had killed his friends.

PAUL: It's completely understandable. If you fought next to your best friend and your best friend was killed by that guy over there and then you captured that guy, you wouldn't be in a charitable mood toward that guy. It takes a lot of understanding to work out that that guy was doing his job and once surrendering should be afforded protection. You can hate him but you now have a moral obligation to protect him. I spoke with Chris Dare about that: how does it work; why is there a moral code? We found out what happens without that code in the trenches of the First World War with mustard gas and crap like that.

SPOTLIGHT: So what is coming up in the next one-shot, *Theater of War: To Soldier On*?

PAUL: The third issue is about my good friend Brian Anderson. He and his friends are the three main characters in the book. Brian is a triple amputee. He was in a Humvee and his navigator and gunner were all in the Humvee and got hit by a roadside bomb. Brian lost both legs and one of his arms. He's one of the finest people I know. He's one of the most honest people I know and he said the most incredible thing to me the first time I met him, and I totally understood it. He said that he has a great job now. He's a wheelchair spokesman and he has a lot of people paying attention to him. But Kenny, the gunner, was not injured, and Kenny has a wife and kid. Brian's honest fear was that he felt worried about Kenny. Kenny was likely going back to Iraq. It was so honest of Brian to say that he was more concerned about Kenny than about feeling sorry for himself. He felt like he could move on. Having said that, there are a great many people injured who suffered a lot of emotional damage as well. In many ways, Brian is a success story.

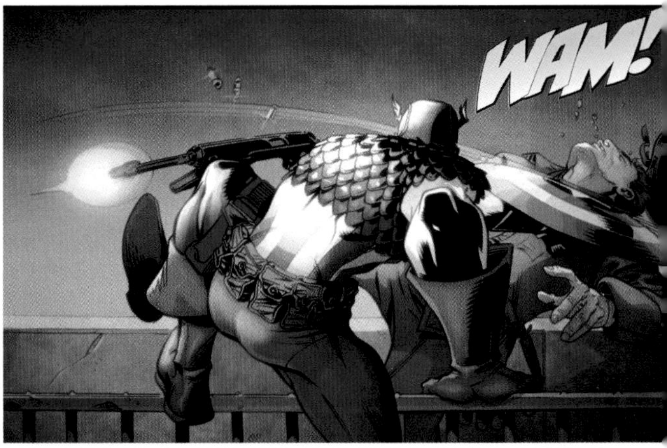
WAM!

BATTLE ACTION: John McCrea's crisply rendered action artwork showcases the realism of *Theater of War.* (Art from *CATOW: A Brother In Arms.*)

SPOTLIGHT: That is amazing. Do you change the setting of this story to WWII?

PAUL: No, this is set in Iraq, during the first invasion of Baghdad. It's the story of Brian encountering Captain America. Cap ends up representing so many different things. He's a soldier, a commanding officer. He's also in a sense a politician, and also an icon. Brian gets to see him through his own ordeal and sees him in many different ways. At times he completely admires him; after being injured, he resents him. The question at the end of the story is, "Who is Captain America?" I think it has an emotionally satisfying ending. My meter for this is editor Jeanine Schaefer. She calls me up when I send in a script and says, "Okay I cried."(*Laughter.*)

Another good thing is – going back to the "America the Beautiful" story – I told Tom Brevoort about how Captain America brings Bobby Shaw's dog tags home and about how Bobby always wanted a beautiful girl and a swimming hole. So Cap brings the dog tags back and makes this speech at the service. He throws the dog tags into the water and says, "I brought you back to your swimming hole, and your girl is a knockout." We pull back and it's the Statue of Liberty. When I first told Tom that he burst out into an involuntary giggle and I said, "You just did that so you wouldn't get all choked up!" (*Laughter.*) But he knew that fit exactly who Captain America was.

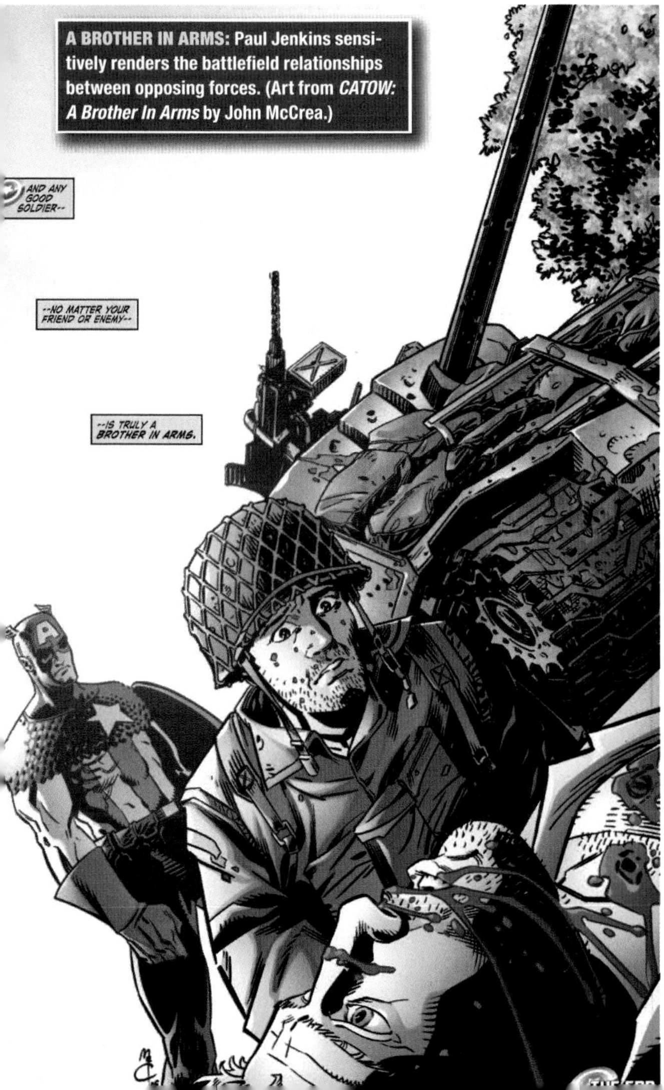
AND ANY GOOD SOLDIER--
--NO MATTER YOUR FRIEND OR ENEMY--
--IS TRULY A BROTHER IN ARMS.

A BROTHER IN ARMS: Paul Jenkins sensitively renders the battlefield relationships between opposing forces. (Art from *CATOW: A Brother In Arms* by John McCrea.)

SPOTLIGHT: Anything you can tell us about the fourth book you have coming out?

PAUL: That one to me is by far the most special. It's my love letter to Captain America. Without giving away too much, it's about what Captain America must really be. When we see him and see his shield and his flag-based uniform, he is the sum total of all of the most important and meaningful and meaning*less* and mundane and intense moments throughout the history of the U.S. He is the personification of America. It's called "Ghost of My Country" and we journey across time to see Cap as the ghost of his country. He exists throughout all of the most important moments of American military history. He was there. And he was there because the sum total of everything that was happening made him come alive. It's kind of a strange concept I suppose, but he is alive because of everything these soldiers did. My friend Brian makes him alive; Doug Huggins and Bobby Shaw bring him to life. Every American soldier brings Captain America alive.

***Thanks to Paul Jenkins for this stirring interview. Be on the lookout for the* CAPTAIN AMERICA: THEATER OF WAR *specials already released, including* AMERICA FIRST!, OPERATION: ZERO POINT, AMERICA THE BEAUTIFUL *and A* BROTHER IN ARMS *– plus* TO SOLDIER ON*, scheduled to ship in August!* ●**